New Industries
from New Places

New Industries from New Places

The Emergence of the Software and Hardware Industries in China and India

Neil Gregory

Stanley Nollen

Stoyan Tenev

A COPUBLICATION OF STANFORD ECONOMICS AND FINANCE,
AN IMPRINT OF STANFORD UNIVERSITY PRESS, AND THE WORLD BANK

Washington, D.C.
Stanford, California

© 2009 The International Bank for Reconstruction and Development / The World Bank
1818 H Street NW
Washington DC 20433
Telephone: 202-473-1000
Internet: www.worldbank.org
E-mail: feedback@worldbank.org

1 2 3 4 12 11 10 09

A copublication of Stanford Economics and Finance, an imprint of Stanford University Press, and the World Bank.

Stanford University Press   The World Bank
1450 Page Mill Road   1818 H Street NW
Palo Alto CA 94304   Washington DC 20433

The findings, interpretations, and conclusions expressed herein are those of the author(s) and do not necessarily reflect the views of the Executive Directors of the International Bank for Reconstruction and Development/ The World Bank or the governments they represent.

The World Bank does not guarantee the accuracy of the data included in this work. The boundaries, colors, denominations, and other information shown on any map in this work do not imply any judgement on the part of The World Bank concerning the legal status of any territory or the endorsement or acceptance of such boundaries.

Rights and Permissions

World Rights except North America   *North America*
ISBN (soft cover): 978-0-8213-6478-9   ISBN (soft cover): 978-0-8047-6281-6
ISBN (hard cover): 978-0-8213-7785-7   ISBN (hard cover): 978-0-8047-6280-9
eISBN: 978-0-8213-7784-0
DOI: 10.1596/978-0-8213-6478-9

Library of Congress Cataloging-in-Publication Data

Gregory, Neil F.
    New industries from new places : the emergence of the software and hardware industries in China and India / by Neil Gregory, Stanley·Nollen, and Stoyan Tenev.
        p. cm.
    Includes bibliographical references and index.
    ISBN 978-0-8213-6478-9 (world bank pbk.) — ISBN 978-0-8213-7784-0 (electronic) — ISBN 978-0-8213-7785-7 (world bank hardback) — ISBN 978-0-8047-6280-9 (stanford university press hardback) — ISBN 978-0-8047-6281-6 (stanford university press pbk.)

    1. Computer software industry—China   2. Computer software industry—India.   3. Computer industry—China.   4. Computer industry—India.   I. Nollen, Stanley D.   II. Tenev, Stoyan, 1961–   III. Title.
    HD9696.63.C62G74 2009
    338.4'70040951—dc22

                                                        2008051221

Cover image: NASA satellite photo of the earth at night.
Cover design by Critical Stages.

Contents

Tables

Foreword

Development is not an abstract concept but a real process of emergence and growth of new industries and economic activities. China and India have recorded extraordinary development success in recent years. The emergence of new industries is not only bringing economic transformation to these countries but is changing the global economic landscape. No industries illustrate better the rising economic prominence of these two countries than the growth of the software industry in India and the growth of the hardware industry in China. Just as interesting for the understanding of industrial development is the relative lack of success of the hardware industry in India and of export success of the software industry in China.

This study seeks to provide an explanation of these remarkable growth stories, based on an empirical analysis of the macro and microeconomic factors underpinning industrial development. In doing so, it sheds a broader light on the economic development paths that China and India have taken since 1990, and also on the process by which developing economies can enter and succeed in new markets.

Several important lessons emerge from the analysis.

First, there is no unique or universal path to sustained development and growth. China and India have followed widely different patterns of economic transformation. Recent trends tend to diminish some of the differences observed in earlier years, reflecting convergence in economic policies and investment climates and the gradual overcoming of the initial obstacles to industrial growth. If these trends continue, China and India may end up at similar destinations, having followed very different routes for the development of their software and hardware industries. Thus sustained growth and development are possible from widely different starting conditions and from following different growth patterns and trajectories.

A second message of the study is that there is no silver bullet for development success. Combined and sustained efforts of private and government actors are necessary to bring positive changes and lasting results. Experiments need to take place to find workable solutions to country- or industry-specific development challenges, but once working formulas are found, the development payoffs can be quick and large.

Finally, countries need not wait to establish perfect business conditions to stimulate growth; a lot can be achieved with imperfect, second-best institutions. Of critical importance, however, are pro-growth government policies to overcome weaknesses in the investment climate, in ways that create space for private investment and innovation. Both China and India rank poorly on World Bank international comparisons of investment climate indicators, yet both have been able to nurture world-beating industries. In both countries, governments continue to work on the first-best solution of improving the overall investment climate—which is a long-term process—while also creating "micro-climates" in the short term that improve the investment climate for specific industries. Creating industrial success stories in this way can help build support for broader investment climate reforms.

I hope that this study will provide all those with an interest in industrial growth and development with new insights into the process by which developing countries can enter and succeed in new industries.

Justin Lin
Senior Vice President and Chief Economist
The World Bank

Acknowledgments

We are grateful to the Government of Norway and the International Finance Corporation for financial support for this study; to the field survey team (Haakon Vennemo, John Skjelvik, and Helen Berg from ECON consulting; Hong Daiyong from Renmin University, Beijing; and G. Srivatsava from the Confederation of Indian Industry); to N.S. Siddharthan, who was at the Institute of Economic Growth of Delhi University and is now at the Madras School of Economics; and others who have contributed to the research for this study (Dilawar Bajauri, Omar Chaudry, Anastasia Gekis, Chendi Zhang, and Qi Lei).

We benefited from discussions with a range of people from the World Bank Group (including Shahid Yusuf, David Dollar, Reyaz Ahmad, Ravi Bugga, Axel Peuker, Andrew Stone, Mark Dutz, Paul Asel, Doug Coulter, and Amitava Banerjee) and elsewhere (including Tarun Khanna, Ramana Nanda, Li Li, Tojo Thatchenkery, Zhang Xuan, and Yasheng Huang). We were also grateful for comments from two anonymous reviewers.

We also thank Irna Das for her help in preparing the manuscript, and Stephen McGroarty, Susan Graham, and Nora Ridolfi from the World Bank Office of the Publisher for taking the manuscript through the publishing process.

Errors and omissions are attributable to the authors. The interpretations are those of the authors, and should not be attributed to IFC or the World Bank Group.

About the Authors

Neil Gregory

Neil Gregory is adviser to the Vice President for Financial and Private Sector Development, World Bank Group. He was previously a manager in the South Asia Department of the International Finance Corporation. He has written on the emergence of the private sector in China and on foreign direct investment to developing countries, and he has lectured on the growth of the private sector in China and India. He holds economics degrees from Cambridge and Oxford Universities and an MBA from Georgetown University; he began his career as an economist with the UK government, and served as adviser to the UK Executive Director of the World Bank Group and IMF from 1993–96.

Stanley Nollen

Stanley D. Nollen is professor of International Business at the Georgetown University McDonough School of Business in Washington, DC. His research includes studies of the growth, intellectual property, and export performance of firms in the information technology industry in India and the success and failure of firms in emerging market economies. He has published books and articles in leading journals. He teaches international business and economics, and has conducted study programs and executive education courses in Belgium, the Czech Republic, Croatia, India, República Bolivariana de Venezuela, and Vietnam and has twice received Fulbright scholar awards. His PhD is from the University of Chicago.

Stoyan Tenev

Stoyan Tenev is chief evaluation officer and head of macroevaluations at the Independent Evaluation Group of the International Finance Corporation. He was previously lead economist for East Asia and Pacific at the International Finance Corporation. His research includes books and articles on China, East Asian economies, transition economies, economic reforms, private sector development, and corporate governance. His PhD is from the University of Maryland.

Abbreviations

CAGR	compound annual growth rate
CMM	Capability Maturity Model
BPO	business process outsourcing
FDI	foreign direct investment
GDP	gross domestic product
GNP	gross national product
IFC	International Finance Corporation
IMF	International Monetary Fund
ISO	International Organization for Standardization
IT	information technology
ITES	IT-enabled services
MNC	multinational corporation
NASSCOM	National Association of Software and Service Companies
OGL	Open General Licensing
PC	personal computer
R&D	research and development
RMB	renminbi
Rs	rupees
S&T	science and technology
SEZ	Special Economic Zone
SOE	state-owned enterprise
STP	software technology park

$ signifies US$ unless otherwise specified

Part I
Foundations

Chapter 1

Context for the Study of the Software and Hardware Industries in China and India

China and India have grown rapidly in importance in the global economy over the past two decades—the same period in which hardware and software have become important tradable products in the global economy. China has reached global scale in the hardware industry but not in software; India has achieved the reverse. These recent developments offer new insights into the ways in which new industries can take root and flourish within the broader context of developing economies. This progress has attracted widespread comment, most of it anecdotal or based on partial explanations of industrial growth. This study seeks to provide a fuller explanation based on an empirical analysis of the macro and micro underpinnings of these contrasting growth stories. In doing so, the study sheds a broader light on the economic development paths that China and India have taken since 1990, and also on the process by which developing economies can enter and succeed in new markets.

China and India, with 38 percent of the global population, are the two largest countries in the world. They rank among the top five countries in purchasing power and are among the fastest-growing economies. China has sustained annual gross domestic product (GDP) growth rates in the 8 to 10 percent range for many years, and India more recently reached the 7 to 9 percent range. As these two economies continue to grow, they will have ever-greater impacts on the global economy. In 2005, they contributed almost half of global economic growth, 40 percent of the working-age population (Ahya and Xie 2004), and 21 percent of output.[1] Their economic development is of worldwide significance.

The differences in development outcomes between the two countries evoke great interest. Although their rates of growth may not turn out to be very different over the long term, the industrial composition of that growth has diverged widely. Nowhere has the contrast been sharper than between China's rise to prominence in the global market for manufacturing and India's parallel rise to prominence in the global market for information technology (IT) services.

This contrast has generated much debate among policy makers and business communities, as well as in the popular press, about the differences in the growth patterns between China and India.[2] The debate has been particularly lively in India—compared with China, manufacturing in India has been an underperforming sector for many years, and China is seen as a threat to India's software services leadership.

The questions this book seeks to answer, key facts about these global industries, and the ways in which this study attempts to answer the questions are the subjects of this first chapter.

Overview of the Software and Hardware Industries

The analysis focuses on two specific sectors: software services and products (*software*) within the broader IT industry, and electronics (*hardware*) within manufacturing.[3]

Three reasons underpin these definitions of the sectors. First, the same underlying technological change—the microelectronics revolution of the past 40 years—has influenced both software and hardware industries, which produce complementary products. By focusing on software and hardware rather than broader industry groupings, the study can simultaneously minimize the effects of differential technological change across industries and discover relationships between the two industries.

Second, because these industries emerged so recently, most of their growth occurred during the period when the Chinese and Indian economies were undergoing market-oriented reforms. Thus, state control influenced the current status of these industries less than it has other sectors. In addition, because the growth in these industries is so recent, it is possible to find data series that track this growth from very early stages as well as to interview participants engaged in the early development of these industries. We can capture more of the total path of the development of these industries than we can for other parts of the manufacturing and services sectors, which will help us explore path dependence.

Third, both software and hardware are sizable industries that are important to economic development in every nation and whose products and services are familiar to most people.

Software Industry Definition

The definition of the software industry is based on the output produced, the value addition in the output (and correspondingly, the skill requirements of labor), and the business function served or the customer for the output (table 1.1). In the software industry, the two main segments are software services and software products. Business process outsourcing (BPO), also known as IT-enabled services (ITES), does not produce software but uses it to perform a range of services for clients. This segment is included in the description of the overall industry, but the analysis in chapter 4 does not include firms that engage in BPO or ITES.

Table 1.1   Software Industry

1. Customized software services
   Programming, testing, maintenance
   Design and engineering
   Systems integration
   Software consulting

2. Embedded software

3. Software products
   Systems software
   Middleware
   Enterprise applications software platforms
   Retail packaged software products

4. Business process outsourcing or IT-enabled services
   Customer and supplier relationships (call centers, inbound and outbound)
   Internal organizational transactions (back office operations)
   Knowledge process outsourcing (professional services)

Source: Authors' compilation.

Software services range from writing lines of code to consulting on business problems. Programming, testing, and maintenance are the entry-level activities. Design and engineering, then systems integration (enabling different software platforms, applications, and hardware to work together), require more labor skill and experience, and more engagement with the client. All software services work is labor intensive, with technical skill, management capability, and value added by labor increasing along the spectrum of activities. Consulting makes the greatest use of general management capabilities and technical skills.

Software services may be performed on-site at the client's place of business by the software developer. Such "body shopping" was typical in the early years of the industry—the software firm abroad supplied people who went to the client's location to do the work for short-term assignments. Software services also may be performed offshore at the supplier's location and delivered electronically to the client. These services, including consulting, are typically customized for the client's needs. They are one-off contracts unique to each client and performed either on a fixed-cost basis or a time and materials basis. Repeated work for similar clients likely embodies some common elements of reusable software.

Embedded software is permanently and unalterably integrated into hardware (for example, controls for automatic clothes washers or internal circuitry for mobile telephones). This segment spans the services-products typology. Embedded software is typically technology intensive and requires close relationships with hardware manufacturers.

Software products can be (1) standardized operating systems, such as Microsoft Windows; (2) enterprise applications platforms, such as customer relations management or business process reengineering platforms from companies such as Oracle or SAP; (3) middleware that links operating systems with applications products; and (iv) retail packaged software products purchased by end consumers in shrink-wrapped packages, such as tax preparation programs, language learning programs, and games. Software products typically require more capital than software services.

Business services that use software but do not create it, such as ITES or BPO, include technical support lines for retail customers (call centers) and back-office operations, such as data entry for bank checks or medical transcription. Some BPO operations deal with external customers or suppliers of the firm, and others manage internal organizational transactions. Some BPO operations are low skill, although demanding in customer service quality; others are high skill and termed knowledge process outsourcing (KPO), for instance, research services such as patent searches and filings. All are labor intensive.

Outsourcing means the services are provided by a different company from the recipient of those services. BPO, however, also includes "insourcing" by captive or company-owned operations conducted offshore. "Offshoring," which is not the same as outsourcing, means that the service is performed in another country: it may be outsourced to another firm, in which case it is also outsourcing, or it may be performed by an overseas location of the client itself. Although this chapter provides data on the BPO segment in its description of industry size and growth, BPO firms are not analyzed in this study because they do not produce software. Some software services firms also have BPO operations, but typically among Indian firms, such operations are spun off into a separate company.

Global Software Industry Size and Growth

Worldwide, software products and services in 2003 (the year of the IFC survey) were estimated to be a $1,023 billion industry (including Internet service providers). Software services and products accounted for more than 60 percent of the industry in that year, and BPO was nearly 40 percent of total industry revenue. By 2007 the software and services industry worldwide had grown in size to $1,527 billion.

Table 1.2 shows the size of the worldwide software industry from 1997 through 2007. The compound annual rate of growth for the worldwide industry over this period, at 15 percent, exceeds the rate of growth of the world's economy by a wide margin. And both Indian and Chinese software industries are growing two to three times faster than the world industry overall.

In 2004, North America accounted for about half of the global market, Europe for 29 percent, and Asia for 17 percent. Both Indian and Chinese software industries are still small compared with the world industry; each country accounts for less than 3 percent of the total world market. However, both China and India are increasing their shares of the world market. If the world market is restricted to the types of products and services that these two countries supply, their market share is much higher.

Table 1.2 Size and Growth of the Global Software and Services Industry Worldwide

($ millions)

	1997	1998	1999	2000	2001	2002	2003	2004	2005	2006	2007
Software and services revenue worldwide	391	453	526	621	735	817	1,023	1,130	1,249	1,382	1,527

Sources: Datamonitor (2003) for 1997–2002; Datamonitor (2008) for 2003–07.

Note: These industry figures include software products and services, software product support and maintenance, information technology services, BPO, and internet software and services.

Table 1.3 Leading Software Services Exporting Countries

($ billions)

Country	Main providers of offshore IT services 2002/03	IT services exports from offshoring 2003/04	Outsourcing providers in 2004	
			IT services exports	BPO exports
China	—	1.7	0.7	0.3
India	9.0	11.5	12.2	5.2
Canada	3.8	2.1	8.2	5.5
Ireland	1.9	3.8	2.2	—
Israel	0.9	0.9	—	—
Philippines	0.6	0.2	0.3	0.8
Russian Federation	—	0.3	0.6	0.1
South Africa	0.1	—	0.2	—

Sources: "Main destinations for offshore IT services" from Evalueserve, reported in NASSCOM, *Indian IT Industry Fact Sheet,* 2004, for April 1 to March 31. "IT services exports from offshoring" from Evalueserve (2004). Outsourcing destinations from neoIT, *Mapping Offshore Markets Update 2005,* 2005, www.neoIT.com. Evalueserve data for Canada, Ireland, and China include software products exports. No official comparable data exist for software services exports from international organizations, and different industry sources of data give different results although the overall conclusions about relative country magnitudes are borne out.

Note: — = Not available from data source.

Software Industry Exports

Exports of software services and products are sizable worldwide, and India's visibility as a software services exporter is a primary motivator for this study. Data on software exports by country come from different sources and are variable and incomplete, but provide a broad-brush picture of the leading exporters. By all accounts, India is the world's leading exporter of software services. Its export revenues range from 1.5 to 3.0 times those of Canada, its nearest competitor, followed by Ireland (depending on the source; table 1.3). For purposes of comparison, U.S. software services exports (not shown in table 1.3) are estimated to be roughly between $2 billion and $6 billion as of 2004.[4] If software products as well

Table 1.4   Hardware Industry

1. Hardware systems
   Mainframe computers
   Workstations and servers
   Desktop and laptop computers

2. Peripherals and components
   Printers, scanners, monitors, keyboards
   Disk drives, pointing devices, power supplies

3. Networking equipment (hubs, routers, switches, modems, cabling)

4. Telecommunications equipment

5. Semiconductors

6. Industrial electronics

Source: Authors' compilation.

as services are included in the measurement, North American and the European Union are the major exporters along with India.

Hardware Industry Definition

Manufactured electronic products in the information technology industry—hardware—include six main segments as outlined in table 1.4.

This description of the size and growth of the worldwide hardware industry and the study's analysis of hardware firms exclude consumer electronics products such as televisions, radios, video cassette recorders, and digital video disk players. Telecommunications services are also excluded because they are not manufactured products. Because of differences between data sources, the worldwide data reported in this chapter include semiconductors; the China and India country data exclude semiconductors, but include industrial electronics products.

Global Hardware Industry Size and Growth

Worldwide, the hardware industry in 2004 was estimated to have a market value of $965 billion to $1,164 billion, depending on the source. Computers accounted for just under one-third of the hardware industry's total size in the late 1990s and just over one-third of the total in 2004. (Data refer to 2004 because this analysis of software firms goes through that year.) Peripherals and components accounted for a constant one-eighth share of the hardware industry throughout the period. Telecommunications equipment, like computers, accounted for roughly one-third of the industry, but its share decreased slightly over the 1998–2004 period (table 1.5). China's share of the world hardware market is substantial, perhaps 20 percent, whereas India's world market share is inconsequential, perhaps one-half of 1 percent.

The compound annual growth rate of the worldwide hardware industry was 6.3 percent over the 1998–2004 period. An absolute decline in the market in 2001 fol-

Table 1.5   Size and Growth of the Global Hardware Industry
($ billions)

Segment	1997	1998	1999	2000	2001	2002	2003	2004	2005	2006	2007
Total hardware sales revenue worldwide[a]	—	668	759	947	861	849	891	965	1,048	1,128	1,207
Computer hardware	191	216	240	308	300	308	321	339	359	379	400
Peripherals and storage devices	75	84	90	107	110	105	113	117	120	129	136
Telecom equipment	216	254	319	409	348	306	295	309	331	357	385
Semiconductors[b]	—	131	159	211	145	147	166	211	238	263	286
Technology hardware and equipment[c]	—	—	—	1,152	1,110	1,075	1,115	1,164	—	—	—

Sources: Datamonitor Industry Market Research reports published in November 2003 for each of the sectors shown for 1997–99; Datamonitor Industry Market Research reports published at various dates in 2005 for each of the sectors shown for 2000–04; Datamonitor Industry Profiles published in February 2008 for each of the sectors shown for 2005–07; except Datamonitor, "Global Telecommunications Equipment Industry Profile," May 2003, for all years (figures for 2003–07 are estimates) for the Telecom equipment data.

Note: — = Not available.

a. Total sales revenue is the sum of the four industries and includes some double counting. Computer hardware includes personal computers, servers, mainframes, workstations, and peripherals; computer storage and peripherals include data storage components, motherboards, audio and video cards, monitors, keyboards, printers, other components, and peripherals; telecommunications equipment includes telephones, switchboards, exchanges, routers, local area networks, and wide area networks.

b. Includes semiconductor equipment in 2005, 2006, and 2007; this subindustry accounted for 24 percent of the total in 2007.

c. Alternative report for technology hardware and equipment from the same source, which includes computers and peripherals, communications equipment, electronic equipment and instruments, and office electronics, gives a different figure from the sum of industries.

lowing the dot-com bust, and again in 2002, plus a slow recovery since then, accounts for this slow growth. The two-year industry recession affected semiconductors and communications equipment more than computers and peripherals; in fact, sales revenues for the latter two segments were flat instead of down from 2001 to 2003, and the compound annual growth rate for these two segments alone from 1998 to 2004 was 7.2 percent. From 2004 to 2007, the most recent year shown, total worldwide hardware industry revenue grew 7.7 percent, a higher growth rate than in the earlier period.

Research Objectives, Methods, and Data Sources

The central questions posed in this study arose directly from two often-asked questions about the differences in the development of the two industries in China and India:

- Why did the Indian software industry achieve such great international success while China's software industry was scarcely noticed outside China?
- Why did the Chinese hardware manufacturing industry grow so large while the Indian hardware industry remained so small?

While seeking to explain these starkly divergent patterns of industrial development, we acknowledge that they are beginning to converge. Chinese software is now noticed outside China, and hardware manufacturing is growing in India (see chapter 7).[5]

Most of the debate about these questions has been based on anecdotal evidence and aggregate data. It is informed by expert opinion, but can benefit from both a more comprehensive approach and more and better facts. We have attempted to ground this debate in a rigorous analytical base, not only by building on the available literature and data, such as that found in the World Bank Investment Climate Assessment surveys, but also by making use of new data gathered directly from interviews with managers in Chinese and Indian software and hardware firms in the International Finance Corporation (IFC) survey.

The analysis begins with the assertion that national differences between China and India can partially explain the differences in these industries' development—differences ranging from macroeconomic and industrial policies to the skills in the labor pool. We also suggest that the differences between the Chinese and Indian firms engaged in these industries (for example, in management practices and technology activity) will also contribute to the understanding of why these industries have developed so differently in the two countries. By analyzing the importance of the various national and firm-level differences, conclusions can be drawn about the reasons for the different growth patterns of their respective industries. We also use these analyses to suggest conclusions about the impact of investment climate and government policies on enterprise development.

The first step was to document the differences and similarities between the Indian and Chinese software industries, and then between the two countries' hardware industries, to determine which among many features are critical in explaining their radically divergent development paths. For the software industries, the objective was to explain why Indian software firms became such successful exporters and why Chinese software firms grew rapidly through domestic expansion, then to identify the factors contributing to the growth of both countries' software firms. For the hardware industries, the objective was to explain the conditions that propelled Chinese hardware firms into world-leading positions and those that kept Indian hardware firms from keeping pace.

Study Approach and Organization of Text

The approach to exploring why the Indian and Chinese software and hardware industries have grown in radically different ways was fourfold. First, the accumulated knowledge offered by those who have already studied these industries was taken into account. We used this information as a stepping stone to a deeper understanding of the issues.

Second, a framework was developed to guide the analysis based on the determinants of performance—factors of production, production processes, and the business environment. Chapter 2 defines and describes this framework.

Third, the analysis marshaled qualitative and quantitative evidence about the political and economic realities whose legacies would affect the development of each country's software and hardware industries. We also drew on data from several sources, including the World Bank Investment Climate Assessment surveys, to paint a full picture of business environment features, such as labor force supply, government policies, and infrastructure, that contributed to the divergence in the industries' growth. Chapter 3 reports the result of this investigation.

Fourth, we adopted a comprehensive and multivariate quantitative approach using new data obtained through the IFC Software and Hardware Firm Surveys (described below) to isolate statistically the differentiating features and to analyze the growth determinants of the firms in each country's industry. Because the Chinese and Indian software industries are similar in size and growth rates but differ dramatically in export intensity, an explanation of differences between these two sets of firms contributes to an understanding of the export performance of the Indian software industry. Chapters 4 through 8 report the analysis and findings for the software industry and chapters 9 through 13 for the hardware industry. Chapter 14 synthesizes the findings and conclusions, and chapter 15 looks at emerging trends since the surveys were completed.

World Bank Investment Climate Assessment Surveys

The World Bank has undertaken extensive surveys of the investment climate in many countries, including China and India (Batra, Kaufmann, and Stone 2003; World Bank 2004b). This study used data from surveys conducted in China and India in 2002. The China survey covered 2,400 software and hardware firms and the India survey 1,827 firms.

These surveys included a common core of questions asked in all countries,[6] plus different sets of additional questions for each country. This analysis used the core questions to compare the investment climates in China and India with each other. It also used the additional questions to shed light on specific issues in the investment climates of China and India.

As indicated both by sales revenue and employment, the World Bank surveys in each country focused on small and medium enterprises, with only a few large enterprises in each sample (table 1.6). The China sample includes a minority of state-owned enterprises and foreign-owned firms, but the majority are domestically owned private enterprises. Almost all the Indian companies surveyed are domestically owned private enterprises.

IFC Software and Hardware Firm Survey

New quantitative data were collected specifically for this study through a survey of senior managers from a sample of software services and products companies and hardware manufacturing companies in China and India. The IFC commissioned the survey, which was carried out using face-to-face interviews. The survey consisted of nine pages of questions answered by checking boxes, marking scales, or

Table 1.6 Size of Firms in the World Bank Investment Climate Survey

Indicator	China	India
Employees (median number)		
Hardware firms	139	15
Software firms	47	—
Sales revenue (median, $ millions)		
Hardware	1.8	3.1
Software	0.5	—

Source: Dollar and others 2003; World Bank 2004b.
Note: — = Not available.

Table 1.7 Number of Firms in the IFC Sample

Type of firm	China	India	Total
Software	60	119	179
Hardware	91	49	140
Total	151	168	319

Source: IFC survey.

filling in blanks. Interview information was cross-checked and supplemented with financial information from company annual reports and other public sources; thus, data on objective variables, such as sales revenue, come from official sources rather than a manager's recollection.

Sample size. The sample consists of 319 firms in the software and hardware industries in China and India, with a larger number of software firms in India and a larger number of hardware firms in China, in keeping with the relative importance of the industries in these countries (table 1.7).

Sampling and data collection methods. The Chinese sample was drawn randomly from a central government statistical report produced by the National Statistical Bureau that identified the set of firms in Beijing and Guangzhou, to which were added firms in Shanghai based on local interviewers' knowledge of the industry. The response rate was 30 percent. Interviews were conducted by Renmin University survey research unit staff members in Mandarin or Cantonese languages.

The Chinese sample of hardware firms covers 31 percent of the industry by sales revenue. The sample of software firms covers only 4 percent of the Chinese industry's revenue because revenue is spread among many very small firms.

Chinese software firms in the sample are slightly larger than the industry mean but broadly represent the products versus services breakdown of the industry.

More firms in the sample are foreign owned and fewer are government owned than is true for the industry, but the proportion of privately owned domestic firms is representative.

For Chinese hardware firms in the sample, median firm size approximates the industry median while mean firm size is larger than the industry average. Computer manufacturers are overrepresented in the Chinese sample, as was true for the Indian sample. (See the annex to this chapter for details.)

The sample of software firms in India was drawn from membership lists of industry associations and an annual trade publication review of each industry.[7] The Indian software industry consists of a small number of medium-to-large firms that account for most of the industry's revenue, plus many very small firms.[8] The sample design included all the medium-to-large firms and a random sample of the small firms. As a consequence, the sample covered 91 percent of the Indian software industry by sales revenue. The response rate from software firms was 62 percent.

A similar sample design was followed for hardware, with a planned smaller sample for the smaller industry; the response rate was 30 percent. The Indian hardware sample covers 53 percent of the industry's sales revenue.

The Indian software sample is representative of the industry but not necessarily of the thousands of very small firms in it. The sample is also representative of industry firm ownership, but it has relatively fewer software services firms and relatively more software products firms than the industry. (See the annex for details of the characteristics of the sample compared with the industry.) The Indian hardware sample consists of firms with higher sales revenue and higher employment than the industry average, and has a greater proportion of firms with computers rather than other segments of the industry as their main line of business.

Questionnaires were completed through personal interviews conducted by staff members of the Confederation of Indian Industry from January through March 2004 in the six leading industry locales—Bangalore, Delhi (including the suburbs of Gurgaon and Noida), Mumbai, Pune, Chennai, and Hyderabad.

Characteristics of the sampled firms

Lines of business and production processes. The main lines of business for software firms in the samples approximate the breakdown of the industry in each nation. In the Chinese sample, software products firms are more heavily represented with 58 percent of the total, mirroring the Chinese software industry overall, in which products probably account for more than half the sales revenue. The main difference in the production process for Chinese compared with Indian software firms is the greater frequency with which Indian firms are engaged in consulting as a main line of business.

In the Indian sample, 85 percent of the firms are software services firms (including embedded software with software services) and 15 percent are packaged software products firms; in the Indian software industry overall, services accounted for 92 percent of sales revenue and packaged products for 8 percent in 2002.

In the hardware sample, 41 percent of the Chinese firms were producers of industrial electronics and 26 percent were telecommunications equipment makers. These figures approximate the makeup of the Chinese industry's sales revenues. More than half the Chinese hardware firms are component manufacturers, whereas only one-quarter of the Indian firms manufacture components as their main line of business.

Among the Indian firms, 43 percent were makers of peripherals and 25 percent were computer makers, which fairly represents the computer intensity of the Indian industry but somewhat overrepresents the peripherals and components businesses, which actually account for one-quarter of the Indian hardware industry's revenues, and underrepresents telecom and industrial hardware products. (See table 1.8 and tables 5.1 and 5.3 in chapter 5 for Indian industry-wide data.)

Firm size, growth, and profitability. The sales revenue of $1,891,000 of the median Chinese software firm in the sample was much smaller than that of the

Table 1.8 Main Lines of Business and Production Processes of Firms in the IFC Sample
(% distribution of firms in sample)

Indicator	China	India
Software: Line of business		
Software services	21.7	75.6
Packaged software products	58.3	15.1
Embedded software	20.0	9.2
Production process		
Programming, maintenance, testing	75.0	89.9
Design, engineering	78.3	77.3
Systems integration	50.0	63.9
Consulting	36.7	60.5
Hardware: Line of business		
Computers	16.5	24.5
Peripherals	15.4	42.9
Telecom equipment	26.4	14.3
Industrial electronic components	40.7	16.3
Production process		
Component manufacturing	58.8	26.5
Assembly of finished products	61.2	75.5

Source: IFC survey.
Note: Figures for production process sum to more than 100 because multiple responses were allowed in the survey.

Table 1.9 Characteristics of Firms in the IFC Sample

	China		India	
	Median	**Mean**	**Median**	**Mean**
Sales revenue per year ($ thousands)				
Software	1,891	6,462	6,451	35,927
Hardware	6,658	104,481	7,140	54,478
Employment (number)				
Software	80	161	225	1,215
Hardware	218	2,392	150	535
Sales growth, 2001 to 2002 (%)				
Software	24.3	79.8	13.6	31.2
Hardware	10.7	4.5	10.0	11.4
Profits (% return on sales)				
Software	8.0	8.2	20.0	16.7
Hardware	4.2	1.4	10.0	13.4
Age of firm (years)				
Software	5	6	11	12
Hardware	9	11	13	15

Source: IFC Survey.

median firm in the Indian software sample, where revenue was $6,451,000 in 2002. Mean sales revenue figures greatly exceeded median figures because of the rightward skew in the size distribution of firms in the software industries in both countries and because of the inclusion of more large firms than small firms in the Indian sample. Average Chinese software firm sales revenue was $6.5 million, and average Indian software firm sales revenue was $35.9 million.

In the hardware sample, Chinese and Indian firms are similar in size as measured by median sales revenue—about $7 million. Both samples have some very large firms that raise the mean sales revenue to $54 million for the Indian sample and $104 million for the Chinese sample (table 1.9).

Employment patterns follow revenue patterns, with Chinese hardware firms having more employees than Indian hardware firms and Indian software firms having more employees than Chinese software firms.

Sales revenue growth was rapid for both Chinese and Indian software firms, but Chinese firms in the sample, with a median growth rate of 24.3 percent for 2002 compared with 2001, outpaced Indian firms, which recorded sales growth of 13.6 percent at the median over the same period. Sales revenue growth for Chinese and Indian hardware firms was similar, with a 10 to 11 percent gain from 2001 to 2002 for the median firm in the sample.

Although revenue growth was slower for Indian software firms, profitability was greater. The median return on sales for Indian software firms in our sample

Table 1.10   Export Intensity of Software and Hardware Firms in the IFC Sample

	China	India
Software		
Median (exports as % of total sales)	0	90.5
Mean (exports as % of total sales)	12.7	71.0
Firms with exports of 10% or more of sales	17.7	88.6
Firms with exports of 50% or more of sales	13.7	73.7
Hardware		
Median (exports as % of total sales)	0	1.0
Mean (exports as a % of total sales)	22.8	16.1
Firms with exports of 10% or more of sales	35.7	22.8
Firms with exports of 50% or more of sales	23.8	14.3

Source: IFC Survey.

was 20 percent compared with only 8 percent for Chinese firms. The Chinese hardware firms in our sample also turned in a weaker profitability record than the Indian firms.

Finally, the greater maturity of the Indian software industry is shown in the mean age of the firms in our sample: 12 years for the Indian firms compared with 6 years for the Chinese firms. Hardware firms are of longer standing than software firms, as expected in the older industry, for both Chinese and Indian firms.

Export intensity. Few Chinese software firms have significant export business (only 18 percent of them have exports as great as 10 percent of their total sales), but most of the Indian software firms in the sample are exporters; 89 percent of them record exports of 10 percent or more of their sales revenue. This pattern replicates the difference in the export performance of the two countries' industries (table 1.10). For hardware firms the pattern is reversed, plus exports are less important overall: 36 percent of Chinese hardware firms earn 10 percent or more of their total sales from exports, while 23 percent of the Indian hardware firms in the sample achieve this level of export intensity.

Ownership. More than three-quarters of Indian software firms in the sample are majority owned by private domestic owners. Majority foreign ownership accounts for 21 percent of the Indian software firms; state ownership is insignificant. Fewer Chinese firms than Indian firms in the software sample are majority owned by private domestic owners, but more Chinese firms than Indian firms (32 percent) are majority foreign owned. Only a small share of firms in the sample are state owned, even smaller than the industry figure of approximately 30 percent (table 1.11). Foreign ownership is also more prevalent among the hardware firms in the Chinese sample than among the Indian hardware firms.

Table 1.11   Firm Ownership in the IFC Sample
(% distribution of firms)

Majority owner	China		India	
	Software	Hardware	Software	Hardware
Private domestic	65	56	78	83
Foreign	32	32	21	13
Government	5	12	<1	4

Source: IFC Survey.

Together, the World Bank and IFC data sets provide important new sources of information on the microeconomic factors influencing the performance of the software services and products industries and the hardware manufacturing industries in China and India. The questions in the World Bank and IFC surveys overlap somewhat, which allows the robustness and freedom from bias of the responses from the two surveys to be checked.

It is hoped that the findings from this study will contribute to understanding the way the business environments in China and India affect the performance of firms and that the findings will identify barriers to private sector growth in general, and in the manufacturing and services sectors in particular. We hope it will also improve knowledge about the dynamics of the growth of the electronics manufacturing and IT services industries in developing countries and more generally show the ways in which variations in the business environment affect the growth of different industries.

Annex 1 IFC Firm Survey Sample Compared with the Industry

This annex reports data on the sales revenue, employment, ownership, and product mix for Indian and Chinese software firms in the IFC sample and compares them with data, where available, on the same dimensions for the industries in each country.[9] The comparison shows how the sampled firms differ from the industry average, with the caution that the definition of the factors being compared might differ somewhat between the industry and the sample of firms.

Software

Sales revenue. The Indian software sample purposely focused on the large firms that account for most of the industry's revenue. The Indian software firms in the sample accounted for 91 percent of the entire industry's sales revenue. The mean sales per sampled firm was $36 million in 2002; the median was $6.5 million.

The Chinese software sample contains firms that are probably similar in size to or somewhat larger than the industry average. In the sample, the mean sales revenue per firm in 2002 was $6.5 million and the median was $1.9 million. The estimated mean sales revenue per firm for the overall industry was between $3 million and $9 million in 2002, calculated from size distribution data.

In the multivariate statistical analysis, the sales revenue of the firm was included as a control variable so that the findings obtained from this analysis take firm size differences into account.

Employment. Indian software firms in the sample were larger than the average firm in the industry. The sampled firms had a mean of 1,215 in 2002 with median employment of 225. For the industry, the average number of professional employees (not all employees) per firm was 186 in the same year.

Chinese software firms in the sample were also larger than the average firm in the industry. Sampled firms averaged 161 employees in 2002 (the median was 80), while the industry average employment per firm was between 115 and 125, calculated from firm size distribution data (although other estimates show smaller figures).

Ownership. The pattern of ownership of Indian software firms in the sample closely follows the pattern for the industry as a whole: 21 percent are majority foreign owned (22 percent for the industry), less than 1 percent are state owned (3 percent for the industry), and 78 percent are privately domestically owned.

Fewer Chinese software firms in the sample are government owned (5 percent) and more are majority foreign owned (32 percent) than in the industry as a whole. The share of privately domestically owned firms, however, is similar to that of the industry.

Product mix. Most Indian software firms in the sample were primarily software services firms (85 percent if we include embedded software with software services as is true for industry figures) as is true for the industry, where the figure is as high as 92 percent.

In China, 60 percent of the sampled firms were mainly software products firms, and in the industry, products probably account for more than half the industry's revenue (estimates range from 44 percent to 85 percent, depending on source).

Hardware

Sales revenue and employment. Three-quarters of the Chinese hardware firms in the sample had sales revenue in 2002 between $1 million and $50 million; for the industry, the average sales revenue per firm in the electronics and telecommunications industry was $24 million. A few very large firms in the sample, however, skewed the sample mean sales revenue up to $104 million, with a median of $6.7 million. Employment per firm in the sample was 218 at the median, and the mean was 2,392, compared with an industry average of 409.

Indian hardware firms in the sample were also larger than the industry average for sales revenue: $54 million for the sampled firms versus $5.1 million for the industry. Industry average employment per firm is not available for comparison.

Ownership. The Chinese hardware firms in the sample represent the industry's pattern of ownership exactly when comparing the numbers of firms in each ownership category. In the sample, 56 percent of the firms were privately domestically owned, 32 percent were foreign owned, and 12 percent were state owned. Whole-industry figures are within 1 to 2 percentage points of those for the sample. Sampled firms that were privately domestically owned, however, had higher sales revenue than those in the industry overall, and foreign owned firms had lower revenues.

Most Indian hardware firms in the sample (83 percent) were privately domestically owned and 13 percent were foreign owned. No industry-wide figures are available for comparison, but a similar ownership pattern is expected.

Product mix. With regard to the number of firms, the Chinese hardware sample contains relatively more computer and peripherals firms and fewer industrial electronics firms than is true for the industry.

A definitive statement cannot be made for the Indian hardware industry product mix because no data are available on the number of firms in each industry subsector. It is expected, however, that the sample also contains relatively more computer and peripheral firms than is evident in the industry.

Notes

1. Data for GDP in 2005 in trillions of U.S. dollars at purchasing power parity rates are as follow: world $60.6, China $8.9, and India $3.7 (U.S. Central Intelligence Agency, World Factbook, www.cia.gov). See also Maddison (2001).

2. For example, Huang (2006a); Chandra, Fealey, and Rau (2006); Khanna and Huang (2003); Mukherji (2002); and Spencer and Sanyal (2002).

3. Hardware includes computers and peripherals, communications equipment, audio-video equipment, electron tubes, circuit boards, semiconductors, printed circuits, and electronic components. It excludes consumer and household electronics.

4. This estimate is based on Moylan (2004). The range depends on an assumed growth rate of U.S. software services exports since 1999 (the latest date given in the source) either at the world average or the Indian average. Data on U.S. trade in services from the U.S. Bureau of Economic Analysis shows "computer and information services" with a value of $8.2 billion in exports in 2005; however, this category is broader than software services.

5. For example, we can find three Harvard Business School teaching cases about Chinese software companies written after 2004 (but no such cases from European Case Clearing House) and two before that, whereas there are still double that number of recent Indian software teaching cases. Scholarly journal articles about Indian software continued to outnumber articles about Chinese software by 1.5 times in the 2005–08 period, as they did previously. Of course, broader searches in the popular literature yield more Chinese references in part because of greater Chinese prominence in international trade and investment generally and issues of intellectual property rights.

6. The standard survey of 82 questions covered regulation, governance, access to finance, and infrastructure services. It also collected data on firm productivity, investment, and employment decisions.

7. Confederation of Indian Industry, NASSCOM, and Dataquest Top 200. For the hardware sample, the sources were the Confederation of Indian Industry, Dataquest Top 200, Electronic Components Industries Association, Manufacturers Association of Information Technology, and Telecom Equipment Manufacturers Association.

8. Firms with sales revenue of more than $50 million constituted only 1 percent of the number of firms in the industry but together had 90 percent of the industry's revenue, while 90 percent of the firms had sales revenue of less than $3 million.

9. **China:** Chen and Hu (2002) for employment, sales revenue, and ownership statistics; CCID (2002) for employment and main line of business statistics; Tschang and Xue (2002); Translations from Chinese to English by Qi Lei and calculations from these sources by Qi Lei and Stanley Nollen. **India:** NASSCOM (2003) for sales revenue and employment; NASSCOM (2002) for sales revenue; Commander and others (2004) for ownership.

Chapter 2

A Framework for Understanding
Industry Performance Differences

The objective of this research is to provide an understanding of the conditions in China and India that led to the strikingly different growth patterns of their software and hardware industries. China's software industry grew rapidly by serving domestic customers; India's software industry grew rapidly by reaching export markets. China's hardware industry grew rapidly in both domestic and export markets; India's hardware industry remained small and slow growing until the early years of the 21st century. How can these differences be explained?

The framework used to guide the analysis makes use of concepts from theories of production economics, international trade, and competitive strategy. While primarily theoretical, the analysis also takes into consideration facts about these industries to create the framework that yields an explanation of the differences in these industries' performances.

Overview: Production Inputs, Management Processes, and Business Environment

The study analyzes the growth and development of a firm according to three sets of determinants. The first is firm-level production inputs about which managers make decisions. These are standard factors of production, such as land, labor, capital, and intermediate inputs. The second is the actions of managers that affect the firm's competitiveness, such as the use of inputs, focus on quality processes, use of technology, and alliances with other firms. The third set of determinants is the environment in which the firm operates and to which the firm's managers respond. The environment includes key features of the firm's industry, the institutions and infrastructure in its business environment, and the regulatory and public policy framework provided by governments. Together these factors establish the investment climate that shapes business growth and development.

Production Inputs and Management Processes

Production of goods and services requires a combination of inputs, and different industries require different combinations of inputs. Some inputs are fixed to a particular location while others are mobile to various degrees. Locations differ widely in their endowments of factors of production, such as quality and quantity of labor, capital, and land, whether these inputs are naturally occurring or created. Locations also differ in the management processes used. Industries become competitive in some locations but not others because of differences in these factors of production and management processes.

Standard international trade theories focus on the supply side of the market, and identify factor productivity, factor abundance, and factor intensity as the drivers of international trade flows. An industry in a locale might have a comparative advantage in export markets if it makes intensive use of the factors of production that are comparatively abundant in that particular locale, and those factors are comparatively productive. (The comparison refers to the same industry in another locale and to other industries in the same locale.) Therefore an analysis must be made of the supply, productivity, and costs of labor, capital, and other inputs for software and hardware production to understand the growth and development of the Chinese and Indian software and hardware industries.

Modern international trade theories also identify factor conditions as determinants of an industry's international competitiveness but stress the importance of created factors rather than natural resource endowments.[1] Created factors are especially important for high technology industries such as software and hardware. The strength of an industry in a locale, and in turn, its export competitiveness, also depends on the strength of other industries that are related to it vertically as suppliers or as customers, or horizontally with technological similarities. Therefore, the production process within the firm must be examined, including its use of technology and its interfirm alliances throughout the supply chain.

A body of knowledge complementary to modern trade theories is the resource-based view of the firm. This view asserts that the firm's competitiveness depends on its tangible resources—physical resources such as land, labor, and capital, plus financial resources. Competitiveness also depends on the firm's intangible resources and the firm's capabilities in using its resources. This viewpoint calls attention to management skill and the firm's organizational culture and reputation.

Business Environment and Investment Climate

Outside the firm, but important to its growth and development, is the industry in which it operates. The key feature of an industry that shapes the competitiveness of its firms is the number and size distribution of firms in the industry, which affect the rivalry among the firms.

The wider regional or national context influences the way in which firms are organized and managed, and their choice of business strategies. The functioning of labor and product markets, the effectiveness of legal and financial institutions, the dimensions of the national culture, and the use of hierarchy in organizations, among others, all contribute to the strategic choices of management. The choices include, for example, the configuration of the firm's lines of business, the organization and location of production, whether to be export oriented or to focus on the domestic market, and whether to forge foreign or domestic alliances. These choices are, in part, managers' responses to the business environment as shaped by national and regional governments.

Governments influence the business environment, and that influence differs from country to country and, for some policies, by the location within a country. Many government policies are general and affect all industries. For example, governments can affect factor quantities and qualities and factor mobility by enabling the creation of human capital and removing barriers to its geographic movement within and outside locations. Governments shape the business environment through the regulatory framework, broad competition policies, and international trade and investment policies. Government policies can also be specific to certain industries but not others. These policies can either promote the development of an industry or hinder it by virtue of how it is regulated. Governments can target particular industries for promotion in many ways, for example, by preferential tax or tariff treatment. Governments can also hinder an industry's growth by imposition of time-consuming and cost-increasing regulations.

The framework developed in this chapter sets out the production inputs, management processes, market features, and business environment features that need to be taken into account in the explanation of Chinese and Indian software and hardware industry growth patterns.

Factors of Production

Industrial development presupposes the availability of critical inputs such as labor, capital, and land as well as other factors such as technologies and infrastructure services, in adequate quantities and of adequate quality. This section describes the input requirements for the software and hardware industries.

Labor

Labor is by far the most important input for software firms. The labor force is the biggest cost component because software firms need qualified workers with specific skills that take substantial education and training to acquire. Labor is also an important factor of production for the hardware manufacturing industry, although to a lesser extent than for software because hardware manufacturing has somewhat less stringent demands for qualifications and specialized skills. Nevertheless, engineers and technical personnel play a critical role. Therefore, an ample supply of qualified workers whose productivity is satisfactory but whose wages are not high should be a major factor in the development of both software and hardware industries. If high-skill, low-wage labor confers comparative advantage for the software industry, then export success might be achieved. If the software industry does not have comparative advantage in a nation (for example, because the hardware industry does instead), high skill and low wages that yield high quality at low cost are still conducive to rapid domestic growth for the software industry even if the industry does not achieve export success.

This framework calls for the analysis of labor supply, labor skill, labor productivity, and labor wages for firms in both the software and hardware industries. Does this constellation of labor variables explain either India's software export success or China's hardware industry growth?

Both China and India are labor-abundant countries although with significant differences in the structures of their labor forces and workers' mobility across firms, industries, and geographical regions. Several elements can affect labor skill and mobility. Some of them are intrinsically linked to the fact that workers are embedded in a multitude of local social relationships through their families and communities. Governments, however, can affect labor skill and mobility in many ways, for example, by providing good higher education institutions with suitable curricula, and by actions within regions affecting availability of housing, institutions for trading land, portability of social safety nets, and access to social services. Labor mobility across national borders is traditionally quite limited, but less so for highly skilled workers and managers than for production workers. Indeed, the mobility of skilled workers was a central feature of the early years of the Indian software industry—software engineers moved from India to client locations in the United States. In addition, mobility of nonresident Indians as managers from outside India back to India has been cited as an Indian software industry advantage. International migration depends on the policies of foreign governments as well as home country governments.

Capital

Hardware manufacturing is a more capital-intensive industry than is software, requiring greater investment in plant and equipment. Hardware also has greater financing needs, and the share of tangible assets that can serve as collateral in bank lending is higher. In the software industry, however, intangible assets play a more important role. Not only do the two industries have different capital requirements, they also demand different financial services. For example, debt financing plays a relatively more important role in the hardware industry. In the software industry, many firms are smaller and use retained earnings or external financing by private equity or venture capital rather than debt finance.

Physical capital is mobile, as is financial capital. In theory, a country does not need to develop a deep and diversified financial system. It can import financial services and physical capital. In practice, however, the behavior of financial flows shows significant home-country bias. Different perceptions about risks, dissimilar business cultures, regulatory limits on foreign ownership, and other factors can impede the mobility of capital. Economic crises have provided governments in emerging markets with strong incentives to deepen and diversify their financial systems to reduce their dependence on external financing.

Both physical and financial capital can be measured and described and included in the analysis of software and hardware industry performance, but neither are expected to be consequential in explaining industry differences.

Land

The software and hardware industries are not heavy users of land (which here includes natural resource inputs). The hardware industry has somewhat higher land requirements than the software industry, but land cannot be considered a critical input in either case. Access to industrial land is important for greenfield manufacturing operations, where transaction costs and the value of the time involved in slow land transfers can be as important as the actual cost of land. Export-oriented hardware manufacturing can benefit from easy access to export markets through geographic proximity and open access to maritime routes. Geographic location, in particular, can affect transportation costs (Krugman 1998), which are more important for hardware manufacturing than for software production. Governments can facilitate the collocation of firms within an industry through policies that create special economic zones or free trade zones, and thus promote the development of industrial clusters in which local labor markets and the suitable talent pool are enlarged, and technology transfer and knowledge sharing are facilitated.

Both China and India have an abundant supply of locations favorable to the erection of manufacturing facilities. Both have long coastlines. China is closer to Japan and the United States while India enjoys better proximity to the countries in the European Union.

The framework suggests that land should not be critical in explaining differential industry performance—not in supply although possibly in cost for hardware firms. Instead, the study needs to take into account two features of land use, both of which are influenced by governments: clustering and special economic zones.

Intermediate Inputs

The hardware industry has a longer supply chain and higher intensity of use of intermediate inputs than the software industry. Localizing the supply chain is a way of leveraging cheap local labor and can confer an important cost advantage in access to cheap manufactured inputs.[2] The breadth of the array of manufactured intermediate inputs in a country is an important determinant of differences in industrial growth; the menu of domestically produced intermediate inputs and capital equipment is often limited in developing, low-income countries. As a result, producers must either make do with imperfect substitutes or import the needed inputs at extra expense. Countries with shallow or nonexistent nonelectrical equipment, electrical machinery, and transport equipment industries are, therefore, disadvantaged. The hardware industry relies more on equipment and machinery than the software industry. The depth of the domestic machine-building industry, allowing for a greater degree of localization, therefore, can be a source of competitive advantage and thus stimulate rapid industry growth. This suggests the presence of a virtuous cycle in industry development: as the industry develops, the supply chain deepens, and more and more inputs can be sourced domestically. This cycle enables a particular country to better leverage its abundant, relatively immobile resources, such as labor and natural resources.

Management Processes

Management is a related factor of production separate from labor, even professional labor, for analytical purposes. A firm's top managers decide which inputs to use and in what proportion. They influence labor costs by whom they employ, how they use the employees, and what complementary inputs are added, not only plant and equipment but also technology and infrastructure. Managers determine the location of the firm, its lines of business, its efforts to export or invest abroad, and its alliances with foreign or other domestic firms. They shape the firm's culture and its business strategy, key factors in its long-term competitiveness. Thus, the availability of managerial talent with the right qualifications and experience should be an important factor for industrial development. Popular and academic literature about Chinese and Indian software and hardware industries suggests four aspects of management processes that are potential discriminators between these two countries' industries.

Quality

Quality is essential for both software and hardware, especially for export success. Both countries' reputations for quality had to be earned over time, and the liability of foreignness had to be overcome for export success. Establishing a reputation for quality is a way to overcome that initial liability. The analysis asks whether quality processes stressed by company managers explain differences in their industries' growth and development.

Corporate Culture

The way in which the workforce of a company is managed may be termed the corporate culture. Corporate cultures vary widely, but firms in a particular industry tend toward similar cultures, driven by alignment with key success factors in those industries. A widely noted feature of the software industry is its distinctive corporate culture, characterized by informality, lack of hierarchy, and greater worker empowerment and flexibility. This culture is seen as well attuned to an industry that succeeds through rapid innovation and short time to market for new products. Manufacturing, in contrast, places greater emphasis on collaboration, consistency, and discipline to ensure low error rates in product development and production. This requirement lends itself to a more formal, hierarchical, and collective corporate culture. Thus, do differences in national culture make it easier for certain corporate cultures to develop in some countries than in others?

Any discussion of culture in a population must recognize that there is wide dispersion around a central tendency. Hence, for a small industry in large countries like China and India, enough people may be in the "tails" of the cultural distribution to create appropriate corporate cultures different from the cultural norms or central tendencies. National culture is therefore likely to have its strongest influence in new industries for which the optimum corporate culture has not yet been discovered. To begin, companies may select staff at random across the distribution of cultural traits, and only from learning by doing move toward identifying the optimum cultural traits, and selecting for these in later staffing decisions.

Successful corporate cultures for a given industry can be seen as one facet of industry technology. As with other facets of technology, the appropriate corporate culture can be acquired by contact with global best practices. Thus, the degree of company exposure to global industry may influence the speed with which corporate culture in the industry in a specific country converges toward the global optimum. The original distance between the national culture and the optimum corporate culture will also influence how quickly the corporate culture approaches its industry optimum.

China and India display important differences in some dimensions of national culture, and production processes for software and hardware are substantially different, regardless of culture. How good is the match between national culture and the optimum corporate culture in each of these two industries? Does the way in which corporate culture fits with national culture contribute to the explanation of differential software and hardware industry performance? Does the degree of exposure to the global industry affect the adoption of optimum corporate culture?

Technology

Software and hardware industries are undergoing rapid technological change. Product life cycles are short, making research and development crucial. In markets at the technological frontier, research and development costs of 10 to 20 percent of revenues are commonplace. However, in developing countries, technological improvements are usually made by adapting innovations that have occurred elsewhere and are typically within the technological frontier. China and India, both latecomers to information technology development, can derive great benefits simply by "catching up" and adapting technologies and ideas developed abroad. Catching up in the technology arena, however, is not a trivial matter. It involves significant innovation in modifying technologies to local conditions and, therefore, requires substantial engineering skills and capacity for learning by doing. Technology transfer calls for mobility of technical knowledge as well as local capacity to absorb and adapt ideas developed elsewhere. For both technology mobility and capacity, the protection of intellectual property rights is an important characteristic of the business environment.

Technological innovations bring rapid productivity improvements, particularly in hardware manufacturing. In general, the services sector shows a slower rate of productivity improvement than manufacturing, and the software services industry is no exception. Nevertheless, the influence of technology needs to be considered in explaining software and hardware industry growth and development, although in China and India specifically the influence might not be great.

International Alliances

Exporting and investing abroad are two well-known methods of achieving international growth. Nonequity strategic alliances can also be employed in conjunction with exporting. Especially for industries in countries that were not well integrated into the global economy in the past—including China and India—industrial growth through alliances is an inexpensive and quick way to reach foreign markets. Chinese hardware firms and Indian software firms both took advantage of such alliances. The firm's top managers can seek to form international alliances as part of a foreign market–seeking strategy. This analysis seeks to determine the extent to which international alliances were formed and the extent to which they contributed to the firm's growth and distinguished it from firms that did not follow the alliance strategy.

Alliances can also be formed with domestic firms to achieve specific production, marketing, or technology objectives. The firms in such an alliance should be more competitive because of their joint activity, but their exporting performance in particular need not be affected.

Business Environment

The quality of policy, regulatory, and institutional factors may have a significant effect on the decisions of mobile factors of production about where to locate, on how effectively firms and industries can make use of available resources, and whether to invest in socially desirable projects. This section looks at the importance of these factors in the context of the hardware and software industries.

Market Competitiveness

Firms operating in more competitive home-country markets can be expected to be pressed to be more competitive themselves, and accordingly to thrive and grow faster than firms in less-competitive home markets. Market-competitiveness indicators are many—among them are the number and size distribution of firms and ease of entry into the market. A firm's protection from international competition through import tariffs or restrictions on inward foreign direct investment also suggests the degree to which the firm faces competition.

Institutions and Infrastructure

Effective institutions—legal, financial, regulatory, educational—underpin well-functioning markets. They supply inputs such as financial services and educated labor, safeguard the firm's contracts and property, contribute to efficient resource allocation, establish fair rules of the game, and, if they function well, reduce transaction costs. Governments are responsible for much of the creation and functioning of institutions, which are important for software and hardware firms equally.

Infrastructure services are both immobile and highly dependent on government policies. Infrastructure can play a catalytic role in the development of particular industries. Software production has modest infrastructure requirements. Software firms need a reliable power supply, urban transportation to bring staff to work, and broadband telecommunications connectivity. Other elements of physical infrastructure—roads, rails, and ports—are relatively unimportant. Electric power needs to be reliable, but the amount of power required is modest. Technological change has led to dramatic declines in the cost of bandwidth while making it less location dependent, which has reduced the importance of connectivity as a differentiating factor in the availability and cost of infrastructure services. International satellite telecommunications protects firms from weaknesses in national telecom infrastructure.

Hardware manufacturing has more requirements than software production: it relies more on logistics, such as ports, road, and rail transportation, but broadband connectivity is not as critical.

Government Policy

In general, government policies that yield macroeconomic stability and regulatory certainty are conducive to industrial growth. Those outcomes are especially favorable for capital-intensive industries that require long-term investments. Firms will distort their capital-labor resource allocations if they face volatility and uncertainty, substituting labor for capital because reliance on cheap labor provides flexibility to cope with uncertainty.[3] The degree of macroeconomic stability and regulatory certainty, therefore, contributes to differences in performance both between countries and between industries. Such policies are more important for the hardware industry, which requires greater commitments of capital and longer payback periods, than for the software industry, which relies more on skilled labor. In addition, the products of the software industry are more mobile across national boundaries. Consequently, the software industry is less dependent on national economic policies and the domestic business environment.

Governments also enact policies specific to industries. Frequently, the policies consist of incentives intended to promote the industries, such as tax relief, research and development subsidies, government procurement of output, and preferential trade or investment regulations, including duty-free imports of components and exemptions from foreign ownership limits. An explanation of the growth of a particular industry must take into account the availability of such policies, and the extent to which the policies are actually effective in achieving their aims.

Demand

The demand side of the market needs to be added to the above supply-side forces affecting industry growth.

Growth in output and incomes stimulates the growth of an industry, especially software and hardware industries. Global spending on these industries' products and services has increased much faster than GDP growth overall for many years. The demand for software and hardware products and services is generally income elastic so that demand increases faster than economic growth (as measured by income). When industries are integrated into the global marketplace, differences in income levels and income growth do not account for cross-country differences. Where domestic markets are protected from international competition, however, the size and the growth of the domestic market can be an important factor for explaining cross-country differences in industry performance. Protection of the domestic industry can result from policy barriers to trade (tariffs, quotas, and the like) or from natural factors such as transportation costs (for hardware) or language barriers (for software).

Government as a major client can affect demand conditions for the development of the industry. Government policies can affect demand conditions in other ways as well. Deliberate policies to increase government purchases of certain products from local producers may have a stimulating effect on the industry. Protectionist measures to reduce import competition are typically intended to divert demand toward domestic products.

* * *

The chapters that follow use this framework to analyze the differential growth patterns of the software and hardware industries in China and India. Because the framework involves macroeconomic factors, including trade policies and the investment climate, the analysis needs to put the development of these industries into the historical context of the evolution of economic policies and the investment climate in each country, the subject of chapter 3.

Notes

1. These paragraphs rely in particular on the work of Porter (1990) and subsequent interpretations applied to the industries studied here, such as that of Kapur and Ramamurti (2001).

2. This argument implies some barriers to trade, such as high transportation costs, import and export duties, or imperfect substitutability between imported and domestically produced equipment and machinery. Otherwise, if cheaper locally produced machinery and equipment are perfect substitutes for imported ones and can be traded at minimum transaction costs, they will be exported at prevailing world prices.

3. Paradoxically, Indian firms substitute capital for labor despite the relative abundance of labor, because of a combination of generous tax depreciation allowances for capital goods and labor regulations that reduce the flexibility of labor (see chapter 4).

Chapter 3

The Legacy of China's and India's Investment Climates

The framework laid out in chapter 2 focuses on the determinants of industrial growth as a combination of micro factors (inputs, management, technology) within a macro context of the business environment and investment climate. This macro context has evolved as a result of government policies that have undergone major changes at various times, especially since 1990. Government policies can have lasting economic impacts on industrial structure. Hence, the context in which growth is currently taking place in these industries differs dramatically from the context in which they first became established in the 1980s, which itself was shaped by government policies of earlier years. The characteristics of China's and India's economies during the period of rapid growth of the software and hardware industries over the past 30 years thus must be placed in a longer historical context. The earlier evolution of these economies created the initial conditions within which the software and hardware industries emerged. This chapter summarizes key aspects of this historical context, highlighting those developments with the most important lingering impacts on the investment climate: the legacy of earlier economic development.

China and India before World War II

The period before World War II was markedly different for China and India. In India, British colonial rule provided government authority and modern institutions that led to economic and political stability and gradual modernization. In contrast, in China the period was violent and marked by major discontinuities. In adjusting to the modern world, China had to cope with enormous problems stemming from lack of strong government, including warlordism, economic dislocation, internal strife, and foreign invasion. China had been under strong foreign influence for more than a century following the first Opium War of 1839–42, but apart from a few foreign concessionary areas along the coast, had borrowed few modern institutions.

Before World War II, the Chinese economy was predominantly traditional. Agriculture accounted for 62 percent of net national product in 1933. In manufacturing, the traditional sector (mostly handicrafts) accounted for 72 percent of overall production. The modern sector (defined as using Western-type techniques) took hold in pockets of the economy, such as banking, pig iron ore and iron ore production, and coal production.

The structure of China's foreign trade reflected the traditional character of the economy. In 1930, for example, agricultural products accounted for 45 percent of exports, minerals for 4.6 percent, semi-manufactured goods for 15.7 percent, and manufactured goods for 34.4 percent. Altogether, machine-made products contributed only 23 percent of exports.[1]

For the economy as a whole, the modern sector contributed very little to total national income in the 1930s. According to various estimates, the total contribution to net national product by the modern sector in mining, manufacturing, transportation, and banking amounted to only 6.6 percent in 1933 (Chi-Ming 1963; Perkins 1975). The modern manufacturing sector was geographically concentrated in Japanese-occupied Manchuria and a few coastal treaty-port cities and linked more with foreign economies than to China's interior. After World War II, therefore, China found itself with a largely dual economy dominated by traditional industries.

In India, the British instituted a common law legal framework supported by independent and competent judicial institutions (World Bank 2004a).[2] The British also provided a stable currency and banking system pegged to the gold standard, integrated India into the international trading system, and built infrastructure (notably ports and railways) and a strong public administration. These policies fostered the development of trade and the institutions that accompany it. As intellectual property became more important during the industrial revolution, India participated in the British intellectual-property framework of patent protection. Perhaps most important, the British economic framework put almost all economic activity in private hands. As a result, India developed a strong base of private enterprises (Roy 2002). At first, colonial corporations dominated many markets, but over time Indian enterprises came to prominence. By the time of independence in 1947, therefore, India possessed a strong base of domestic private enterprises. Between 1850 and 1938, India experienced rapid industrial growth (Srinivasan and Tendulkar 2003). In 1945, India was the seventh largest industrial country by volume of output (M. Desai 2003).

Experiments with Socialism and Planning Post–World War II

Both China and India experimented with socialism and central planning in the years following World War II. The approaches taken and the results achieved differed widely. India followed a gradual approach, introducing more state control but keeping its private sector and capitalist institutions intact. China pursued a radical revolutionary approach in which old social and institutional structures were swept away by social engineering. Nevertheless, the country saw a major improvement compared with the preceding period of chaos and strife: it had a strong government with the capacity to design and implement ambitious social and economic programs.

China

In the period between 1952 and 1975, China adopted and implemented a Soviet-type economy. Markets were replaced by central planning as the means for allocating resources and investments. Banks, domestic and foreign trade, and enterprises of any importance were nationalized and placed under the control of managers appointed by the state. Central planners set production targets that determined the output of enterprises. The plan also determined how outputs should be produced and who was to receive them. Prices remained in use but mainly served accounting purposes. Prices were the instrument and outcome of policy decisions rather than parameters of economic decision making. The main objective of the system was to achieve economic growth by mobilizing forced savings under the control of the planners. These elements represent the orthodox Soviet economic system, but China introduced several modifications that made it quite different from the norm. In contrast to the Soviet Union's "lop-sided stress on heavy industry to the neglect of agriculture and light industry" (Mao 1956), China attached more importance to agriculture and light industry based on the belief that such an approach would lead to a greater and faster development of heavy industry over the long term (Mao 1956).

China also resisted the temptation to follow the example of the Soviet Union in concentrating everything in the hands of the central authorities, which shackled local authorities and denied them the right to independent action. As early as 1957, the Chinese introduced a considerable degree of decentralization whereby the central directives were used as guidelines for lower levels to interpret and implement in light of their specific conditions. As a corollary to administrative decentralization, more autonomy and independence were given to the units of production in China than had been the case in the Soviet Union.

On the negative side, however, decentralization led to some extreme forms of self-dependent economic development nationally, regionally, and within enterprises. This policy limited China's participation in the worldwide economy just when global technological developments and economic growth were generating tremendous benefits to developing economies pursuing export-oriented policies.

Mobilization campaigns and mass movements to achieve a rapid transition to true socialism were important aspects of China's evolution during this period. Two leading examples of this strategy were the Great Leap Forward (1958–59) and the Cultural Revolution (1966–69), both associated with enormous social and economic costs.

Despite the counterproductive economic policies of the Maoist period, the Chinese economy during 1952–75 achieved some important accomplishments. Foremost among these was a record of impressive economic growth and rapid restructuring of the economy. From 1952 to 1975, China's GDP grew at an average annual rate of 6.7 percent and industry increased its share of GDP from 20.9 percent to 45.7 percent.

India

In India, the Nehru government, which came to power following independence in 1947, set the economic framework the country followed for 40 years, through the mid-1980s. The mid-century framework, therefore, had as strong an influence as the colonial period on the structure of the modern Indian economy. Significantly, the government did not seek to replace the market-economy institutions established by the British or (as in much of Chinese- and Russian-ruled Asia and Eastern Europe) to entirely replace private enterprise with public enterprise. Rather, it worked within the framework of a mixed economy, with public and private enterprises functioning alongside each other, using public administration and law to direct the economy through a process of both public ownership and regulation of the activities of the private sector.

However, a marked shift occurred in the direction of economic policy from that of the colonial period. Emphasis was placed on national economic self-sufficiency and import substitution rather than on free trade. In place of domestic laissez-faire capitalism, the government intervened extensively to shape the pattern of economic activity. These interventions had an explicit bias in favor of small and rural industries and toward labor rather than capital, seeking to restrict the scope of large enterprises. The law of unintended consequences took hold, however, and policies intended to promote small enterprises served to keep enterprises small, thus suppressing growth. Tight regulations on the terms of labor in enterprises employing more than 100 employees served to discourage employment of more than 99 workers and pushed labor into unregulated informal enterprises. Likewise, regulations aimed at clipping the wings of large enterprises were most effectively navigated by large enterprises, leading to an expanding role for large industrial houses, such as the Birlas and Tatas, particularly in areas that were not reserved for the state.

Another unintended consequence of government intervention was that as policies were developed to foster agriculture and industry, the services sector was neglected, thus leaving the services sector the most free to grow unconstrained by government regulation. The industrial workforce stagnated: it constituted 10.5 percent of the total workforce in 1901 and 10.2 percent in 1991. From the perspective of its labor force, India failed to make the transition from an agrarian to an industrial economy. As a percentage of GDP, industry grew slowly from 11.1 percent in 1900–10 to 16.4 percent in 1940–46 to 27 percent in 2000 (Roy 2002). India went from being the leading developing-country exporter of manufactured goods in the 1950s to the 11th largest in 1999 (Lall 1999).

The impact of Nehruvian economic policies was to decouple India from the global market and to restrain the growth of agriculture and industry. Growth from 1946 to 1986 averaged 3.5 percent a year—respectable, but only half what other developing countries achieved at similar stages of development or what India achieved following economic liberalization. India's share of world merchandise trade fell from 2.2 percent in 1948 to 0.5 percent in 1980 (Srinivasan and Tendulkar 2003). Trade as a percentage of GDP fell from about 20 percent in 1914 to 8 percent in 1970 (Roy 2002; IMF statistics).

Domestically, the private sector faced investment licensing as well as direct discretionary controls, which resulted in a private sector that had difficulty responding to a changing business environment and new technological advances. Foreign investment was discouraged, thus blocking a channel of technology transfer and market access. Rent-seeking behavior drove domestic investment choices to the detriment of the most productive use of capital. Exporting withered because profits were greater in the protected home market (Ahluwalia 2002).

The early five-year plans illustrate the Indian government's approach to development during the initial postindependence years. These plans clearly focused on two main goals:

- The first goal was to ensure state control over the economy through the expansion of public ownership of production in India. Basic and heavy industries were reserved for development by the public sector. Fiscal and monetary policies were used to mobilize private financial savings for public investments, supported by the government's insistence on high statutory liquidity levels and cash reserve ratios for commercial banks. Moreover, commercial banks were required to allocate credit to specified priority sectors. To facilitate this policy, life insurance companies were nationalized in 1955, and commercial banks faced the same fate in 1969.

- The second goal was to encourage private sector participation in government-determined priorities. Multiple controls over private investment characterized industrial policy. The policy limited the areas in which private investors were allowed to operate and often determined the scale, location, and technology of these operations. This policy resulted in a highly inefficient industrial structure, supported by a protective trade policy that often was sector or even subsector specific. Moreover, during the 1960s and 1970s, protection against foreign competition was a central component of the government's strategy to achieve self-reliance. Protecting priority sectors and offering them adequate access to foreign exchange became the dominant government position. The way these priority sectors were chosen was never clear, however, resulting in a regime dominated by bureaucratic discretion and vulnerable to rent-seeking.

Trade policy during this period supported the government's approach to economic development, effectively limiting India's participation in world trade. From 1940 to 1992 in India, general controls in some form prevailed on all imports and exports. Import controls were relaxed through the expansion of the Open General Licensing (OGL) list after independence, but the 1956–57 foreign exchange crisis resulted in the restoration of comprehensive import controls until 1966. As a result of the foreign exchange crisis, India devalued the rupee and introduced some liberalization of import licensing and cuts in import tariffs and export subsidies for about one year. In 1968, however, domestic animosity toward the devaluation resulted in the reversal of all liberalizing initiatives and the tightening of import controls, which continued until the beginning of a period of phased liberalization in the late 1970s.

In fact, in the early 1970s, trade policy in India returned to being highly restrictive. Most imports were subject to discretionary import licensing or were channeled through government monopoly trading organizations (except commodities on the OGL list). The government's import-substitution policies resulted in an extremely diverse industrial structure with a high degree of self-sufficiency, but many industries exhibited high production costs and poor quality because of technological inadequacy. In the mid-1970s, India attempted to address the increased demand for capital equipment and technology through extensive import substitution in the capital goods industries and through promotion of domestic research and development. These efforts made the need to upgrade outdated capital stock and technology in many industries increasingly apparent. As a result, there was a move to slowly liberalize imports of capital goods and technology.

The policies that India followed after 1947 had a significant impact on subsequent performance. India's emphasis on tertiary education and policy distortion created a bias toward skill-intensive industries. Heavy government involvement in capital goods production promoted development of industries that required scale and capital. Rigid labor laws as well as constraints on the scale of private enterprises limited the development of labor-intensive industries (Kochhar and others 2006).

Divergence in Growth Paths

About 1950, China and India had almost equivalent national income per capita ($50–$60 in 1952 U.S. dollars). Agricultural output per person in China was higher than in India, but China was closer to the limits of its cultivable land and of yields per hectare given the technology of that time. India's industrial output was more modern and diverse and, judged on the whole, greater per person than China's (Malenbaum 1982).

From these beginnings, China and India followed widely divergent growth paths from 1950 to the end of the 1970s. GNP per capita in India increased 1.5 times, whereas in China GNP per capita increased 3.75 times (Malenbaum 1982). A look at the structural changes in the economies of the two countries suggests some of the sources of the divergence in growth performance.

The structure of national output in China changed dramatically over the period. Agriculture's share of output declined from 51 percent in 1950 to 19 percent in 1980. The services sector also declined in relative importance but more moderately, from 34 percent to 26 percent. The big shift was in industrial activity, in-

Figure 3.1 Manufacturing as Percentage of GDP in China and India, 1968–2002

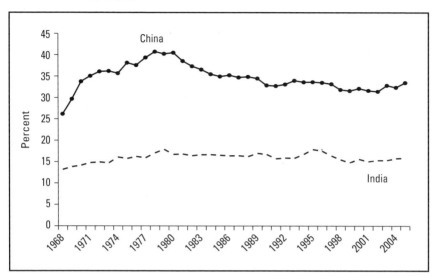

Source: World Bank World Development Indicators database.

creasing from 15 percent of GDP in 1952 to 55 percent in 1980. The same sectoral ratios show much less dramatic change in India, where agricultural output declined from 62 percent in 1950 to 42 percent by 1980/81, industry increased from 14 percent to 24 percent, and services expanded from 24 percent to 34 percent.

Industrial growth thus explains the divergent growth paths in China's and India's economies. From 1950 to 1980, China expanded industrial GDP per person to 7.5 times the level of 1952 and India to 2.5 times. China's record not only exceeds India's but also is unique in the world in the history of national growth. As Malenbaum (1982) argues, no developing country has achieved so rapid an expansion of industry as was recorded for China in this period. Similarly, records of Western development going back a century and more offer no comparable rates of industrial expansion over a three-decade interval (Malenbaum 1982). Thus, rapid growth of industrial output was a much more important force in the development of China than of India, where manufacturing remained stable at about 15 percent of GDP compared with China's expansion from 25 percent to 35 percent of GDP (figure 3.1).

The differences in labor productivity among the major sectors (agriculture, industry, and services) explain some of the divergence between China and India in overall growth performance. These sectoral differences in labor productivity were once much higher in China than in India. By 1975, the ratio between value added per worker in industry and in agriculture was 16:1 in China but only 3:1 in India

(Malenbaum 1982). With such large differences in labor productivity, shifting of labor resources from agriculture to industry in China brought much larger economic gains than the corresponding shift in India. Sundrum (1985) decomposes the 8.6 percent industrial growth over the period 1957–75 in China to find that 5.7 percent was due to labor allocation and 2.8 percent to labor productivity. The 5.5 percent industrial growth in India over the period 1951–71, however, was almost equally divided between labor allocation and labor productivity.

The much greater annual increase in capital stock in China than in India also contributed to the diverging growth paths of the two countries. From about the same ratio of investment to GDP at the beginning of 1950s, investment in China increased much more rapidly in the following decades than it did in India. In the 1960s and 1970s, the ratio of investment to GDP was between 26 and 30 percent in China and between 17 and 24 percent in India. Faster capital accumulation thus supported faster growth in China.

Market Reform

In both countries, dissatisfaction with the pace of economic growth and poverty reduction led to the adoption of market reforms that unleashed faster growth. This process began earlier in China than in India, but China started from a position where markets played a smaller role in economic life.

China

The years immediately following Mao's death in 1975 were marked by poor economic performance and a post–Cultural Revolution crisis of confidence among the elites (Shirk 1993). In this environment and beginning with the Third Plenum of the Eleventh Communist Party Central Committee in December 1978, Deng Xiaoping and his allies initiated a set of far-reaching policies designed to reform the structure of the Chinese economy. In subsequent years, these reforms transformed all aspects of the economy: agriculture, private and collective industry and commerce, work incentives, foreign trade and investment, and state industry.

Reform began with decollectivization of agriculture. The household responsibility system, pioneered in Anhui province, spread through rural China during 1978–81. Under this system, the land was divided and leased to households who became responsible for providing a certain amount of product to the collectives. In effect, Chinese farmers became sharecroppers with the collectives as their landlords. The reorganization of agricultural production was complemented by an increase in the purchase prices for major farm products. The decollectivization of agricultural production and gradual marketization of food distribution contributed to the emergence of private and collective industry and commerce in the countryside.

A private enterprise boom began in rural areas. The contract responsibility system evolved into a fundamental reform in agriculture because economic management devolved to households. Some households then shifted to nonagricultural activities and became "specialized households" (*zhuanyehu*). Many of these were in fact private nonagricultural businesses. Because they originated within the collective agricultural economy, however, their private nature could be ignored for the time being, thus obviating the need for guidelines or regulations to deal with them. In 1983, China introduced a series of central and local regulations for the licensing and control of individual businesses, taxation, product quality and hygiene, and free markets.

The legalization of the nonstate economy led to the emergence of privately run enterprises (*siying qiye*) distinct from the smaller individual enterprises (*getihu*). Such enterprises, defined as privately owned enterprises employing more than eight people, began to develop as early as 1981 but did not come under regulation until 1988. Larger private enterprises developed in various ways. Some were *getihu* that grew and took on more employees; others emerged from the leasing of state or collective enterprises to individuals. Private firms could obtain a collective license by paying an "administration fee" to a state or collective unit or local government organization and thereby receive its stamp on the application for registration. Such firms were called "red hat firms," meaning that the private owners put on a collective ownership hat to evade the government's prohibition of private firms and its ideological harassment.

The greatest change in official attitude toward private ownership may have come at the Fifteenth Party Congress held in September 1997, when private enterprise was recognized as an important component of the economy. The forum also stressed the rule of law and its crucial role in enabling a modern market economy to work well. Private ownership and the rule of law were incorporated into the Chinese constitution in March 1999. The fourth revision of the 1982 Chinese constitution in March 2004 included for the first time protection of private property and human rights.

Beginning in 1978, a major focus of the reforms was on reintroducing work incentives. China was the first of the transition economies to introduce performance agreements involving a contractual relationship between the enterprise, usually represented by its director, and its supervisory agency, in which the directors' rewards were linked to enterprise performance. Under many such contracts, enterprises had greater autonomy over sales and managers and were permitted to give bonuses to their employees and to hire temporary labor. From 1986 on, most newly hired workers in state-owned enterprises (SOEs) were given fixed-term, usually three-year, contracts. These measures were intended to put an end to the "iron rice bowl" system, under which workers were effectively guaranteed the right to keep their jobs for their entire careers, regardless of their performance. Under the new system, workers whose performance was unsatisfactory could, in principle, be terminated when their contracts expired.

Perhaps the most radical element of the reform initiatives begun in 1978 was the decision to open China to foreign trade and investment. To attract foreign investment, the government allowed certain geographic areas to offer concession-ary customs and tax treatment to potential investors. These privileges were granted to four export processing zones, or Special Economic Zones, located in the provinces of Guangdong and Fujian (1979), to 14 coastal cities and the island province of Hainan (1984), and to three coastal river deltas—the Pearl River Delta, Yangtze River Delta, and southern Fujian (1985). These regions benefited tremen-dously from their special foreign investment status, thus creating increased demand from other regions to have the special status extended to their territories as well.

The government promoted exports in several ways, including through the gradual decontrol of foreign exchange. When reform began in the late 1970s, the Chinese currency was highly overvalued at 1.5 yuan to the U.S. dollar. By 1986, the currency was devalued to 3.7 yuan to the dollar. Three rounds of devaluation in 1989, 1990, and 1991 brought the nominal value of the currency to 5.3 yuan to the dollar. In the mid-1980s, the Chinese government also established foreign ex-change markets for joint venture and local firms.

The measures to open the economy were highly successful. Exports expanded dramatically from $9.8 billion in 1978 to $762 billion in 2005. China became a major magnet for foreign direct investment (FDI) and has attracted more than $400 billion since the beginning of reform (World Bank data). FDI and export success were valued not so much for the foreign exchange they brought in as for the advanced technologies and market disciplines of foreign competition that they introduced. Success in attracting FDI and increasing exports are intrinsically linked. Foreign-invested enterprises account for more than half of China's ex-ports. The "Open Door Policy" attracted advanced foreign technology and man-agement techniques in return for access to China's domestic market.

Finally, since 1995 privatization has become an important focus of reform in China. Privatization began in earnest after Deng Xiaoping visited southern China in 1992. In 1995, after extensive discussions, the central government decided on the policy of *zhuada fangxiao* or "keep the large and let the small go." The state de-cided to keep between 500 and 1,000 large state firms and to allow the rest to be leased or sold. Estimates suggest that by 2005 more than 50 percent of industrial SOEs in existence in 1996 had been privatized and 26 percent merged or liqui-dated (Garnaut and others 2005). Privatization and the growth of new private en-terprises have transformed the structure of the Chinese economy. (See table 3.1.) The private sector has become the dominant sector of the Chinese economy, ac-counting for 37 percent of GDP in 2003 (Garnaut and others 2005).

India

India started its experiment with market reform later than China. The first break-point in Indian economic policy is generally acknowledged to have come in 1984, when Rajiv Gandhi succeeded his mother as prime minister and embarked on limited economic liberalization. Many early reforms focused on industrial and trade policy. An inefficient industrial structure supported by protectionist trade

Table 3.1 China: GDP and Investment Trends

Indicator	1980s	1990s	2000–04
GDP growth (annual avg. %)	9.5	9.5	9.2
Primary sector growth	5.4	4.2	3.4
Industrial sector growth	10.4	12.2	10.3
Services sector growth	12.3	8.2	8.3
Annual investment rate (% of GDP)	26	32	38
Public investment rate	17	18	16
Private investment rate	9	14	22

Source: World Bank World Development Indicators database.

policies resulted in the early realization within the government that industrial policy in India required greater liberalization and openness.

Major liberalization of regulations that controlled industry gained momentum only in the second half of the 1980s. The result was stronger growth in exports (annual growth of 14.4 percent during 1985–90) as well as accelerated GDP growth. Panagariya (2004) notes five broad liberalizing steps:

- The OGL list, reintroduced in 1976 with 79 items, had increased to 1,339 items by April 1990. Additions mostly included machinery and raw materials for which no substitutes existed in India.
- The government substantially reduced the share of canalized[3] imports in total imports from 67 percent to 27 percent between 1980/81 and 1986/87.
- Several export incentives were introduced or expanded, particularly after 1985, including replenishment licenses, which allowed exporters to import, provided income tax deductions on profits attributable to exports, lowered interest rates on export credit, and permitted duty-free imports of capital goods for selected export industries.
- Industrial controls and related reforms were relaxed and included de-licensing, moderation of requirements for licenses, introduction of broader definitions of goods covered by licenses, liberalization of the Monopolies and Restrictive Trade Practices Act, abolition of price and distribution controls on cement and aluminum, and tax reform.
- A realistic exchange rate was introduced, with the nominal depreciation of the rupee, thus ensuring that the real exchange rate did not negatively affect India's competitive relationship with other developing countries.

In general, the impact of the reforms of the 1980s resulted in stronger trade flows with increased imports, particularly during the fast-growth periods, as well as increased exports. From 1985 to 1990, exports grew by 12 percent as measured

Figure 3.2 GDP Growth in India

Source: CEIC database (www.ceicdata.com).

in U.S. dollars and 7 percent in volume (constant prices) compared with worldwide export growth of 4 percent in volume. In addition, industrial output showed solid gains, with industrial GDP growth increasing from 4.5 percent per year in 1985/86 to 10.5 percent per year in 1989/90.

"Growth during the 1980s was fragile, highly variable across years, and unsustainable," and it was only "once the 1991 reforms took root that growth became less variable and sustainable with even a slight upward shift in the mean growth rate" (Panagariya 2004). Data for GDP growth during the 1980s illustrate this point (figure 3.2). Average GDP growth from 1981/82 to 1990/91 came in at 5.6 percent (compared with 5.7 percent from 1991/92 to 2001/02), with much of this attributed to the strong growth between 1987/88 and 1990/91 when average growth for the three-year period came in at 7.6 percent. Annual GDP growth between 1981/82 and 1987/88 averaged a far lower 4.8 percent.

Policy changes introduced under the government of Rajiv Gandhi in the mid- and late 1980s contributed in some measure to the acceleration of growth, even though these policy reforms appear small in retrospect (Panagariya 2004).

Although economic growth accelerated as a result of these early reforms, fiscal imbalances began to emerge as both external borrowing and government expenditure at home increased. External borrowing helped to bridge the gap between exports and imports; the total imports-to-GDP ratio exceeded the total exports-to-GDP ratio by 2.5 to 3.0 percentage points during the 1980s. Foreign borrowing helped the Indian economy achieve higher levels of investment and imports, but foreign debt also rose substantially, with the external debt-to-GDP ratio rising

Table 3.2   India: Average Effective Rate of Protection
(unweighted average tariff rate %)

Indicator	1980–85	1986–90	1991–95	1996–2000
All industries	115.1	125.9	80.2	40.4
Intermediate goods	147.0	149.2	87.6	40.1
Capital goods	62.8	78.5	54.2	33.3
Consumer goods	101.5	111.6	80.6	48.3

Source: Das 2003.

from 17.7 percent in 1984/85 to 24.5 percent in 1989/90. Rising government expenditure led to large fiscal deficits, with the combined fiscal deficits at the state and central level increasing from 8.0 percent in the first half of the 1980s to 10.1 percent in the second half. The result was an increase in current account deficits, falling reserves, and a balance of payments crisis in 1991.

In 1991, Iraq invaded Kuwait, causing a spike in oil prices and disruption of remittances. This was the last straw for the fragile balance of payments position created by the prevailing economic policies in India. The ensuing balance of payments crisis gave rise to a strong commitment to progressive economic liberalization, which has become a cross-party consensus surviving numerous changes of government since 1991. Although the pace of economic reform has varied, the move toward dismantling government restrictions on trade, investment, and private enterprise has remained consistent.

The exchange rate system was transformed from a discretionary basket-pegged system to a market-determined, unified exchange rate over the two-year period 1991–93. The heavy anti-export bias in the trade and payments regime was substantially reduced by a phased reduction in the exceptionally high customs tariffs and a phased elimination of quantitative restrictions on imports, which was finally completed in 2001. Reduction in tariff protection has been less far-reaching (see table 3.2). During 2004/05, the unweighted average protective tariff for industrial goods was slightly below 20 percent. Although India's tariff levels are significantly lower than in 1991, they remain among the highest in the developing world. China's import duties, for example, averaged 9.8 percent in 2007.

The government also reformed the tax structure, which, according to the Ministry of Finance, "had become unduly complex, economically unjustifiable in many respects and administratively unsatisfactory. Special exemptions and preferences had proliferated; nominal rates were high, and evasion widespread. Tax rates and procedures changed frequently, and tax policies encouraged economically unsound investment and production choices" (Kelkar 2003). The government focused on reducing and removing the complexities and inconsistencies of the Indian tax system. This action resulted in fundamental changes to the income tax structure that included decreases in individual and corporate tax rates and improved tax administration measures.

Figure 3.3   Foreign Investment in India: 1993–2004

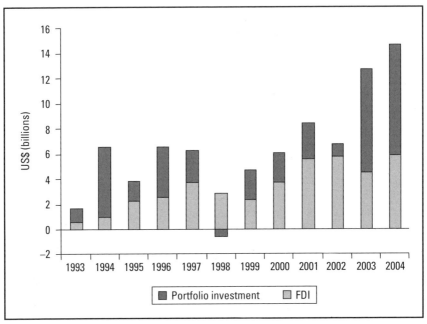

Source: CEIC database.

The financial sector underwent substantial reform during the 1990s to improve the efficiency and quality of intermediation. These reform measures included the partial privatization of several banks and financial institutions and the entry of private (including foreign) banks, mutual funds, and other financial intermediaries into financial sector activities (Basu 2005). The reforms also allowed financial institutions to set lending and deposit rates, abolished controls on capital issues, and improved regulation of capital markets under a newly established independent regulator, the Securities and Exchange Board of India.

FDI was significantly liberalized over time with 100 percent foreign ownership allowed in most sectors (although restrictions remain in some key sectors, such as retail and banking). As a result, FDI inflows increased from $97 million in 1990/91 to $5.6 billion, or nearly 1 percent of GDP, in 2004/05 (World Bank World Development Indicators). As a result of remaining high levels of protection, FDI into India has been oriented mainly to the protected domestic market rather than to the use of India as a base for exports.

Capital account liberalization also facilitated greater flows of foreign portfolio investment, although until 2004 these investments were concentrated in a small number of blue chip companies that met international investor requirements for corporate governance, shareholder protections, liquidity, and the like (see figure 3.3).

Table 3.3   India: GDP and Investment Trends

Indicator	1970s	1980s	1990s	2000–04
GDP growth (annual avg. %)	3.2	5.6	5.8	5.8
Agriculture, Fisheries, Forestry sector growth	2.0	3.4	3.0	2.2
Industrial sector growth	4.0	7.0	5.8	5.8
Services sector growth	7.2	6.9	7.6	7.3
Average investment rate (% GDP)	—	22.0	23.0	24.8
Public investment rate	—	10.0	7.8	5.8
Private investment rate	—	12.1	15.2	19.0

Source: World Bank database.
Note: — = Not available.

As a result of economic reform, the pace of growth picked up, particularly during the five years following the balance of payments crisis. Lifting controls on licensing, technology import, and foreign investment resulted in a significant increase in industrial investment driven by the private sector, thus spurring growth in the first half of the 1990s (table 3.3). Private investment grew by 16.3 percent per year between 1992 and 1996. For the decade of the 1990s, however, GDP remained only marginally above the average for the 1980s, because of weaker growth after 1996. Several interpretations have been proffered about why growth slowed. One of the most plausible explanations is that Indian industry, operating largely in commodity sectors, responded to the boom years of the early 1990s by substantially increasing capacity on the expectation that profits would continue to be dependent on production increases meeting traditional domestic shortages (Krueger 2002). By 1996, however, overcapacity, combined with a liquidity crunch and domestic political uncertainty, which translated into tempered economic expectations, resulted in the economic slowdown of the late 1990s.

The reform triggered an export boom, with total exports of goods and services increasing from $18 billion in 1990/91 to almost $65 billion in 2003/04, but the boom was uneven. Following substantial growth in the early 1990s, trade reform slowed, and firms faced increased competitive pressure and shrinking profit margins. Export growth slowed as a result. In the next few years, Indian corporations pushed to improve competitiveness and productivity. Efforts intensified as the Indian government moved to liberalize FDI rules and allow the entry of multinationals. After 1999, export growth resumed its upward trend, spurred by exports of services and, to some extent, manufactured goods. In fiscal year 2004/05, Indian exports grew to $80.8 billion, a 50 percent increase over 2002/3 (see figure 3.4).

The largest 10 exporting industries remained fairly stable from 1993 to 2003, except for the rise to prominence of software. All of the more competitive sectors (for example, chemicals, textiles, computer software) have increased their shares. The export shares of the state-dominated sectors—air transport services and

Figure 3.4   Annual Exports of Goods and Services from India: 1990–2004

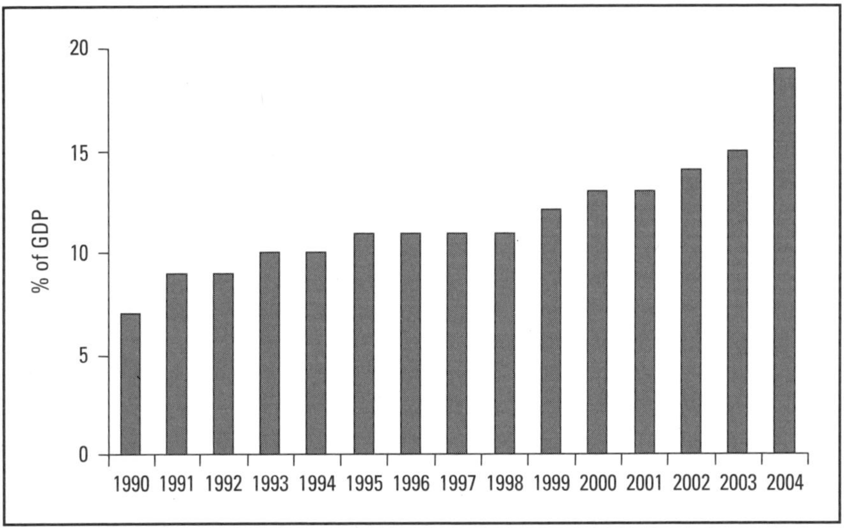

Source: CEIC database (www.ceic.com).

petroleum products—declined in the period 1993–2003. According to the World Trade Organization, India had the fastest growing services sector in the world over this period—sales of services expanded at a 17.3 percent compound annual growth rate and accounted for nearly half of the country's total exports as of 2003.

Some areas have remained relatively untouched by reform, such as the provision of infrastructure, which remains dominated by public utilities. Infrastructure user charges do not reflect the cost of supply, and theft and misuse are major problems. Telecommunications is the exception to this situation. Progressive liberalization of telecommunications led to rapid growth of private cellular and, more recently, fixed-line providers, driving tariff levels to among the lowest in the world (approximately two cents per minute for mobile service) and improving service levels dramatically (see figure 3.5). The government has invested heavily in some aspects of infrastructure (notably roads) and private investment in ports has been significant, but infrastructure provision as a whole remains subject to weak management and underinvestment.

Reform has been insufficient for small scale industries (SSIs), too. The policy of reserving production of certain items for this sector persists, which restricts investment in plant and machinery in any individual SSI unit to a narrowly defined investment ceiling. Since the late 1970s, this policy has encompassed about 800 items. Despite 1997 and 2001 government reports suggesting that the policy of reservation be abolished, about 590 items remain reserved. Small firms that produce goods classified as reserved cannot expand, achieve economies of scale, or

Figure 3.5   Average Telecommunications Tariff Rates in China and India

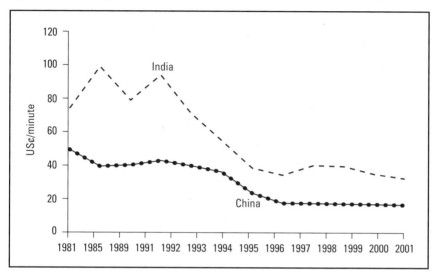

Source: CEIC database (www.ceic.com).

improve efficiency. Labor regulations also have not been reformed and continue to affect firms employing more than 100 staff. Firms are increasingly finding loopholes in these laws, particularly with regard to services sector workers (who may be employed on contracts or classified as "essential workers" exempt from many labor regulations, a practice endorsed by the state government of West Bengal).

More generally, political opposition has resulted in limited progress in privatizing SOEs and reforming public sector services, such as health and education. In addition, the efficiency of private investment in the agricultural sector has been hampered by minimum support prices for agricultural products, input subsidies, and laws and procedures that create barriers to trade and movement of agricultural commodities and prevent corporate investment in agriculture.

Comparison of Approaches to Reform

This section emphasizes the salient similarities and differences in India's and China's approaches to reform. In both countries, crises triggered shifts in policies, orienting them toward reform. In China, the painful memories of the Cultural Revolution shaped the approach to reform. In India, the 1991 macroeconomic crisis provided the major impetus.

Political considerations also played a role in these reforms. In China in the aftermath of the Cultural Revolution, the legitimacy of the ruling Communist Party became predicated on delivering growth and shared prosperity. According to Rodrik and Subramanian (2004), the attitudinal change in India that triggered the transition to a higher growth path was motivated by the perceived need by the ruling Congress Party to counter the threat posed by the Janata Party.

Similarities also extend to the speed of reform. Both countries adopted a gradual approach to reform and liberalization, a politically feasible approach because it avoids creating significant losers in society.

Significant differences appear in reform approaches. India had a modern regulatory and legal framework, which was rendered ineffective by a negative attitude toward business. Once the attitudinal change occurred, the response by the private sector and the economy was robust, leading to India's crossing the 5 percent growth level. China did not have an adequate institutional framework but, like India, engineered a major change in attitude toward business and development.

China followed a different regulatory approach, which has been called "first develop then regulate." A key feature of this approach was reform of the administrative system. Despite the lack of political liberalization, China reformed its bureaucracy substantially and early in the reform process. The government encouraged bureaucrats to become businessmen, aligned incentives for bureaucratic promotion with market-based indicators of growth and development, undertook a major drive toward decentralization that shifted responsibilities and resources to lower levels of the government, and forced government agencies to sell their services to make up for cuts in budget allocations (see box 3.1). The reforms created local governments with strong incentives to promote development of their economies.

The administrative reforms also created a congruence of interests between the emerging private sector and the government. Local governments wanted jobs, which the private sector was best at providing. This congruence of interests provided protection of private property rights in effect, even in the absence of a legal and regulatory framework.

The process of administrative reform also led to intense interjurisdictional competition in China to attract private investment. This competition made local governments responsive to the needs of private investors and thus created incentives among local governments to learn, innovate, and improve the business climate. China created an environment in which incentives were aligned to support development first and in which laws and regulations only gradually caught up with reality. India gave less local discretion, with most key policies determined at the national level.

Legacy: The Conditions for Industrial Growth

The paths taken by China's and India's economies left each one with marked strengths and weaknesses. On the positive side, China has a system in which local governments have strong incentives to support growth and development. On the negative side, however, this approach has led at times to government interference, corruption, segmentation of the domestic market, and difficulties in macroeco-

---

Box 3.1 China's Early Approach to Science and Technology (S&T)

Before the mid-1980s, political and administrative confusion continued to hamper research and development (R&D). Even when technological innovations did occur, the R&D establishment had little incentive to introduce them into the economy. The organizational structure prevented interchanges between the different spheres of production and research, and an undefined ownership structure ensured that few products moved into production. In a socialist commodity economy, no one could be sure if an innovation was the property of the scientist, the scientist's home institution, or the state. Most enterprises treated technology as a public good and refused to reimburse S&T units from which the technology was transferred.

By the mid-1980s, the Chinese became increasingly aware of the need for fundamental reform of the S&T system. Some measures first developed in the course of economic reform were applied to the S&T system. In March 1985, the Communist Party issued a document clarifying the reforms believed necessary to create the organizational structures capable of ensuring that the S&T system made contributions to economic growth. The "Decision of the Central Committee of the Chinese Communist Party (CCP) Concerning the Reform of the Science and Technology Management System" reformed the system for funding allocation and decreased state budgets for research institutes, expanded technology markets, and encouraged cooperation between research and production units.

The decision encouraged universities and independent research institutes, which were faced with increased financial pressure and reduced budgets, to take advantage of the broadening of the parameters of accepted ownership structures to launch their own commercial ventures. As long as they fulfilled their primary work tasks and did not encroach on the technical or economic interests of their original work units, S&T personnel were allowed to "engage in spare time technological work and consulting services." They were entitled to payment for such work but would be required to hand over part of their income if they used technological results, data, or equipment drawn from their home units. Practices along these lines actually predated the decision by about five years, but the decision legitimized the practice and provided additional incentives. Many of the most famous and successful *minying* (private) enterprises originated from the Chinese Academy of Sciences (CAS) during that time. With budget reductions of almost 70 percent, branches of the academy established dozens of spin-off enterprises. The CAS acted as an incubator for the first spin-off companies, granting permission for commercial initiatives through sometimes very ambitious policies that dictated the relationship between central institute and the company. The CAS typically advanced capital to these enterprises to be repaid once the company became commercially successful. In many cases, the CAS also provided office space in its buildings.

Sources: Baark 1987; Kennedy 1997.

---

nomic control. China's industrial sector remains heavily dominated by SOEs, and the banking sector by state-owned banks. However, China's approach has led to synergistic development, with the government able to channel financial resources through the banking sector to support industrial growth; but the late development of a domestic private sector in both the industrial and banking sectors reduced the dynamism and responsiveness of these sectors. To a large extent, FDI has filled the gap left by lack of domestic private investment.

Table 3.4   Comparative Performance, 2004

Indicator	China	India
Exports of goods and services (% annual growth)	28.4	28.1
Exports of goods and services (% GDP)	34.0	18.1
High tech exports (% manufactured exports; 2003)	29.8	4.9
Gross fixed capital formation (% GDP)	43.3	31.6
ICT expenditure (% GDP; 2003)	7.8	4.6
Manufacturing value added (% GDP)	32.4	15.8
Manufacturing value added (% annual growth)	9.0	8.7

Source: World Bank World Development Indicators database.
Note: ICT = Information and communication technology.

Consequently, China has among the highest investment rates in the world, and an economy that is heavily industrialized (32 percent of GDP) with a strong outward orientation (exports at 34 percent of GDP and growing 28 percent a year in 2004). It has benefited from strong domestic research and the transfer of technology through FDI. As a result, high technology accounts for nearly 30 percent of exports (see table 3.4).

For its part, India possesses the deeply entrenched institutions necessary for the effective functioning of a market economy, including an independent central bank, tax administration, legal framework and judicial system, transparent accounting and public disclosure, and well-functioning equity and debt markets. It also has several strong private corporations with good corporate governance, and a large, unified internal market with a functional transport infrastructure, despite its limited quality and capacity. Rodrik and Subramanian (2004) analyzed data from China and India on output per worker, physical capital per worker, education, and total factor productivity, and concluded that Indian institutions are better than China's, but India's growth has underperformed relative to institutional quality.

The constraints on economic opportunity in India over the past 50 years have also encouraged outward migration of skilled labor, leading to the creation of important networks of nonresident Indians. These networks are particularly concentrated in medicine and engineering in the United States and the United Kingdom.

On the negative side, SOEs continue to dominate several important markets (for example, banking, oil and gas, railways, and international aviation), and the functioning of public institutions has become slower and more costly as a result of pervasive rent-seeking behavior. Mid-size firms in the public and private sectors are missing from the economic activity equation. In both manufacturing and services, economic activity is split between a small number of large, formal enterprises and a large number of very small, informal enterprises. In manufacturing, the share of informal enterprises is about 43 percent as measured by value added and more than 90 percent as measured by employment. Because of the lack of government regulation of services, the software sector does not show the same duality between formal and informal sectors. Even the smallest software companies function in the formal sector.

The long period of inward orientation and restrictions on foreign investment resulted in a lack of access by Indian companies to international trade and investment networks. In 2004, India's exports of goods and services were only 18.1 percent of GDP, compared with 34 percent in China, but were growing at a similar rate. Indian manufacturing companies are less integrated into global supply chains. In 2004, the manufacturing sector in India accounted for approximately 16 percent of GDP, compared with 32 percent in China and 20 percent to 35 percent in Southeast Asian economies.[4] India's share of nonagricultural exports in world exports increased marginally from 0.5 percent in 1990 to 0.9 percent in 2003. India's services exports fared better, accounting for 1.2 percent in 2003 of global exports in services. This growth took place, however, on the back of a narrow set of subsectors, primarily software exports, which grew at an annual average rate of 49 percent during the second half of the 1990s.

Notes

1. The structure of the Chinese economy was undergoing a rapid transformation at the end of the 19th and the beginning of the 20th centuries, as indicated by the fact that in 1873 the share of machine-made products was not quite 2 percent (Chi-Ming 1963).

2. There is circumstantial evidence to suggest that common law is a favorable framework for the growth of private enterprise.

3. Canalization refers to the monopoly rights of the government to import certain items.

4. In 2005, the formal industry and services sectors in India together accounted for about 27 million jobs or less than 7 percent of total employment; some 70 percent of organized jobs are in the public sector. Formal manufacturing provided just 7 million jobs or less than 2 percent of total employment.

Part II
Software

Chapter 4

Software Industry Performance in China and India: An Introduction

The software industries in both China and India are among the fastest growing in the world. The distinction between the two, however, lies in the basis for this size and growth. India is the world's leading exporter of software services; China's software industry is mainly oriented to the domestic market. This chapter describes the software industries of these two countries, explains which features account for the differences between them, and offers answers to two questions about their performance:

- What conditions led to India's outpacing the rest of the world in capturing the software export market?
- What conditions enabled the Chinese software industry to grow quickly by serving a domestic market while failing to compete in export markets?

The analysis is based on new survey data from the IFC Software and Hardware Firm Survey (described in chapter 1 and the annex to that chapter), in addition to previous empirical studies and the published opinions of experts. The analysis is grounded in the investment climates of the two countries, which help explain how the divergent paths of economic development, supplies of factors of production, and government policies affected the growth of their software industries. Some of the findings accord reassuringly with common beliefs, but only partially. Other answers suggest new insights into the performance of these two industries.

Overview of the Industries

To describe the essential features of the Indian and Chinese software industries, this section provides data on the size and growth of the two industries as mea-

The empirical analysis of the survey data in chapters 4 through 8 was conducted jointly with Professor N. S. Siddharthan of the Delhi University Institute of Economic Growth until 2007 and the Madras School of Economics since 2007, whose contributions the authors acknowledge with gratitude.

sured by revenue and employment, describes the types of software services and products supplied by the firms in these industries, and compares their export revenue with their domestic sales. (See chapter 1 to place this discussion in the context of economic growth worldwide and in China and India.)

Industry Size

Sales revenues for India's well-known software industry are not greater than those of China's less internationally prominent software industry. The Indian industry reached about $40 billion in sales revenues in the Indian fiscal year 2006/07 (April 2006 through March 2007), and $22.2 billion for 2004/05, the end of the growth period in this retrospective comparison. These revenues include the estimated value of the output of foreign-owned, captive software development centers in India that produced for their home country parents but did not record export revenue. Sales revenues for the Chinese software industry were $64 billion in 2006 according to government statistics, and $29 billion in 2004. Table 4.1 provides details and sources for these and other data reported below.

Employment figures and number of firms provide an additional perspective on industry size. The Indian software industry employed 1,630,000 people in 2006/07, and 1,058,000 people in 2004, one-third of whom were in the especially labor-intensive information technology–enabled services (ITES) or business process outsourcing (BPO) segment. In 2004/05, India's firms numbered about 3,170, distributed between a few large firms (the largest five accounted for 44 percent of the industry's revenue) and many smaller firms (NASSCOM 2005). In China, total employment in the software services and products industry was estimated at 1,667,000 in 2004, of which about 500,000 were professionals. Estimates of the number of firms from different sources vary widely: 6,282 in 2002 (Tschang and Xue 2005) and more than 8,000 in 2005. This diversity in firm size and the consequent industry heterogeneity can be explained by the way in which government policies were implemented (see chapter 2 for the theoretical argument).

Industry Growth

Both countries' software industries have grown very rapidly and sustained this growth over a lengthy period. From 1990/91 to 2004/05, the Indian software industry grew at a compound annual growth rate (CAGR)[1] of 40 percent, and from 1994 to 2004, the Chinese software industry grew at a CAGR of 38 percent (figure 4.1). Because China's exchange rate system changed in 1994, that year is used for the beginning of the growth calculation. Calculating growth rates in local currencies does not materially affect the results.[2]

Employment. Growth in employment in the Indian software industry has been considerably slower than growth in sales revenue. Over the 1990–2004 period, the number of professionals increased at a CAGR of 24 percent per year. In China during a shorter and more recent time period (2002–05), employment growth

Table 4.1 Software Industry Revenues in China and India

($ millions)

India	1990/91	1991/92	1992/93	1993/94	1994/95	1995/96	1996/97	1997/98	1998/99	1999/2000	2000/01	2001/02	2002/03	2003/04	2004/05	2005/06	2006/07
Software and software services	209	289	382	545	803	1,182	1,798	2,929	4,009	5,538	8,280	9,965	12,455	15,574	22,193	30,300	39,600
Domestic	99	123	161	222	330	471	724	1,150	1,379	1,537	2,020	2,280	2,580	3,374	4,973	6,700	8,200
Exports	110	166	221	325	473	711	1,074	1,707	2,599	3,962	6,204	7,653	9,875	12,200	17,220	23,600	31,400

China	1990	1991	1992	1993	1994	1995	1996	1997	1998	1999	2000	2001	2002	2003	2004	2005	2006
Software services and products	—	—	517	1,077	1,294	1,753	2,478	3,147	3,296	5,006	6,772	8,893	13,360	18,116	29,060	48,400	64,000
Domestic	—	—	—	—	—	—	—	—	—	4,754	6,373	8,167	11,860	16,304	26,260	44,810	57,940
Exports	—	—	—	—	—	—	—	—	—	254	399	726	1,500	1,812	2,800	3,590	6,060

Worldwide	1990	1991	1992	1993	1994	1995	1996	1997	1998	1999	2000	2001	2002	2003	2004	2005	2006
Software and services industry	—	—	—	—	—	—	—	391,358	452,870	526,298	620,749	735,057	817,380	1,023,000	1,130,000	1,249,000	1,382,000

Sources:

For India, NASSCOM, "Software Industry in India 1995–96," for 1991/92 through 1995/96; www.nasscom.org for 1996/97 onward; see also NASSCOM, "Strategic Review: IT Industry in India," annual editions.

For China, Hu, Lin, and Foster (2003); see also http://zlin.ba.ttu.edu; Ministry of Information Industry and State Statistical Bureau of China (2006); Gong and Cao (2002).

For China 2003, Hu and Sheng (2004). For China 2004, 2005, and 2006, Chinese Ministry of Information Industry Statistics Report.

For Worldwide, Datamonitor (2003) for 1997–2002 and Datamonitor (2008) for 2003–2007.

Note: — = Not available.

Years for India are fiscal years from April 1 to March 31.

Indian software and services include packaged software products, IT-enabled services, software consulting, and software services delivered on-site and offshore.

For India, the value of software exports from overseas software development centers of foreign companies was estimated at 66,840 million Indian rupees or $1,474 million

(19 percent of software exports) in 2002/03; this ratio is used for subsequent years (*Dataquest* 2003, p. 120); an estimated $570 million or 40 percent of this amount that comes from cost centers is not reported as export revenue and if added to the figures in the table, raises export revenue to about $10,430 million and total Indian software market size to about $13,025 million in 2002/03; for 2003/04 this adjustment might add $900 million to yield export revenue of $13,100 million and total revenue of $16,500 million.

For China, software products include platforms, systems, middleware, applications, and maintenance software.

Exchange rate system in China changed in 1994 so 1992 and 1993 data are not consistent with 1994 and later data.

For worldwide data, the industry includes software products and services, software product support and maintenance, information technology consulting and training, business process outsourcing, and Internet service providers.

Figure 4.1 Software Industry Revenue over Time for China and India

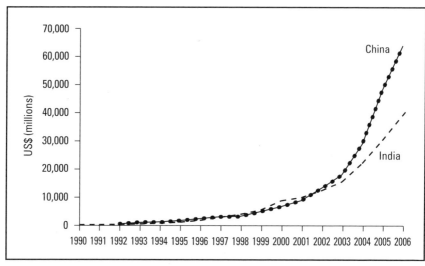

Sources: India: NASSCOM; China: China Software Industry Association, China Information World (February 2004), China Center for Information Industry Development.

was about 30 percent per year, also somewhat slower than the industry's revenue growth.

Entry. Growth in the size of an industry can result from both the entry of new firms and the expansion of existing firms. From 2002 to 2005, the number of firms in the Chinese software industry increased 2.2 times, and the industry's revenue increased 3.0 times. Average firm size increased by 37 percent, which is similar to the annual rate of growth of the industry's revenue (Chen and Hu 2002). These data imply that the overall growth in the Chinese software industry was accounted for in roughly equal proportions by entry of new firms and by expansion of existing firms.

Worldwide software industry revenues grew 15 percent per year over the 1997–2004 period. Both Indian and Chinese software industries grew two to three times faster than the world industry overall.

Types of Products or Services

The difference in the services-products mix is an important distinction between the Indian and Chinese software industries (table 4.2).

India's software industry concentrates predominantly on software services. Although Indian software services began as body shopping (see chapter 1), since the early 2000s the trend has been to do western clients' software development work offshore in India, where costs are lower. In 2001/02 for the first time, more

Table 4.2 Contribution to Software Industry Revenue by Product and Service Type

Country and software type	Percentage of total revenue
India	
Software services exports in 2005	100
Project-based engagements	55
Custom applications development and maintenance	51
IT consulting	2
Systems integration	2
Network consulting and integration	1
Outsourcing engagements	35
Application management	31
IS outsourcing	4
Support and training	9
China	
Total industry in 2005	100
Information technology services	62
IT planning	9
Implementation	33
Maintenance and support	14
Operations	2
Training and education	5
Packaged software	38
System infrastructure software	11
Application development and deployment	7
Applications	19

Sources: For India, NASSCOM (2006); for China, IDC (2006b).
Note: Percentages may not add exactly because of rounding. BPO is not software services and is not included in this table.

than half of the Indian software industry's revenue came from offshore work. In 2004/05, 71 percent of Indian software revenue was generated offshore. Indian software companies did most of this work in India, but some work was conducted at the Indian companies' operations in China or Europe. This trend is consistent with the strategic plans of Indian software companies to move toward higher–value added and higher-skill lines of business, especially systems integration and software consulting. Software consulting services were the fastest-growing segment of the Indian software industry, registering a 51 percent gain in 2004/05 over the previous year. In 2004/05, BPO also grew faster than the Indian industry overall, with a 40 percent increase. Over the longer span of time from 1999/2000 to 2004/05, BPO achieved a CAGR of 57 percent, and in 2004/05, BPO accounted for about 26 percent of the industry's revenue (*Dataquest* 2005; NASSCOM 2005).

Some Indian software companies are attempting to increase their products businesses, but the products-services mix had not changed appreciably for the industry as a whole as of 2005. In 2004/05, packaged software products accounted for only 5 percent of the Indian industry's revenue, while software services made up 68 percent of the industry and BPO brought in another 26 percent (*Dataquest* 2005). Much of the Indian software services consisted of production of customized software (about half the total Indian software industry's export revenues).

Differences in the services-products mix and in the types of data reports make it difficult to compare China's software activities with India's, but any comparison between Chinese and Indian software firms needs to account for the services versus products heterogeneity in the firms' lines of business. The multivariate work in this analysis explicitly introduces the services versus products businesses of the firms to control for effects that might be unique to each line of business.

China's industry is much more oriented to software products than India's. According to some sources (NASSCOM 2003; Tschang 2003), China's software services accounted for less than half of its software industry revenue in the early 2000s, declining from more than half in 1999 (Saxenian and Quan 2005; Tschang and Xue 2005). (The "information technology services" figure in table 4.2 includes nonsoftware services and thus underestimates China's software products orientation.) Chinese software products consist mostly of systems software and supporting software, including software for databases, communication, languages, and anti-virus uses. There is no discernible trend over time in the relative importance of these lines of business (Tschang 2003).

A majority of Chinese software activity, whether products or services, consists of less-skilled entry-level work, although high domestic demand resulted in substantial systems integration work requiring higher knowledge capital. Indian software services exports, which dominate the Indian industry, consist mostly of customized software applications development, both from project-based engagements with clients and from outsourcing engagements. This work mainly involves programming, testing, and maintenance, and in total probably more than three-quarters of Indian software services production was at the low end of the knowledge capital continuum.

Exports

Despite the industries' similar total sizes, the two countries' industries differ radically in their export intensity (figure 4.2). The Indian software industry is mainly an export industry, whereas the Chinese software industry is domestically oriented with nearly 90 percent of its 2004 revenues accounted for by the home country market. In 2003/04, India's software industry earned 78 percent of its revenues from exports—up from 58 percent in 1997 and just over 50 percent in 1990 (NASSCOM 2005). The export intensities for customized software services and BPO are

Figure 4.2   Software Industry Domestic and Export Sales Revenue over Time for China and India

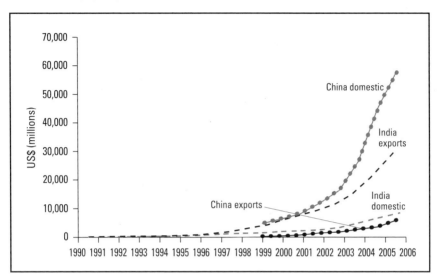

Source: See table 4.1.

higher still, well over 80 percent, while the small Indian packaged software products business is mainly domestic (*Dataquest* 2005). By far the largest single customer country for Indian software exports was the United States, which accounted for 68 percent of all exports; Britain, with 15 percent of all export sales, was a distant second. No other country exceeded 3 percent. Europe in total, including Britain, imported 23 percent of India's software, and Japan accounted for 3 percent. Exports to China in 2004/05 were 0.1 percent of the Indian industry's total.

Basis for New Analyses

Results of the IFC Software and Hardware Firm Survey provide the multivariate statistical basis for the explanation of the differences between the software industries of China and India. To give a historical and institutional background, this study relates its findings to the economic evolution in these two countries, described in chapter 3. To give further substance to the quantitative analysis—that is, to help understand the numerical findings—and to contribute qualitative insights, the analysis delves into the supply conditions for factors of production and the features of the business environment within which firms operate in each country.

The firm is the unit of analysis for the survey data. To the extent that firms in the surveys represent their industries, averages, medians, and frequencies refer to the industries, and simple comparisons that are statistically significant can represent differences between the two countries' industries. The multivariate analysis of the firm-level data is constructed so that the interfirm differences obtained also represent differences between the industries. To consider the effects of the investment climate on the firms in an industry, the analysis uses country-level information, such as government policies, which are usually industry specific.

To organize the analyses of the Indian and Chinese software industries, the study follows the framework set forth in chapter 2: factors of production in chapter 5; production processes in chapter 6; the business environment including market competitiveness, followed by observations about special features, such as English language and Y2K, as they relate to the differences between India's and China's industries, in chapter 7. Chapter 8 concludes with a brief summary of the findings on India's success in the export market and China's domestic-market success.

Notes

1. The use of the compound annual growth rate allows a single annual growth rate figure to be expressed for the entire period of years, smoothing out annual fluctuations in growth rates. It is calculated from the revenue levels at the ending and beginning years and the number of years between them.

$$\text{CAGR} = \left(\frac{\text{ending value}}{\text{beginning value}} \right)^{\left(\frac{1}{\text{\# of years}} \right)} - 1$$

2. The Chinese renminbi was pegged to the U.S. dollar beginning with a devaluation in 1994, until the 2 percent revaluation and adoption of a basket of currencies as the benchmark in July 2005. The renminbi had appreciated somewhat in real terms while its exchange rate was pegged to the U.S. dollar (and it appreciated nominally about 2 percent with the July 2005 revaluation, although that event postdates the market size and growth data reported here). The Indian rupee depreciated gradually nominally during this period but remained nearly constant in real terms.

Chapter 5

The Influence of Factors of Production on Differences in the Software Industries of China and India

This chapter examines the traditional economic factors of production—labor, capital, and land—that are available to the firm to use in producing output. Differences in either the quantity or quality of these inputs in China and India will influence the development and performance of the software industries of the two countries.

Labor Force

Characteristics of the labor force can distinguish one country's industry from that of another country's industry, and contribute to the performance of its firms. Labor that is low-wage but also reasonably productive, and important to the production of the product or service, confers a cost advantage.

Supply

In the software industry, the labor force, especially technically educated professionals, is by far the most important input, accounting for more than half and up to 70 percent of the total cost of software production, according to the IFC survey results and previous analyses (Ghemawat 2002). Accordingly, this analysis examines the size and characteristics of the labor forces in China and India.

China. China has the largest labor pool in the world—about 776 million people in 2005—and has achieved major improvements in the quality of its labor force. The level of illiteracy declined from a third of the labor force in 1983 to less than a tenth by 2000. China has become by far the largest producer of engineering and science graduates in the world. At the beginning of reforms in 1978, China was producing about 56,000 engineering graduates per year. The number of postgraduate degrees granted in science and engineering fields during the 1990s provides an example of the substantial increase in the availability of workers with requisite skills. Between 1995 and 2000, science and engineering doctorates granted in China increased 240 percent, from 518,000 to 1,247,000, and computer science as a discipline began adding faculty and students. In 2005 alone, China graduated 1.1 million engineers, implying average annual growth of 11 percent over the last 28 years up to 2005. Of course, engineers and science graduates work in many industries, not only information technology (IT). However, China produced more than 50,000 IT graduates in 2004 and had a stock of about 350,000 IT professionals (Contractor and Kundu 2005).

Although China has many technically skilled workers, more have lower-end and fewer have higher-end competence than workers in India (NeoIT 2005). Historically, technical education in China lagged behind that of other countries, but it is catching up fast. The Chinese government began to focus attention on software education in its 10th Five-Year Plan (beginning 2001). The Ministry of Education in 2001 authorized the launch of 35 model university-based software institutes, with financing from China's banks and domestic and foreign companies. The first six software institutes in Beijing were associated with elite universities, such as Peking University, Beijing University of Aeronautics and Astronautics, and Tsinghua University. Such institutes admitted approximately 5,000 students in 2002. In recognition of the limitations of an educational system in which memorization has been the dominant method of learning, these institutes use international textbooks and a corporate management model. The institutes are also allowed to offer courses and hire faculty based on market demand—unlike China's traditional, government-controlled educational institutions. The creation of these institutes demonstrates the Chinese government's ability to redirect resources quickly and on a large scale. These efforts focus on resolving the brain drain problem (box 5.1).

Both the government and private firms are developing specific new software training and English-language programs as part of an effort to build outsourcing capabilities. For example, Jade Bird, a leading Chinese software company, established a software-engineer training program that attracted more than 12,000 trainees as long ago as 2001. Foreign corporations and educational institutions are also involved. Carnegie Mellon University, for example, has contracts with several large Chinese cities for training courses based on its software system development model. Indian IT training schools are also competing aggressively in the China market: NIIT has opened more than 100 branches in China, and Aptech has close to 90 branches as well as a joint venture with the Chinese Ministry of Science and Technology.

India. Like China, India's large labor force and large number of engineering and science graduates (large in absolute terms, although small relative to the population as a whole) provided the necessary supply conditions for labor-intensive ser-

Box 5.1 The China Brain Drain Problem

China's software industry faces a serious brain drain problem. An estimated 30 percent of the students earning computer science degrees from China's elite universities, such as Tsinghua and Peking Universities, went abroad to pursue higher degrees in the 1990s—a substantial increase over the prior decade. It is difficult to find accurate data on the number of students who return to China after graduation, but most sources estimate very limited rates of return, particularly among those studying in the United States, the foremost destination for Chinese postgraduate students. Between 1978 and 1999, for example, the return rate from the United States was estimated at 14.1 percent, and a U.S. National Science Foundation study in the late 1990s found that 88 percent of Chinese science and engineering doctorates in the United States reported that they planned to stay abroad.

China's provincial and central governments recognize the severity of the loss of human capital. Accordingly, they have developed programs that aggressively court talented returnees. For example, the Hundred Talent Program developed by the Chinese Academy of Sciences offers scholars higher salaries than they might earn in the United States, generous housing packages, extensive research funding, and research teams. Despite these incentives, anecdotal evidence suggests that scholars who do return accept positions in multinational firms or in local start-ups rather than in university or government research programs.

Chinese policy makers have devoted substantial resources to promoting technical and business exchanges that involve overseas Chinese students, events such as conferences, investigation tours, joint research projects, and exhibits. Such activities enable scientists and researchers, business people, and policy makers to exchange know-how and informa-

tion and provide opportunities for overseas Chinese professionals to build relationships with their counterparts at home in China. In some cases, a government agency develops a program that directly funds such events; in others the agency subsidizes nongovernment organizations and the private sector to sponsor them. In the late 1990s, Chinese academic institutions, technology companies, and the government increased their commitment to improving external communications with overseas Chinese in the United States. In addition, the Ministry of Education established the Chunhui Program to finance short-term trips to China by overseas Chinese who were trained abroad to participate in technology-associated activities, such as conferences and research projects.

Government agencies in China also compete to recruit students to return home to start technology enterprises. Representatives of cabinet-level ministries and municipal governments from large cities, such as Shanghai and Beijing, as well as cities in more remote western provinces, pay regular visits to Silicon Valley to encourage Chinese technology professionals to return home. The visiting Chinese officials use the occasion to publicize China's favorable policy and business environment. Many municipal governments have established Returning Students Venture Parks within the Special Enterprise Zones. These parks are reserved exclusively for enterprises run by returnees. In addition to the infrastructure and financial benefits available in all science parks, the Returning Students Venture Parks address returnees' special needs, such as accelerating bureaucratic processes for establishing residency or obtaining access to prestigious primary and secondary schools for their children.

Source: Saxenian 2005.

vices as well as the skilled labor required for more complex software production. According to the National Association of Software and Service Companies (NASS-COM), the Indian IT industry's influential industry association, "India's key advantage in the global IT . . . industry is the availability of an abundant, high-quality, and cost-effective pool of skilled knowledge workers" (NASSCOM 2003,

p. 137). NASSCOM's experts are not alone in making this assessment. Pandey and others (2004, 16) state that a "large and talented labor pool has been the most prominent factor that has contributed to the Indian IT industry's reputation and success." Worldwide, the World Economic Forum ranks India third on availability of scientists and engineers, and eighth on quality of management schools (World Economic Forum 2003). The IFC survey shows that, on average, Indian firms fill vacancies for managers and professionals within seven weeks, suggesting good availability of suitable candidates.

India has strong higher education institutions focused on engineering and mathematics skills, notably the Indian Institutes of Technology, as well as engineering colleges. The growing private higher education institutions that offer IT education, such as NIIT and Aptech, complement the output of public education institutions (Contractor and Kunda 2005). Karnataka and Andhra Pradesh were among the first states to allow such private institutions. Karnataka played a leading role in setting standards for them, which helped Bangalore attract IT companies by increasing the supply of trained labor. In the IFC survey, Indian company managers rated government education policies as quite beneficial to their growth (3.4 as the mean on a 5-point scale where 1 = little impact and 5 = great impact). Many Indian graduates received postgraduate degrees in the United States or the United Kingdom, often in IT.

India's annual output of newly accredited engineers rose from 60,000 in 1987/88 to 340,000 in 2003. Between 1992 and 2002, the number of Indian graduates with engineering or IT degrees and diplomas tripled (Commander and Kundu 2005). In 2002, India added more than 70,000 IT graduates to increase its stock to more than 400,000 IT professionals.

Because domestic employment opportunities for scientists and engineers were limited, India began exporting its skilled technical labor in the form of on-site contract workers in the 1980s. In the late 1980s, approximately 75 percent of export earnings came from such body shopping. This exporting of skilled labor overcame the domestic weaknesses in the investment climate. As the business environment improved in India, firms moved from being body shops, whose role was simply as an intermediary managing the supply of skilled labor, to playing a larger role in project management (A. Desai 2003). Thus, India's abundance of this factor of production prepared the way for the emergence of its domestic software industry (Heeks and Nicholson 2004).

Labor Supply-Demand Balance

Does the Indian software industry face a labor shortage? The labor supply-demand balance question is frequently raised. Will there be sufficient numbers of technically educated graduates to join the workforces of software companies whose demand for new employees is growing rapidly? In China, a similar question arises: is the supply of technically educated labor that is qualified for software work, especially in the international software business, big enough and growing fast enough?

An idea of the employment supply-demand balance can be obtained by comparing data on employment (demand) with data on graduates in technical fields of study (supply) over time. The data are not comparable across the two countries, however, and even if they were, they are too aggregate to permit firm conclusions to be drawn.

In the view of industry observers, "Both China and India are suffering from acute skill shortages at the more sophisticated end of their economies" (*Economist* 2006, p. 11). Table 5.1 shows growth in both demand and supply (2002–05 time period for China and 2000–05 for India).

India. The increase in potential supply is much larger than the new demand. Most new employees—80 percent in 2005—in Indian software firms, however, are engineering graduates, not science graduates, although recruitment of science graduates is increasing (*Dataquest* 2006). The most rapid rate of growth in the Indian software industry is in BPO, which is less skill intensive than software services or products; therefore, much of the new employment demand may not require engineering graduates. Nevertheless, an analysis of the labor supply-demand balance by NASSCOM (2005) forecasted a slight deficiency of total labor supply to the Indian software industry beginning in 2008. The NASSCOM analysis used data and forecasts of new engineering graduates, the numbers of these graduates who would enter the industry, and the number of others (such as science graduates) who would enter the industry.

China. The increase in the potential supply of professionals in China has been much greater than the increase in demand. Not all software employees are educated in technical fields, however, and only some of the new technically educated young people go into employment in the software industry. A look at the rate of increase in demand and potential supply abstracts from these problems. The compound annual growth rate (CAGR) of engineering and computer science graduates from 2001 to 2005 was 33 percent, and the CAGR for all new technically educated persons (including science and mathematics diploma-qualified persons) was 28 percent. These rates of increase in supply are close to the rate of growth of the industry's revenue.

The Chinese software workforce picture might not be so sanguine as these data suggest. A recent study argues that only a fraction—as low as 10 percent—of China's science graduates who seek employment in a range of occupations including engineering and quantitative analysis are suited to work for multinational corporations (MNCs; Knowledge @ Wharton 2008). Although China has many engineering graduates, both absolutely and as a share of all university graduates, MNC managers claim these graduates lack the practical skills or teamwork

Table 5.1 Labor Demand and Supply
(thousands of persons)

China	2000	2001	2002	2003	2004[a]	2005
Demand: Employment in software services and products						
Total demand	—	—	1,067	1,567	1,667	1,883
Professional	—	—	320	470	500	550
Other (based on 3:7 ratio of professional to other employees)	—	—	747	1,097	1,167	1,283
Yearly change in demand	—	—	n.a.	500	100	166
Supply: Change in potential supply of technically educated persons, new graduates						
Engineering and computer science	—	—	161	185	217/352	265
Physical sciences and mathematics	—	—	206	237	278/103	339
New diploma-qualified persons						
Engineering and computer sciences	—	—	152	200	242/293	296
Physical sciences and mathematics	—	—	194	257	310/70	379
Yearly addition to supply	—	—	713	879	1,046	1,279
India	**2000**	**2001**	**2002**	**2003**	**2004**	**2005**
Demand: Employment in software services, including ITES and BPO, and products						
Total demand[b]	430	522	670	830	1,058	1,287
IT services, engineering and R&D services, and software products	360	416	490	614	742	878
ITES and BPO	70	106	180	216	316	409
Yearly change in demand	n.a.	92	148	160	228	229
Supply: Change in potential supply of technically educated persons, new graduates						
Engineering degree (4-year)	—	—	—	139	170	222
Engineering and computer diploma (3-year)	—	—	—	177	195	219
Sciences degree	—	—	—	—	540	505
Postgraduate sciences degree	—	—	—	—	—	50
Yearly addition to supply	—	—	—	—	—	996

Sources: For China, Chinese Ministry of Education, www.moe.gov.cn/edoas/website18/info14477.htm; for India, NASSCOM (2006).
Note: — = Not available; n.a. = Not applicable; ITES = IT-enabled services; BPO = Business process outsourcing.
a. Employment figures for China are not comparable between 2003 and 2004 because of a change in data coverage in the Chinese data source beginning in 2004; when two numbers appear in a cell, the first number belongs to the older source and the second number belongs to the newer source.
b. Indian IT employment figures exclude hardware-related employment.

experience needed for MNC employment, especially in services and export businesses. (More of India's technical graduates are deemed suitable for these types of employment.) Furthermore, the rapidly growing demand for labor in Chinese manufacturing industries means that many of the new university graduates are not available to the software industry.

From these data for both China and India, it appears that China's new potential supply of technical graduates available to the software industry exceeds India's supply (Wadhwa and Gereffi 2005). However, the claimed inferior suitability of new Chinese graduates tends to diminish any raw numerical advantage held by the Chinese software industry.

Labor Skill and Cost

The skills that a firm's workers and managers contribute to the performance of the firm are especially important in a skill-intensive business such as software. It is widely believed that one of the most important factors responsible for the rapid growth and export success of the Indian software industry was the abundance of skillful, technically educated workers who received low wages. Because of its importance, this belief warrants close analysis. This study analyzed labor and management in Chinese and Indian software firms to glean insights into the features of these firms that relate to their differential performance in export markets. The analysis investigated the skill of the workforce and the way in which labor was deployed in the firm, and examined the productivity of labor in the firm.

Education, experience, and occupations of the workforce. To understand the skill composition of a firm's workforce, the study analyzed the education embodied in its workers and managers, the experience they brought to the firm, and the occupations into which they were deployed.

> *The workforces of Indian software firms were more highly skilled than the workforces of Chinese software firms, mainly because Indian software firms employed more professionals who were more highly educated.*

In a simple comparison, Indian software firms exceeded their Chinese counterparts on most education and experience indicators of the skill of labor and management. Indian software firms had higher entry-level qualifications for professionals, and more Indian professionals had postgraduate educations. A postgraduate degree was required of newly hired employees in Indian software firms, and nearly 40 percent of all professionals in the firms had achieved this level of education. In contrast, a first university degree or lesser diploma was sufficient for professional employment in the median Chinese software firm, and between one-quarter and one-third of all professionals had postgraduate degrees (table 5.2).

More Indian professionals were educated abroad (although the numbers were small for both countries), and more had work experience abroad, whereas hardly any Chinese professionals had foreign work experience. (The predominance of export business among Indian software firms that was and still is to some extent conducted by Indian employees relocating temporarily to their Western client's workplace was surely a major source of this experience; whether professionals' work experience abroad preceded or caused export success has not been determined.)

Table 5.2 Labor and Management Skill Features of Chinese and Indian Software Firms

Finding: *The typical Indian software firm is distinguished from the typical Chinese software firm by having higher entry-level educational qualifications for professional employees, having more professionals with postgraduate education, and employing more professionals.*

Professionals	China	India
Entry-level qualification (median firm)	Diploma or 1st university degree	Postgraduate degree
Postgraduate education (mean percentage with)	*28.5*	*39.4*
Education abroad (mean percentage with)	2.7	5.5
Work experience abroad [b] (mean percentage with)	1.4	26.0
Share of total employment (median percentage)	*29.2*	*69.1*

Finding: *Indian software firm managers had more education and experience abroad than Chinese software firm managers, but these differences are not significant distinctions between the two countries' firms when other labor skill factors are considered.*

Managers	China	India
Postgraduate education (mean percentage with)	42.7	55.6
Top manager completed postgraduate education (mean percentage)	88.1	99.2
Education abroad (mean percentage with)	5.8	11.7
Work experience abroad [b] (mean percentage with)	2.4	36.0
Years experience of top manager in this industry[a] (mean)	17.2	18.4
Share of managers in total employment[a] (median percentage)	10.0	8.7
Skilled and unskilled labor		
Share of skilled labor in total employment[a] (median percentage)	33.0	21.8
Share of unskilled labor and support staff in total employment[a] (median percentage)	23.9	19.9

Source: Authors' calculations based on data from IFC survey.

Note: The methodology for these two analyses was logistic regression analysis where the dependent variable was binary with value = 1 for China and value = 0 for India. All variables are statistically significant univariate differences between Chinese and Indian software firms at the 0.05 percent level or better unless indicated otherwise. Variables in italics indicate statistically significant differences between Chinese and Indian software companies when many other features of the firm are accounted for in a multivariate analysis. For occupational distribution, differences between means for each country are in the same direction as differences in medians except for skilled labor, for which the Indian mean is 32.4 and the Chinese mean is 31.4.

a. Not statistically significant at the 0.05 percent level.

b. Statistically significant differences between Chinese and Indian software companies only when other skill factors are accounted for.

Indian software firms employed relatively more professionals than Chinese software firms; professionals accounted for 69 percent of employees in the median firm in India (the mean was 59 percent). In the typical Chinese software firm, professional employment was much less, at 29 percent of the workforce (the mean was 35 percent).

The characteristics of managers also differ. Managers in Indian software firms embodied more education, more education abroad, and vastly more experience abroad (some of the Indian managers with work experience abroad might have been nonresident Indians who returned to India). These are all statistically significant simple comparisons.

A more rigorous test of the workforce skill differences between Chinese and Indian firms can be achieved with a partial analysis. Accounting for all of the skill features at the same time, which features shine through to distinguish one country's software firms from the other's? Because the notable difference between the growth and development of Chinese and Indian software firms is India's relative export success, these partial differences are inevitably associated with export performance. A further analysis asks which skill features remain statistically significant when other factors that might separate the two countries' software firms—technology factors and international links—are also included.

The strong partial test of workforce skill differences between Chinese and Indian software firms showed that professional labor mattered most. Indian software firms had more and better professional labor than Chinese software firms. The Indian firms required higher educational qualifications for entry, had higher educational attainment among professionals altogether, and assembled a professional workforce that was larger relative to the size of the firm's total workforce. This outcome is a tribute to Indian software firm managers, who themselves were more educated than their Chinese counterparts. However, it was not the qualifications of management that mattered ultimately but rather how they managed the workforce, for which further evidence is presented next.

Labor productivity. A firm's labor productivity and labor wage rate taken together yield its unit labor cost. If the firm's production process is labor intensive, then its unit labor cost is indicative of its cost competitiveness. While low cost is not enough to yield overall competitiveness in product markets, it is thought to be crucial for Indian software exports. The productivity of Indian software labor is widely believed to be sufficient to yield a unit labor cost, and accordingly a unit total cost of production, far below that which could be achieved in the United States (Ghemawat 2002; Kapur and Ramamurti 2001). Consequently, Indian software firms can produce software services at prices below those of U.S. suppliers. Chinese software products firms can also compete in export markets for software on the basis of price, if their labor productivity is sufficient and wage rates low enough. This section reports a fine-grained analysis of labor productivity and unit labor cost among Chinese and Indian software firms based on the IFC survey data.

Labor productivity can be measured in a variety of imperfect ways, either in the aggregate—for nations or industries—or at the firm or work-unit level. A standard measure is output per worker—a crude measure affected by several forces simultaneously. Measured output per worker can increase if the skill of labor increases, if

Figure 5.1 Framework for Explaining Labor Productivity and Unit Labor Cost for Firms

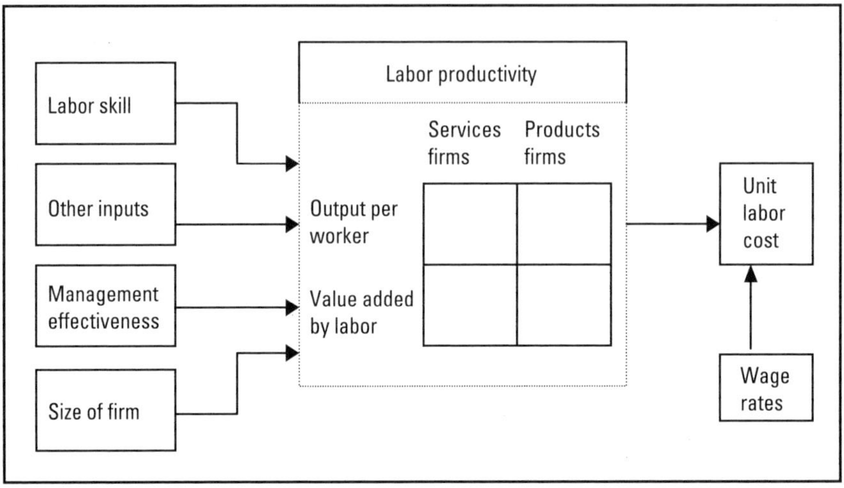

Source: Authors.

more capital and other complementary inputs are employed, if managers use labor more efficiently, or in the long run if firms grow and scale economies can be exploited. Capital-intensive industries typically have high output from little labor and hence high measured output per worker.

Value added is another imperfect measure. Value added by labor refers to the contribution of labor to the value of output produced. It is measured by subtracting from revenue the costs of all purchased inputs such as raw materials, components, supplies, and equipment. This measure varies with the labor intensity of production: industries whose inputs are mostly cost of goods sold, such as retail stores, typically have low value added by labor, and industries whose inputs are mostly labor, such as consulting firms, typically have high value added by labor.

The first step in the analysis is to report labor productivity by both measures for Chinese and Indian software services and products firms. The second step is to understand the observed differences according to the countries' possession of the expected determinants of labor productivity, that is, to explain why the productivity differences occurred. The third step is to report wage rate data, and the fourth and last step is to calculate unit labor cost for the software firms in China and India in the IFC survey (see figure 5.1).

The labor productivity of software firms is explained according to the potential determinants of that productivity—labor skill, other inputs (complementary inputs such as capital, and intermediate inputs such as raw materials), management effectiveness, and size of firm, which affects scale economies.

The analysis measures labor productivity in two ways: as output per worker, and as value added by labor per worker. Software services and software products firms have different labor intensities, use of capital, and use of intermediate inputs; therefore, labor productivity for each type of firm is measured separately. Finally, labor productivity combined with wage rates determines unit labor cost:

$$\text{Unit labor cost} = wL/Q$$

where w = wage rate, L = number of workers, and Q = output.

Because most Indian software firms are services firms and more than half of Chinese software firms are products firms, the analysis measures labor productivity separately for product and services firms in each country.

Before the analysis of productivity at the firm level is presented, labor productivity measures for the software industries as a whole in China and India are examined.

Labor productivity in the software industries as a whole. Labor productivity can be determined very roughly for the Chinese and Indian software industries as a whole simply by dividing each industry's total sales revenue by its total employment in each country. The calculation is very rough because the two countries' industries are not the same and because of concerns about data comparability, on both the sales revenue and employment sides. Nevertheless, it is a preliminary and suggestive indicator.

Using the revenue data in chapter 4 and employment data in this chapter for the two countries' industries for 2004 (tables 4.1 and 5.1), labor productivity for the Indian software and services industry was $20,976 per worker (the figure includes BPO; it approximates the figure from NASSCOM (2005) that average revenue productivity for the Indian software and services industry was $23,000 per person in fiscal year 2004. The corresponding labor productivity figure for the Chinese software industry was lower, at $17,432 per worker. These results, which show an Indian advantage, could be due to several differences between the industries, including differences in the price level for outputs that would favor the Indian figure. Most Indian firms are exporters and receive Western prices, whereas most Chinese revenue is earned from the domestic market where prices surely are somewhat lower for similar products; however, Indian software exports were in the past mostly low-value, entry-level services that commanded only low prices.

The aggregate country difference does not necessarily mean that individual Indian software firms are better performers or more competitive than their Chinese counterparts. For a more micro view, the firm-level data from the IFC survey are explored. (See Arora and Athreye 2002; Arora and Gambardella 2005; and Contractor, Hsu, and Kundu 2005 for discussions of labor productivity in Indian software.)

Labor productivity and value added at the firm level. Labor productivity was calculated simply as output per worker (sales revenue in U.S. dollars divided by total employment). Value added by labor—defined as revenue minus the cost of non-labor purchased inputs—was calculated as net profit plus labor cost (both measured in U.S. dollars).[1]

These calculations reflect translations of rupee- and renminbi-denominated sales revenue figures into U.S. dollars, which was done using market exchange rates prevailing at the date of the figures (2002). If either exchange rate is a disequilibrium exchange rate, the dollar figure is distorted. The Indian rupee was a flexible (but managed) exchange rate after the economic reforms of 1991, but the Chinese renminbi was pegged to the dollar in 1995. The real effective exchange rate, which considers countries' price inflation rates as well as the market exchange rate, gives a truer picture of a currency's effect on the export competitiveness of the firms in the country. Over the period from the early 1990s to 2002, the rupee real exchange rate depreciated, then appreciated, so that it was about the same at the end of the period as it was at the beginning—nominal depreciation was roughly offset by price inflation. For China during this period, the renminbi real exchange rate weakened, then strengthened, and was roughly constant toward the end of the period, ending up about the same or slightly appreciated from where it started.[2] (The date of the exchange rate translation in this study precedes concerns about undervaluation of the renminbi.) Although the analysis cannot judge if either currency was under- or over-valued, it can be inferred that neither country gained or lost trade competitiveness because of its exchange rate during the period of software industry growth under study.

A mixed picture of labor productivity emerges. Chinese firms in the IFC sample had higher labor productivity but Indian firms had higher value added (although the value added difference was not statistically significant). Variation among firms in the Chinese industry was greater (table 5.3).

However, the two countries' software industries are not strictly homogeneous in their lines of business (and the samples are not strictly representative of the industries). For example, most Indian firms are software services firms, whereas more than half the Chinese firms are mainly software products firms; these two types of firms have different production technologies and face different markets. Most Indian software services are exported to Western markets whereas most Chinese software (services and products) is sold domestically. Software services firms are more labor intensive than software products firms, and relatively more Indian firms are software services firms. This means that Indian software firms are more likely to have higher value added by labor than Chinese firms because the Indian firms use fewer purchased inputs (labor costs accounted for 53 percent of total costs among Indian firms in the sample whereas labor costs were 40 percent of total costs for the Chinese firms). Therefore, the analysis needs to describe labor productivity and value added by labor for software services separately from its description of labor productivity and value added by labor for software products firms.

Table 5.3   Labor Productivity and Value Added by Labor for Chinese and Indian Software Firms

All software firms (services and products)	China	India
Labor productivity ($/worker, 2002)		
Median	29,625	25,557
Mean	45,383	31,381
Standard deviation	48,339	26,095
Value added ($/worker, 2002)		
Median	11,796	13,873
Mean	18,035	18,498
Standard deviation	21,796	19,144
Software services firms (median $/worker, 2002)		
Labor productivity	10,000	24,138
Value added	11,761	14,431
Software products firms (median $/worker, 2002)		
Labor productivity	32,400	26,189
Value added	11,796	9,956

Source: IFC survey.
Note: Differences are statistically significant for labor productivity but not for value added; sample size for Chinese software services is only 13.

Differences in labor productivity and value added by labor in Chinese and Indian software firms were probably due to the services versus products difference in their lines of business. Indian software services firms probably had higher labor productivity and value added by labor than Chinese software services firms, but Chinese software products firms probably outperformed their Indian counterparts in these measures.

The result of analyzing services separately from products is that the median Indian software services firm had somewhat higher labor productivity and value added by labor than its median Chinese counterpart, although the sample sizes are small for this disaggregation and the difference for value added was not statistically significant. Conversely, Chinese software products firms showed somewhat higher labor productivity and value added by labor than their Indian counterparts (but again, the sample size is small and the difference in value added lacks statistical significance).

Why do Indian software services firms appear to achieve better labor productivity and value added results than their Chinese counterparts? The answer depends on the features of a firm's inputs and management that determine its labor productivity. Both labor productivity and value added by labor should vary with the skill of labor; the amount of complementary inputs such as capital and technology; the efficiency of management in using labor, capital, and technology; and perhaps the size of the firm, if scale economies are present. More-skilled workers means that each worker produces more output, and more capital and technology employed mean that output is greater without greater labor input. Management that more efficiently combines inputs means that more output is achieved with the same amounts of inputs. If scale economies apply, output increases faster than inputs as firms grow.

Most of these anticipated results hold true for the firms in the sample. In a multiple regression analysis, firms with more labor skill achieved both higher labor productivity and higher value added by labor (labor skill was represented by a single summary indicator, labor cost per employee).[3] Firms with more use of capital (indicated by the firm's capital-labor ratio) also achieved both higher labor productivity and higher value added by labor. However, technology input (indicated by research and development [R&D] spending) did not contribute. This result is not unexpected because Chinese software firms spent more on R&D than did Indian firms, but most of that spending is believed to have been adaptive rather than innovative and therefore would not lead to greater productivity. The size of the firm (indicated either by revenue or total employment) was marginally significantly correlated with value added but not with labor productivity. This analysis accounted for the firm's line of business so that the effects of labor skill and the capital-labor ratio are independent and separate from the services or products business of the firm. (Table 5.4 shows these results, with the nonsignificant variables omitted.)

Table 5.4   Explaining Labor Productivity and Value Added by Labor in Chinese and Indian Software Firms

	Effects of potential labor productivity and value added determinants			
Dependent variable	**Labor skill**	**Capital-labor ratio**	**Software services versus products**	**Country**
Labor productivity	Positive and significant but small; elasticity is < 0.1	Positive and significant and substantial; elasticity = 0.5	No significant partial effect	No significant partial effect
Value added by labor	Positive and significant but small; elasticity is < 0.1	Positive and significant and substantial; elasticity = 0.8	No significant partial effect	Indian firms are higher

Source: Authors.

Note: The findings are based on multiple regression analysis of IFC survey data. The four independent variables explain 64 percent of the variation in labor productivity and 74 percent of the variation in value added by labor among software firms in the sample. The sample size is 149 for labor productivity and 145 for value added. Labor productivity is output per worker; value added by labor is revenue minus costs of purchased inputs. Labor skill is labor cost per worker; capital-labor ratio is value of capital per worker.

Software firms were more productive if they had more labor skill and more capital intensity, whether they were services or products firms. In addition, the analysis leads to the inference that Indian software firms achieved both higher productivity and value added in part because of greater management efficiency.

The analysis that explains labor productivity and value added differences among software firms included a country dummy variable. The effect of the firm's country is significant for value added by labor. Indian software firms had higher value added by labor after other determinants were accounted for. Of course, country cannot determine value added; rather, the country variable picks up unmeasured contributors to value added that vary systematically by country. The prime candidate among these contributors is the efficiency of management in using inputs. (Other candidates would be other inputs not measured or included in this analysis, except the technology and scale economies already considered, but because software production relies mostly on labor and equipment, the influence of other inputs is doubtful.) By inference, the management of Indian software firms, in particular software services firms, was more efficient than Chinese management in using labor and capital. The analysis below pursues the ways in which management affected the performance of Indian and Chinese software firms.

While the effect of management efficiency can only be inferred from this analysis, the amounts of labor skill and capital that software firms in India and China possessed can be documented. Looking separately at software services and software products firms indicates that Indian software services firms had significantly more skilled labor (using the summary labor cost per worker indicator). This finding mirrors the one reached earlier in this chapter using different indicators of labor skill (education, experience, and occupational distribution). In addition, Indian software services firms were slightly but not significantly more capital intensive, and their firm size in the IFC sample was much larger (although firm size is not important to labor productivity). However, among software products firms, Chinese firms had an edge over Indian firms in labor skill (table 5.5).[4] These differences in the resources of the firms in the two countries match up with the differences in labor productivity and value added by labor revealed in the analysis.

From the detailed analysis of labor and management skill, productivity, and value added in the software firms in the sample, the analysis concludes that

Indian software firms relative to Chinese firms had more labor and management skill, and these capabilities contributed to somewhat higher labor productivity and value added by labor in Indian software services firms. However, the same is not true for Chinese software products firms that had some advantage in labor skill compared with their Indian counterparts and thus, in turn, had higher productivity.

Table 5.5 Differences between Chinese and Indian Software Firms in
Determinants of Labor Productivity and Value Added in 2002

Feature	China	India
Software services		
Labor skill		
Labor cost per worker (median, $)	6,374	8,867
Capital-labor ratio (median, $/worker)	8,400	9,369
Firm size		
Revenue (median, $)	1,200,000	6,615,000
Number of employees (median)	110	225
Software products		
Labor skill		
Labor cost per worker (median, $)	8,844	6,328
Capital-labor ratio (median, $/worker)	4,347	10,807
Firm size		
Revenue (median, $)	1,982,400	5,339,226
Number of employees (median)	68	150

Source: IFC survey.
Note: Differences for firm size indicators are highly statistically significant, but differences for capital-labor ratio and labor cost per worker are only marginally significant. Sample size for China software services is small at 13 firms.

This conclusion accords with the observed growth and development of the two countries' industries. Software services dominated the Indian industry, but software products were more important to the Chinese industry.

These conclusions do not suggest a negative outcome for Chinese software services firms. An additional piece of evidence permits a further understanding of the labor and management differences between the two countries' firms. If differences in labor skill between the two countries' firms are accounted for, and if other differences between the firms are also accounted for in a multivariate logistic regression analysis that distinguishes between Chinese and Indian software firms (quality certifications and international links were included as additional explanatory variables), Chinese firms end up exhibiting higher labor productivity. This finding has intriguing implications: Given the labor skill in the firm and given its capital, given its services versus products main line of business, and given the quality certifications and international links of the firm, the median Chinese software firm had higher labor productivity than its Indian counterpart. Thus, some of the Indian labor and management advantage consisted of superior quality certifications and international links; once the latter variables are measured and included in the analysis, higher labor productivity was no longer a feature of Indian firms.

Wages. One of the several ways in which companies can compete in export markets is on the basis of price. Indian software companies successfully did so in the

Table 5.6 Wage Rates in Chinese and Indian Software Firms

Starting median monthly rate for new employees	China		India	
	Wages ($)	Benefits (%)	Wages ($)	Benefits (%)
Professionals	330	25	315	15
Skilled workers	240	25	168	15
Unskilled workers	120	20	78	15

Source: IFC survey.
Note: Wage rate differences for professionals and skilled workers in China and India are not statistically significant.

past in the U.S. market for customized software services. Making very rough calculations from aggregate market wage rates and illustrative firm-level labor productivity from 2002, it appears that wages in Indian software firms were about 20 percent of their U.S. competitors' while labor productivity in the Indian firms was about 50 percent less, thus yielding a unit labor cost that was much lower than that achieved by U.S. firms (the data were extracted from Ghemawat 2004). Indian software firms possessed an absolute advantage and were able to do software development work at lower prices than U.S. software firms.

Comparisons of wages in the software industry across countries are fraught with difficulties. Reported wage data depend on employees' jobs and their experience, the region of the country in which the firm is located, and exchange rates and purchasing power parities for cross-country comparisons. Wage data for Indian software services can be distorted by the inclusion of the earnings of Indian software firm employees located abroad at a client's place of business (body shoppers) who are paid according to export market wage scales. To make these wage comparisons as valid as possible, this analysis uses the starting wage rate for entry-level professionals in India and China.

The raw wage data reported by firms in the IFC survey are similar but slightly higher for Chinese software firms (table 5.6). The differences were not significant for entry-level wage rates paid to either professionals or skilled workers. These two occupations accounted for a large majority of the total workforce in the firms. Similar results were reported by Aggarwal and Pandey (2004) for the entire IT industry: annual salaries of $5,375 to $8,960 in India and $6,360 to $9,540 in China. The cost of benefits is also somewhat higher for Chinese firms: 25 percent of wages for Chinese firms as the median for professionals and 15 percent of wages for Indian firms. The multivariate analysis of differences between the firms in the two countries finds that differences in wage rates are not statistically significant. Because trade in software services and products is liberalized, factor prices—even the wages of immobile labor—are expected to be equalized (see chapter 2 for the theoretical basis of this claim). Furthermore, differences among firms in starting professional wages do not contribute to either faster or slower growth in either Chinese or Indian software firms.

Unit labor cost. A critical element in the comparison of labor-intensive Chinese and Indian software firms is unit labor cost. That figure depends not only on wages and benefits, but also on labor productivity. If Chinese software firms pay roughly equal or slightly higher wage and benefit rates than Indian firms but also have somewhat higher labor productivity overall, then Chinese unit labor cost will be equal to or lower than that of Indian firms. Unit labor costs of $0.31 for Chinese firms and $0.40 for Indian firms were derived from the IFC sample. (The Indian figure means, for example, that Indian software firms spent $0.40 on labor for every dollar of output produced and sold.)

Software services production is more labor-skill intensive than software products production (which is more capital intensive); accordingly, the unit labor cost for software services is higher than it is for software products. For China and India combined, the figures from the sample are $0.42 for software services and $0.30 for software products. The same held within countries; thus, Indian software services unit labor cost was higher than Indian software products unit labor cost, and similarly for China (but because of small sample size for Chinese software services, this result can only be suggestive). Most important, the unit labor cost of Indian software services appeared not to be lower than the unit labor cost of Chinese software services.

Another measure of the cost of labor is the overall average labor cost per worker (rather than per unit of output), which encompasses both wage rates and the distribution of occupations. This measure was higher for Indian firms; again, however, the difference was not statistically significant. (Labor cost per worker for the firm also reflects benefits and other nonwage costs attributed to labor.) This result is as expected because Indian software firms employed more professionals compared with Chinese firms, and professionals were paid more than skilled workers.

Indian software services firms did not achieve more export success than Chinese firms on the basis of lower labor cost.

Capital

Economic theory distinguishes between two types of capital: physical capital and financial capital. While obviously related, they are independent of each other when determining availability and impact on a firm's performance. However, neither physical nor financial capital is a major input into software production; thus, a more thorough discussion of the financial sectors of China and India takes place in chapter 10, in the next part on hardware industries.

Physical Capital

Software production does not require much physical capital (factories and equipment). Fixed physical assets of companies are mainly offices, which can be leased, and computers, costs for which have been dropping. Physical capital requirements

Table 5.7   Physical and Financial Capital Needs

Finding: *Capital intensity is greater for software products than software services firms.*

Physical capital	China	India
Capital-labor ratio (fixed assets per employee, $)		
Software products firms		
Mean	$27,164	$43,282
Median	$4,347	$10,806
Software services firms		
Mean	—	$16,346
Median	—	$9,369

Finding: *More Indian software firms have bank loans and more have equity or venture capital finance than do Chinese software firms in a simple comparison, but these differences are not statistically significant in a multivariate analysis.*

Financial capital	China	India
Have bank loans (percentage yes)	23.3	37.3
Have equity or venture capital finance (percentage yes)	16.7	34.5

Source: IFC survey.
Note: — = Not available because the sample size is small. The mean capital-labor ratio is much higher than the median for software products, and the mean has a high standard deviation, which indicates a few firms have very large capital-labor ratios and many firms have much lower ratios.

are lower for software services than software products. Because the services-products mix differs substantially between the Indian and Chinese software industries, the analysis does not compare the two countries as a whole but disaggregates each country's industry into services firms and products firms. From the IFC survey data it appears that Indian software products companies were more capital intensive than their Chinese counterparts (table 5.7). In the multivariate analysis, controlling for the services versus products business of the firms, the capital-labor ratio is not statistically significantly different between one country's firms and the other's.

Financial Capital

Although such firms have a modest need for externally obtained financial capital, Indian software firms were more likely than Chinese firms to have bank loans, and to have external equity or venture capital finance, but this is not a statistically significant difference between the two countries' firms

At the outset, software firms require financial capital to pay start-up costs (see box 5.2). Sometimes these costs can be met by the pooled savings of the founders. Infosys Technologies is the usual example of this type of finance. Until its initial public offering in 1993, Infosys grew without significant external financing. A

Box 5.2 Infosys Technologies: Software Startup with Early Self-Financed Growth

In 1981, seven young Indian entrepreneurs founded Infosys Technologies as a startup with initial equity of $1,000 from their pooled savings. Infosys today, with sales revenue exceeding a billion dollars, is India's second (or third, depending on the year) largest software company. Because of restrictions on imports of computers to India in 1981, the company began by providing onshore work (body shopping) in the United States, where Infosys employees worked on clients' computers. Because virtually no capital investment was required, Infosys quickly had a positive cash flow and was able to grow organically with very limited external financing. In 1993, just 12 years after its founding, the company made an initial public offering (IPO) on the Bombay Stock Exchange followed by a private placement in 1995. Before this private placement, Infosys had borrowed a total of $725,000 from local banks for various capital expenditures. The company made minimal use of debt financing. As the Indian government eased restrictions on the IT industry in the 1990s, Infosys moved toward offshore production, with most of its staff based on a large campus in Bangalore, paid for from the proceeds of the IPO. Infosys obtained ISO 9000[a] certification early in 1993 as a way to assure U.S. customers of high-quality performance. In 1998, it became the first Indian company to achieve CMM[b] Level 4 quality certification and achieved Level 5 in 2000.

Infosys has continued to grow organically, listing its American Depository Receipts on NASDAQ in 1999, the first Indian company to be listed on an American exchange. The amount of capital raised was only $75 million, but the listing further enhanced Infosys's reputation among key U.S. clients.

Sources: Nanda and DeLong 2002; Kuemmerle and Coughlin 2004.

a. ISO = International Organization for Standardization, a network of international standards institutes; ISO 9000 is a family of standards for quality management systems.

b. CMM = Capability Maturity Model and refers to a company's ability to manage the software development process.

2001 survey of 40 Indian software firms found that more than half had relied on friends and family financing for establishing a startup (Arora and others 2001).

Some software firms, especially software products firms, require financial capital from external sources to cover the development costs of new products, even after the start-up of the firm itself. India has a well-developed financial sector that includes banking services, equity markets, and venture capital (see chapter 10). Production cycles, however, are short for software services, and working capital needs are limited. The rapid growth of India's software industry, with its ample profits, means that Indian firms have been generating sufficient cash flow from operations to fund expansion from retained earnings.

Less than one-quarter of Chinese software firms in the IFC sample had bank loans, and only 37 percent of Indian IT companies in the survey had taken out bank loans. Of the companies without a loan, 93 percent said that they did not need one. Software services firms are more likely to have bank loans than software products firms, which accounts for part of the greater frequency of bank borrowing by Indian firms, more of which are software services firms. Indian software firms are on average older and bigger than Chinese software firms and, therefore, more likely to have greater borrowing capability. Some of the Chinese software firms report that cumbersome bank procedures and collateral requirements were reasons for not applying for bank loans. Indeed, software firms typically have little collateral to offer. The greater prevalence of bank borrowing by Indian firms is a statistically significant simple difference from Chinese firms, but this difference does not survive the multivariate analysis.

Many firms require capital to reach a critical scale of operations to compete in international markets. Because of the nature of the risks, the primary need is for equity. Just over one-third (34.5 percent) of surveyed software companies in India had venture or equity capital. In the two years previous to the survey, 27.8 percent had sought equity or venture capital financing, and of these, two-thirds were successful. These data suggest that many Indian software firms were able to finance their growth from (tax-free) retained earnings, having used venture capital for seed capital. The reported profitability of software companies, with gross profits averaging 20 percent of revenues for services and products among firms in the IFC survey, supports this conclusion.[5] A smaller portion of Chinese software firms (16.7 percent as compared with 34.5 percent for Indian firms) had external equity financing. State-owned Chinese software firms typically can use retained earnings as well as capital transfers from the government as sources of finance.

In China, despite the rapid development of small private software companies, opportunities for raising capital domestically were traditionally limited. Chinese software companies thus turned to foreign investors to fill the void. Foreign investors responded aggressively. In recent years, the initial public offerings of a growing number of Chinese companies and the sale of still more companies to foreign software companies proved to investors that they could exit from their investments in China. As a result, the pace of investment accelerated.

Land Use

As mentioned in chapter 2, software industries are not heavy users of land and natural resource inputs. Software firms do benefit, however, from collocation with other firms, known as agglomeration or clustering. Geographic clustering is internationally recognized as important for the development of the software industry. The industry's high reliance on the intellectual capital embodied in skilled staff, the value creation that comes from the intermingling and recombination of these assets, and the ability to sustain supporting business services and capital providers contribute to the importance of this factor. Clustering is advantageous for knowledge-intensive industries because it facilitates the transfer of tacit knowledge. When firms in the same industry collocate, their employees can learn from others, and collocation allows firms to take advantage of the larger local labor market that develops.

Special Economic Zones (SEZs) in China played an important role in making land available to domestic and foreign manufacturing and services companies and in facilitating clustering. The first SEZ was established in 1979; by 2003, China had well over 100 investment zones recognized by the central government, as well as hundreds of zones run by local governments without explicit central government support (Naughton 2007). The SEZs in many ways exemplify China's commitment to market opening through its dual-track approach, with one set of liberal policies for SEZs that do not apply elsewhere. The SEZs tend to subsidize the price of land for industrial uses compared with market allocations, aside from their international trade benefits. Although less special than before (Naughton 2007), the economic zones continue to play an important role in China's expansion drive, in promoting the development of the high tech sectors.

Nearly 83 percent of Chinese software firms in the IFC survey were located in SEZs. The Chinese SEZs, usually in coastal areas, have attracted foreign direct investment and resulted in clusters of similar firms and their suppliers. The Chinese firms surveyed reported somewhat greater importance of both the labor pool and knowledge-sharing advantages of geographical collocation than did the Indian firms, with scale scores of 4.7 and 4.2, respectively, out of 5.0. The importance of clustering, both for fostering innovation and enlarging the labor pool, has been noted in particular for Chinese software firms (Yang, Ghauri, and Sonmez 2005).

Government promotion of high tech firms indirectly by mitigation of land use problems applies also in India, where market allocation of land did not work well. The policy instrument was software technology parks (STPs). Disputes about ownership that take decades to settle, restrictive tenancy and rent control laws and land use regulations, and high stamp duties kept a large part of urban real estate off the market (Lall and Mengistae 2005; World Bank 2004b). Access to suitable land is seen as a constraint to the growth of companies, particularly in urban areas (Bhide 2004). McKinsey estimated that land market distortions reduced GDP growth by 1.3 percentage points a year (McKinsey Global Institute 2001). The creation of STPs mitigated the effect of this constraint for software companies: because of their export orientation and lack of input supply links, software companies were less dependent on particular locations and could make use of greenfield, peri-urban locations.

In India, the first clusters were established in STPs in Bangalore, Bhubaneshwar, and Pune in 1990 (Bajpai and Shastri 1999), and by 1998, there were 25 clusters (Saxenian 2000). Initially, the STPs were concentrated in the south and west to take advantage of proximity to engineering colleges, including the Indian Institutes of Technology (Arora and others 2001). Other early clusters were located in Hyderabad, Mumbai, Pune, and the Delhi suburbs of Gurgaon and Noida to take advantage of the availability of engineering skills. As the industry grew and labor became scarcer in these locations, the industry expanded to other centers of population and education.

Table 5.8   Importance of Geographic Location

Finding: *Indian software firms benefited less from the talent pool and knowledge-sharing effects of clustering than Chinese firms; this is a statistically significant difference between the two countries' firms.*

Clustering or agglomeration, Importance of firm's geographical location	China	India
Knowledge sharing among employees	4.7	4.1
Availability of talent pool	4.2	3.3

Source: IFC survey.
Note: Mean of 5-point scales; higher score means more importance.

Among India firms in the IFC survey, 88 percent were located in STPs. These firms rated the geographical location of the company as important for availability of skilled labor (scale score of 4.1 out of 5.0) and informal knowledge sharing (3.3), and also for special infrastructure facilities (3.9). These results indicate that the STPs were effective both in offering clustering advantages and in providing infrastructure.

Most of the Chinese software industry is concentrated in the largest cities, particularly Beijing, Shanghai, and Guangdong. Chinese clustering equals or exceeds that in India, with 71 percent of all firms located in those three leading cities (Saxenian 2005); 35 percent of the industry's revenues are from firms in Beijing alone. The clustering pattern reflects the concentration of Chinese universities and research institutes. Shenyang in the northeast and Hangzhou are also gaining recognition for their strong software firms. Characteristics of these locations include the presence of universities with strong IT programs, government support for the industry, and vibrant industrial or commercial activity. In some cases, such as Neusoft in Shenyang, or TOP in Chengdu, a single large firm rather than a concentration of firms dominates the industry in the city.

Among the 600 largest Indian software firms, 61 percent were located in Bangalore, Delhi (including Gurgaon and Noida), and the Mumbai-Pune corridor in 2002, and 81 percent of all these firms were accounted for when Chennai and Hyderabad were included (Basant and Rani 2004).

Locating software firms in clusters is a management decision that is beneficial because it creates and then takes advantage of larger talent pools and informal knowledge sharing among employees—but it is also clearly the result of location incentives by governments in both countries (table 5.8).

The clustering edge that Chinese software firms have does not necessarily give them an edge over Indian firms in export performance, however, because the benefits of clustering are not export biased. In addition, the greater prevalence among Indian software firms of on-site workers at the customer's place of business diminishes the realized benefits of clustering in the home-country location.

Notes

1. Value Added = Revenue – Purchased Inputs; and Profit = Revenue – Purchased Inputs – Labor Cost. So Value Added = Profit + Labor Cost.

2. The India data come from the Reserve Bank of India and use wholesale prices and export weights. The China data and conclusions are reported in Tyers and others (2006) and in Wang (2005). Each country's real effective exchange rate is export or trade weighted and does not refer to its exchange rate against the U.S. dollar alone.

3. Labor cost per employee reflects both the occupational distribution of the workforce and the wage rates paid to workers in each occupation. To be a valid measure of labor skill in a cross-country sample, similar wage rates must be present in the two countries' industries, and this is true in the IFC sample. When converted to U.S. dollars at market exchange rates, the entry-level median monthly wage for professionals, which is the largest single occupation, was $315 in India and $330 in China. This difference was not statistically significant, but if anything, its use understates the Indian firms' labor skill.

4. A comparison of capital-labor ratios across countries requires a similar cost of capital, and for software firms we refer mainly to equipment. Because China had a low-cost hardware manufacturing industry to supply equipment to Chinese software firms, but Indian software firms made more use of imported equipment, the calculated capital-labor ratio probably understates the Chinese figure.

5. This figure corresponds closely to the net profit of Indian software companies in 2001, reported in A. Desai (2005).

Chapter 6

The Influence of Management on the Software Industries in China and India

Management is part of the production process that affects a firm's and industry's performance (see chapter 2). This book offers data and draws inferences about management's impact on labor as analyzed in the "labor skill and cost" section of chapter 5. Indian software services firm managers appear to have used inputs more efficiently than their Chinese counterparts. This chapter develops this topic further and adds new management dimensions. It begins with a focus on managers themselves—the skills they possess and the practices they adopt. It continues with an analysis of two domains of business activity that are the ultimate responsibility of top managers and deemed important to the software industry—technology and international links. In this way this chapter seeks to provide a comprehensive picture of the importance of management in the explanation of software firm export performance.

Management Skill Practices

A firm's top managers can lead its growth and development in several ways, three of which this section analyzes. First is the objective skill of managers as indicated by their experience. Second, and perhaps most important for these countries' software industries, is management of the process of producing software for customers that is high quality, on time, and within budget. The success of this process can be represented by quality certifications. The third management process has two related components: the fit of key characteristics of the firm's professional workforce—represented by features of the national culture—to the needs of the software production process and the entrepreneurial orientation of the firm.

Management Experience

As seen in table 5.2, Indian software firm top managers had slightly longer experience in the industry than did their Chinese counterparts, although the difference

Table 6.1   Management Experience and Firm Growth

Finding: *Among Indian software firms, those whose top managers have greater length of experience in the software business also show faster revenue growth.*

Experience of top managers	China	India
Contribution of one more year of experience to revenue growth (percent)	−26	+7

Source: IFC survey.

was not statistically significant. Indian top managers had vastly (and statistically significantly) more work experience abroad (also in table 5.2). A comparison of two countries' industries that differ radically in their export success might be expected to yield differences in the foreign experience of managers. (However, while significant in a simple comparison, this difference does not remain important as a differentiator between the two countries' software firms when other variables are taken into account.) This section adds one further finding about management experience.

A manager's longer experience in an industry, up to a point, should produce better management of complex processes and systems, which, in turn, should contribute to more success in obtaining externally awarded, process-oriented customized software development business. In the IFC sample of firms, Indian firms whose top manager had more experience also showed faster revenue growth. Firms whose top manager had one additional year of experience turned in 2 percentage points faster revenue growth, which was a 7 percent advantage over the average revenue growth for Indian firms (table 6.1). The same cannot be said for Chinese software firms. In fact, the results suggest an opposite effect: Chinese firms whose top managers had longer experience turned in slower revenue growth. This contrast implies that Indian firms whose markets are primarily export markets benefit from more-experienced top managers, but Chinese firms whose markets are primarily domestic benefit from top managers who are newer to the industry.

Quality Certification

More Indian than Chinese software firms had quality certifications and Indian firms had more of them. Indian firms with more quality certifications grew faster, but Chinese firms with more quality certifications did not.

The ability of a firm to grow internationally, especially a services firm from a developing country, depends on the ability of its management to enter new markets abroad. When the service is quite new, as software services were, and the developing country has a negative country of origin reputation, as India did, the goal is to build confidence among potential export customers by ensuring services and products are delivered on time, in full, and within budget. Obtaining internationally recognized quality certification was the most effective way of achieving this goal for Indian software firms.

Table 6.2   Quality Certifications

Finding: *Many more Indian software firms had CMM quality certification than did Chinese software firms; this is a statistically significant difference between them even when accounting for other differences.*

Finding: *Indian software firms with CMM quality certifications showed faster revenue growth than did those without these certifications, but there was no effect for Chinese software firms.*

Quality certification	China	India
Share of software firms with a CMM quality certification (percent)	7	47
Average number of CMM certifications (for those with a certification)	1.0	2.1
Effect of having CMM certification on revenue growth	No effect	90% faster

Source: IFC survey.

In the software industry, the Capability Maturity Model Integration (CMMI) certification from the Software Engineering Institute at Carnegie Mellon University is the standard measure of quality.[1] Like the well-known International Organization for Standardization (ISO) certifications for manufacturing firms, CMMI certifications communicate to customers the level of advancement of the firm's software services capabilities and the best practice processes that the firm uses for managing software services production. These quality certifications indicate the level of management skill as well as the firm's technology level.

Indian companies have made great use of external certification to signal the quality of their processes to customers. As table 6.2 indicates, Indian software firms scored much higher than Chinese software firms on the number of firms with CMMI certifications. All of India's top 30 companies were CMMI-certified to Level 4 or 5, compared with only 6 out of 30 firms in China (De Filippo, Hou, and Ip 2005). Motorola's Bangalore subsidiary was the second company in the world to achieve CMMI Level 5 certification. In 2004, 60 out of 80 firms globally with CMMI Level 5 (highest) certification were from India (Heeks and Nicholson 2004). As early as March 2001, half of all CMM[2] Level 5 software developers were in India, and 196 of the 400 top Indian information technology (IT) firms had ISO 9000 certification (Kapur 2002).

Chinese firms do not have many quality certifications because, some observers claim, their managers do not have the skills that matter for CMMI certification. They have less exposure to process management or systems integration and consequently less "ability to organize large scale and complex software projects involving the development of separate but linked modules by multiple development teams" (Saxenian and Quan 2005, p. 117).

Indian managers promoted the development of CMMI quality certifications to introduce best practices into their products and services, to reassure foreign customers about the quality of the firms' services and thus expand their foreign markets, and to compete against other Indian software companies to secure American export contracts (Athreye 2005; personal interviews by the authors with Chinese software managers). Chinese software managers, in contrast, viewed CMMI certification as only a marketing tool rather than a tool that could improve quality control and reduce costs through standardization of processes. The Chinese disregard for CMMI certification no longer applies, however, as it is now mandatory for some government software contracts.

Some of the difference in numbers of certifications could be explained by the fact that more Indian firms than Chinese firms are software services firms—for which the CMMI certifications are more useful. However, Indian software services firms are more likely to have these certifications than Chinese software services firms; thus, the quality certification difference is an Indian firm trait as well as a services firm trait.

In addition, among Indian software firms, those with quality certifications turned in faster revenue growth than did those without such certifications. In contrast, for Chinese software firms, quality certification had no effect on revenue growth.

Management within National Cultures

To add to an understanding of the successful but divergent development of the Indian and Chinese software industries, this analysis examines two intangible features of managers and professionals: the influence of national culture on the way they manage, and their entrepreneurial orientation. Many previous studies have indicated that national culture influences management practices, and current research has suggested links between national cultures in India or China and the information technology (IT) industry in particular (Cater-Steel and Toleman 2008; Neelankavil, Mathur, and Zhang 2000; Perlow and Weeks 2002).This section relates features of Indian and Chinese software firm management drawn from their national cultures to some of the essential elements of the software production process.

Software production is a creative and innovative process—at least some parts of it are. Testing lines of code and maintaining established programs, which Indian software firms did plenty of, can be dull and routine. However, most Indian software production was for customized services; every job was new and different in some way. Furthermore, Indian software firms pursued export markets, and had to deal regularly with foreign firms and foreign ideas. Customized software development for Western clients by Indian firms often required ingenuity and inspiration, and benefited from initiative and quick decision making.

Much of the business of Chinese software firms consisted of adapting Western software products to Chinese language and business conditions—more routine work. Chinese software firms also developed new products but they were fairly standardized and focused on the already-familiar domestic market. This work required innovation, too, but may have benefited from a more habitual and ordered management style than would have been found in India.

According to the widely used research findings by Hofstede (1980, 1991) on the link between national culture and management styles, Indian national culture diverges the most from that of other countries of the world in its tolerance for ambiguity and ability to cope with uncertainty (India's score is 40 and the world average is 65, where a lower score means less uncertainty avoidance).[3] This implies that workers within this cultural setting are unusually open to novel and unstructured situations, are comfortable with few rules and open-ended work situations, and accept innovative ideas and behaviors.[4] Of course, these are generalizations about the national culture to which individuals belong, whereas in fact there is a distribution of behaviors around a central tendency (see chapter 2). Culture is not deterministic, and one can find Indians who do not behave in this way and Chinese who do, but there will be many fewer Indians who do not match the generalization and many fewer Chinese who do. A further proviso is that national culture–influenced behaviors are less manifest in more-educated professionals than for the population as a whole, and they diminish with the individual's international exposure.

Software development has been observed to fit with national cultures that tolerate uncertainty, such as those of India and the United States. "Indian teams 'go with the flow' and work with moderate levels of uncertainty" (Borchers 2003, p. 543). Furthermore, Indian culture has been described as more specific in contrast to the more diffuse (high context)[5] culture of China, and customized software production benefits from greater specificity (Schneider and Barsoux 2003).

India and China show the greatest difference in measures of national culture on "individualism." Although India is at the world average, China is the outlier in its collectivism, or lack of individualism (China's score is 20, India's score is 42, and the world average is 43; a lower score means less individualism). In a more individualistic culture, workers are more inclined to speak their mind, and put greater weight on accomplishing tasks in the workplace than on relationships. In such a culture, managers manage individuals. In contrast, in a highly collectivist culture, harmony and relationships are important. Various researchers have commented that the Chinese pay great attention to how to interact with others in a proper manner, and note that virtuous interpersonal behavior is a core Confucian value (Chen 1995; Child and Warner 2003). In this cultural context, managers manage groups. Tsang (2007) noted that many Chinese software firms are managed with practices that derive from collectivism.

India's greater international links (discussed later in this chapter) meant that Indian software companies obtained greater exposure to other national cultures, particularly that of the United States. To the extent that there is a dominant corporate culture in the software industry, it has been heavily influenced by West Coast American culture, and the specific subculture of Silicon Valley. The emphasis on ambiguity and individualism, and the lack of rigid corporate structures in this culture exhibits less cultural distance from the Indian national culture described by Hofstede than does the Chinese national culture he described. This finding is consistent with the high levels of success attained by Indian emigrants in Silicon Valley; indeed, this subculture has to some extent been influenced by its Indian participants.

The greater, earlier exposure by Indian companies to this successful corporate culture, and the shorter cultural distance, enabled Indian managers to fashion their corporate cultures more quickly after this model (as a visit to the campuses of Infosys or Wipro quickly confirms).

The contrasts between Indian and Chinese national cultures are consistent with the Indian focus on exported customized software services and the Chinese focus on domestic standardized products. Together with greater exposure to the corporate culture of software companies in the United States, India's national cultural attributes facilitated more rapid adoption of global best practice in corporate culture for software production.

Entrepreneurship

Entrepreneurship is expected to be related to growth in the software industry, which is new and populated by many startups and small firms (Contractor and Kundu 2004; Mitra and Li 2002). Entrepreneurship appears to be linked to national culture. For example, successful entrepreneurs appear to embody characteristics such as tolerance of ambiguity and comfort with uncertainty, as well as creativity (see box 6.1) (Timmons 1994; www.businesstown.com/entrepreneur/article1.asp). Culturally determined personal traits can be manifested in concrete workplace behaviors. Software companies, especially those that export, "require entrepreneurial, open, xenophilic, creative values," whereas hardware companies do not (Contractor and Kundu 2004, 9).

Nanda and Khanna (2007) have claimed that entrepreneurship is an area in which India has an advantage over China.[6] Indian entrepreneurs include both new business entrants and members of incumbent (often family-owned) firms who start new businesses. Huang and Khanna (2003) claim that entrepreneurship is a flourishing tradition in India, but not in China. However, other evidence suggests little difference between China and India in entrepreneurship. The two countries are in the same "above average" group based on survey data, interviews, and standardized national data from 40 countries (Global Entrepreneurship Monitor 2004). India had greater total entrepreneurial activity from startups and new businesses than China, but China had more firm entrepreneurial activity (activity within established firms). In several measures of the prevalence rates of entrepreneurial activity, Chinese figures were slightly larger than Indian figures. For example, new business owners were 10.5 percent of the adult population in China in 2006 and 5.3 percent in India; early-stage entrepreneurial activity was exhibited by 16.2 percent of the Chinese population and 10.4 percent of the Indian population (Global Entrepreneurship Monitor 2006). A recent report claims that China has more entrepreneurs per capita than any other country in the world (*Economist* 2007a).

Attitudes of university students in the arts and sciences toward entrepreneurship were favorable and similar in both China and India. Indian young people held more positive attitudes on several aspects of entrepreneurship (for example,

Box 6.1   UFIDA Software Ltd.: Risk Taking Pays Off

UFIDA Software Ltd. (UFIDA), one of the leading suppliers of management and accounting applications software in China, can trace its fast growth to three factors. Two of these factors fit with the usual explanations for Chinese software industry growth—technological strength and growth-promoting government policies. The third contributing factor is not so commonplace—the innovative and risk-taking behavior of its founders.

Two enthusiasts with only one PC, a rented apartment, and a loan of 50,000 Chinese renminbi (about $6,000) from a relative's savings established UFIDA in December 1988. At the time, a government officer job was the best job in China, but the two founders left these prized jobs to strike out on their own. Qiqiang Shu, one cofounder, was an aggressive and risk-taking entrepreneur who subsequently founded two other software companies after he left UFIDA in 1994. Wenjing Wang, the other cofounder and the CEO of UFIDA, transformed himself from technical expert to businessman. The antitraditional character of the cofounders enabled UFIDA to achieve a culture of innovation.

While other IT companies in China were focusing on hardware or translating foreign software packages into the Chinese language, UFIDA launched its Chinese accounting software package, which was developed internally, and provided customer training and service. The timing was propitious: the Chinese government was promoting the computerization of accounting in the entire Chinese economy, and UFIDA's early start gave it first-mover advantage in a growing market.

Despite competition from numerous domestic companies, UFIDA focused on building a core competence of technological superiority, spending roughly 16 percent of its revenue per year on R&D. It launched a 32-bit management accounting software package in 1994. It created new generation products—the first accounting/management software of its type in China—and extended its product line from enterprise resource planning, customer relations management, and human resources applications to industry vertical solutions such as e-government, finance, and asset management solutions. According to reports from independent market surveys such as CCID Consulting and IDC, since 2000 UFIDA's management solutions software has ranked first in China.

In 2001, UFIDA's management took a major step. It launched a successful initial public offering (IPO) on the Shanghai Stock Exchange. Private companies in China face many difficulties when trying to obtain permission for an IPO in the domestic stock market. UFIDA's good relationship with the government and its leading position in the Chinese accounting software market helped it win this opportunity. Using capital raised from its IPO, UFIDA quickly acquired Anyi Software Co. and entered the e-government arena. It also acquired 34 distribution channel companies to reach the entire Chinese market. From its strong domestic base, UFIDA entered international markets, opening branches in Hong Kong, China and Japan in 2004, and began delivering versions of its products that were suitable for the international market. UFIDA continuously upgrades these products, tailoring some to customers who are entering the greater Chinese region from outside locations.

Source: Contributed by Zhen Wu, Georgetown University graduate business student.
Note: See also a description of UFIDA's relationship with the Chinese government in Saxenian and Quan (2005).

76 percent of Indian students agreed that entrepreneurship is better than working for others, while 67 percent of Chinese students agreed with that statement), but not on all aspects (for example, 79 percent of Indian students agreed that entrepreneurship was respected in their country, while slightly [and not significantly] more Chinese students—83 percent—agreed) (Goel and others 2007).

Table 6.3 Entrepreneurship and Independence of Action

Finding: *Professionals in the Indian software industry were not more entrepreneurial overall than professionals in the Chinese software industry, but Indian software products firms were more entrepreneurial than Indian software services firms. The combination of entrepreneurial orientation and greater Indian independence of action is a statistically significant difference between the two countries' software firms.*

	China	India
Entrepreneurial orientation (mean score on 3-item, 15-point scale)	11.1	11.2
Independence of action (percentage of managers who say professional employees have to be convinced to follow instructions when they do not fully agree)	7	47
Entrepreneurial orientation $\times$ independence of action (regression interaction)	*6.9*	*10.4*

	China		India	
	Services firms	Products firms	Services firms	Products firms
Entrepreneurial orientation (mean score on 3-item, 15-point scale)	11.2	11.1	10.9	12.1

	All services firms	All products firms
Entrepreneurial orientation (mean score on 3-item, 15-point scale)	10.9	11.4

Source: IFC survey.
Note: The variables in italics are statistically significant, differentiating between Chinese and Indian software firms in a multivariate analysis.

Evidence from the IFC survey shows little or no difference between Chinese and Indian software firms in the sample: scores on a standard entrepreneurship scale were 11.2 out of 15.0 for Indian firms and 11.1 for Chinese firms (table 6.3; higher scores indicate more entrepreneurial orientation). These scores were not statistically significantly different. (The scale was formed from factor analysis of questions about the firm's propensity to take on risky projects, to experiment with and use alternative approaches to problem solving, and to emphasize R&D and new processes.) However, entrepreneurial orientation was slightly higher in software products firms than in software services firms, especially in Indian software products firms, of which there are proportionately fewer than in China. In a multivariate analysis of the two countries' sets of firms that accounted for the services versus products main line of business of the firm and other potential discriminators, entrepreneurial orientation was not a statistically significant differentiator.

The next section, on technology, asks whether firms—Chinese or Indian—that are more entrepreneurial are also more innovative.

If the failure to find an Indian entrepreneurial advantage in software services is puzzling, it might be explained by observations heard from Indian software managers in personal interviews: "'Indians don't follow the rules,' we were told, whereas in China, 'Decisions are not challenged'" (Parnell and others 2003, 127). These reports from the field led to the analysis of differences between the management of professionals in Indian and Chinese software firms. The difference that emerged is the interaction of entrepreneurial orientation with the independence of action exhibited by professionals, as reported by top managers. Professionals had to be convinced to follow instructions with which they did not fully agree in many more Indian firms (47 percent) than was the case in Chinese firms (only 7 percent), which may be a manifestation of a national cultural difference between the two countries, as identified by Hofstede (1991).[7] The interaction means that the entrepreneurial orientation of Indian professionals is reinforced or strengthened by the observed greater tendency to question instructions, and the combination of the two tendencies rather than either one alone is a statistically significant difference between Indian and Chinese software firms.

Because entrepreneurial orientation and independence of action are cultural traits, they are stable long-term features, and whether one firm has more or less of these characteristics did not influence its one-year revenue growth in the multivariate analysis.

Technology

The software industry is a high technology industry, but until recently few Indian or Chinese firms were at the technological frontier. Therefore, it is unclear whether technology inputs were important to the performance of the Indian and Chinese firms. Even if technological primacy was not important to the achievement of rapid growth in the past, the continued growth of each country's software industry will likely depend on the ability of software firms to innovate and move up the value chain. The analysis of technology in software firms considers R&D inputs; new products, patents, and royalty earnings as outputs; and intellectual property (IP) in the firm.

The quantity and quality of technology in a software firm can be influenced by the firm's own in-house R&D activity, and by relationships with foreign sources of technology through direct imports of equipment, movement of its employees to foreign firms, and either equity or nonequity strategic alliances with foreign firms. Indian software firms in particular might have gained technology experience by having employees working on-site at client sites outside India; the technology experience was then transferred back to India by the return of the bodyshopping employees or through moving the work itself offshore to India. In the late 1980s, around 75 percent of software export earnings came from on-site work, but by 2003 on-site work was reduced to 50 percent as offshore work increased (Heeks and Nicholson 2004). One survey reported that 60 percent of Indian software firms believed that migration of skilled labor to work for IT firms in the United States and the United Kingdom benefited their firms by providing contact with new technology, changing working habits, and facilitating access to new markets and customers. However, the amount of technology transferred depends on the level of advancement of the work, which usually was not very high.

FDI can be a source of technology transfer. In the Chinese software industry, FDI was greater than in the Indian industry (see the next section on international links); nevertheless, FDI was potentially important in India, too. The National Association of Software and Service Companies (NASSCOM) estimated that in 2001/02 multinational corporations (MNCs) accounted for 26.6 percent of Indian software sales. Some of India's domestically owned IT companies had non-equity links to foreign hardware companies in their early years because of the bundling of software and hardware (for example, TCS/Burroughs, Datamatics/Wang, and Patni/Data General) (Athreye 2005). This facilitated technology transfer even in the absence of FDI.

Research and Development

R&D activity is greater in China overall than it is in India, by several measures, and the same result is found among the two countries' software firms:

> *There was more R&D activity among Chinese firms than Indian firms, and this was a statistically significant difference between the two countries' industries; although software products firms had more R&D activity than software services firms, the country difference persisted.*

As table 6.4 shows, almost all Chinese software firms incurred R&D expenditures, and R&D expenditures of Chinese software firms as a percentage of total costs were very much higher than the corresponding share for Indian software firms. Software products firms were more likely than services firms to spend money on R&D, and a greater proportion of Chinese firms are software products firms. Nevertheless, whether the firms were products or services producers, Chinese software firms spent more on R&D than did their Indian counterparts. The legacy of strong research institutes in engineering fields developed in the Nehru era in India, which yielded top-flight software professionals, appears not to have translated into an R&D tradition in software companies. In contrast, the university origin of some Chinese software companies might have led to a culture more conducive to R&D in these firms.

The greater Chinese R&D spending did not translate into a Chinese advantage in the marketplace because much of the R&D focused on adapting foreign software to Chinese language and business conditions—an expenditure that Indian software firms did not have to incur. Moreover, firms that spent more on R&D did not have faster revenue growth than firms that spent less, whether in China or in India.

New Products, Patents, and Royalties

> *Chinese software firms had a technology output edge over Indian software firms; they introduced more new products, a statistically significant difference*

Table 6.4   Technology Inputs and Outputs

Finding: *Fewer Indian software firms spent money on R&D than Chinese firms, and this is a statistically significant difference between the firms in the two countries; Indian firms with R&D expenditure spent less, whether they were products or services firms.*

Technology input: R&D spending	China	India
Percentage of firms with R&D expenditure[a]	93	72
R&D costs as percentage of total costs (median)	*22.5*	*5.0*
Software services firms	15.0	3.5
Software products firms	30.0	15.0

Finding: *Indian software firms made fewer new product introductions than Chinese software firms, and this difference between them is statistically significant. Indian firms were also less likely to file for patents (without regard to their services or products business), but this difference is not statistically significant in a multivariate analysis.*

Technology outputs	China	India
New product introductions in the one year before the survey (average number)	*2.66*	*2.23*
Patent filings in the three years before the survey[b] (percentage with filings)	34	20
Royalties and technology fees earned abroad in the three years before the survey		
Percentage of all firms with such earnings	12	21
Amount of such earnings if any received (median)	$120,000	$85,744

Intellectual property	China	India
Number of competitors' products that do not comply with intellectual property rights laws (percentage)		
Mean	28.0	9.3
Median	20	0

Source: IFC survey.

Note: The variables in italics are statistically significant, differentiating between Chinese and Indian software firms in a multivariate analysis.

a. In China and India combined, 92 percent of all products firms and 70 percent of all services firms had R&D expenditures.

b. In China and India combined, 35 percent of all products firms and 17 percent of all services firms filed for patents in the three years before the survey.

from Indian firms. They also filed for patents more frequently, but this difference was not statistically significant. Although products firms in both countries were more innovative than services firms, the Chinese advantage persisted without regard to their line of business.

Creation of new products represents one of the most tangible outcomes of technology activity, and Chinese software firms introduced more new products and processes than did Indian software firms: 2.66 versus 2.23 per year. Two findings can explain this difference: (1) more Chinese firms introduced new products

(63 percent) compared with Indian firms (58 percent), and (2) the rate of new product introduction among those Chinese firms that introduced new products was greater (3.74 compared with 3.10 for Indian firms). The difference in the rates of new product introductions, although small, is statistically significant in the multivariate analysis.

Using a simple comparison of software services firms, the analysis found that software products firms, whether Chinese or Indian, were more likely to introduce new products and to introduce more of them, but the difference between the types of firms was small and not statistically significant. This finding leads to the conclusion that the greater amount of new product introduction by Chinese software firms is mainly a feature of the location (country), not of the line of business.

Patent filings and awards, and royalties and technology fees received, are other technology outcomes. China's software firms showed higher raw numbers for patent filings and awards, but the differences with India are not significant in a multivariate analysis of the two countries' firms. China awards software patents, but the Chinese firms in the IFC sample filed for patents only in China, not in the United States. Because local markets comprise the main outlet for Chinese software, most of Chinese firms' products and R&D are China-specific. India does not award patents for software; patent filings by Indian firms occur mostly in the United States.

Copyright registration is another measure of technology output, and is available for software even when patenting is not. The analysis found no significant difference in copyright activity between Chinese and Indian firms, and no significant difference between products and services firms. Between 25 and 30 percent of all firms reported copyright registrations in the three years before the survey.

Few software firms earned royalties or technology fees from abroad (21 percent in India and 12 percent in China), and this difference was not significant.

China's overall technology output edge may be due to the fact that Chinese software firms are younger and smaller; normally, high tech firms incur a higher proportion of R&D costs in the early phase of the development life cycle.

Innovation and Entrepreneurship

Will businesses that are more entrepreneurial also prove to be more innovative? Do new businesses create more new technologies and more new products than businesses that have been in existence for some time? It is easy to assume that the answer is yes. However, evidence from the Global Entrepreneurship Monitor (2006) indicates that the majority of entrepreneurs are not especially innovative. In middle-income countries, 79 percent of entrepreneurs in established businesses were not using any new technology and 13 percent were using technology that was one to five years old; only 5 percent were using the very latest technology. Some 61 percent had no new products, 20 percent had products that were new to some customers, and 16 percent had products that were new to all customers. For early-stage entrepreneurial activity, the figures were somewhat but not much more tilted toward new technology and new products.

What is true for all industries in middle-income countries worldwide might not be true for the IT industry in China and India. Evidence from the IFC survey, on which most of this study is based, indicates there is a link between entrepreneurship and innovation, but it is small. Software firms that spent money on R&D (a measure of potential innovative activity) were more entrepreneurially oriented than firms that did not—the correlation was small (0.174) but statistically significant. The positive association between R&D spending and entrepreneurship held for Indian firms (the sample of Chinese firms without R&D spending was too small to test the relationship), and it was true for both software services firms and software products firms. Similarly, software firms that introduced new products (a measure of potential innovative output) were more entrepreneurially oriented, but this association held for Indian firms only; it did not hold for Chinese firms. Whether firms received technology fees from abroad, another measure of innovative output, was not quite significantly associated with entrepreneurial orientation. The absence of a stronger relationship between entrepreneurial orientation and innovative activity or output for Chinese software firms offers evidence that the R&D conducted by these firms was mostly adaptive rather than innovative.

More-entrepreneurial software firms were also more innovative, but just slightly so; this is true for Indian software firms but probably not for Chinese software firms.

Overall, Indian software services firms were less entrepreneurial than other software firms (either Indian software products firms or Chinese software services or products firms); but among Indian software firms, those with a more entrepreneurial orientation were more innovative. The net effect for the Indian software industry—that it is less technologically active than the Chinese software industry—reveals that the relative lack of entrepreneurship outweighed the tendency toward innovation. It also means that if entrepreneurship in India can be boosted, for example, by government policies to enable it, if not by culture change, the Indian software industry might achieve technological activity and output that matches that of the Chinese software industry.

Intellectual Property

Poor protection of IP in both China and India remains a problem for firms in the software industry. Chinese software firms estimated that 28 percent of their competitors' software does not comply with IP laws and regulations. The percentage indicated by Indian software companies was much lower, at 9 percent. Piracy rates in China remain at more than 90 percent across all industries dependent on copyright protection. In business software applications, trade losses from piracy are estimated at $1.6 billion or a level of piracy of 92 percent, which is among the worst in the world (IIPA 2005). Consequently, a Chinese company with a new

Table 6.5   Entrepreneurial Orientation Score and Technology Activities

Finding: *Indian software firms, software services firms, and software products firms that had R&D input were slightly more entrepreneurial than those without R&D input. Indian software firms that introduced new products were slightly more entrepreneurial than firms that did not introduce new products.*

	Firms with R&D spending	Firms without R&D spending
All software firms	11.4	10.2
Chinese firms	11.1	—
Indian firms[a]	11.6	10.0
Services firms[a]	11.3	10.1
Products firms[a]	11.5	10.3

	Firms that introduced new products	Firms that did not introduce new products
All firms	11.4	10.3
Chinese firms	11.1	11.0
Indian firms[a]	11.6	9.9
Firms that received royalty payments from abroad		
All firms	11.7	11.0
Chinese firms	11.6	—
Indian firms	11.7	11.0

Source: IFC survey.
Note: — = Not available because the sample size is small. Entrepreneurial orientation scores are mean scores on a 3-item, 15-point scale. All differences are statistically significant at the 0.025 level.
a. Variables in italics show statistically significant differences at the 0.025 level.

product idea is more likely to have the idea stolen than to become a market leader. A recent survey of Chinese software enterprises reports that more than one-quarter of respondents consider unauthorized copying, sharing, and installing of software to be the most significant barrier to the industry's growth (Saxenian 2005). Software piracy is especially destructive in the consumer market. Enterprise applications that require large-scale implementation and training are less affected because they are more customized; consequently, Indian software firms are less adversely affected than Chinese firms. Pirated software sales in China were estimated at $2.5 billion to $5.0 billion in 1999, compared with only $2.1 billion for legal software; a majority of the installed software base in the country is pirated software (Saxenian 2005). More Chinese software firms than Indian firms do not comply with laws and regulations governing IP rights, according to managers in our survey (table 6.5).

Significant progress has been made in China in developing a regulatory and legal environment for IP protection, but enforcement remains difficult. While raids and seizures continue at high levels, low administrative fines and the lack of criminal enforcement against piracy have meant that the copyright enforcement system has little deterrent effect. Despite continued government expressions of concern and commitment to root out piracy, many admissions of the seriousness of the problem, and a major anti-piracy campaign begun in September 2003, piracy rates have not decreased (IIPA 2004).

International Links

Relationships with foreign firms can contribute to a firm's performance by providing access to scarce inputs, such as technology (discussed above), or access to markets abroad as well as an introduction to management best practices. The analysis explores three types of links the firms in the IFC survey developed: foreign ownership, nonequity alliances, and contact with overseas residents of the home country. Table 6.6 shows the numbers and types of alliances among the software firms in the survey and their impact. The analysis shows that nonequity alliances, mentioned by Vedwa (2004) but in few other studies, are among the most important features of Indian software firms. Contact with overseas residents is frequently mentioned in the literature, but its role was probably more important in the early years of the industry than in later years.

Nonequity Strategic Alliances

Nonequity strategic alliances are long-term relationships between firms with specific purposes, such as to conduct joint R&D, marketing, or production. These alliances involve close cooperation and knowledge sharing for mutual benefit without ownership stakes of one firm in the other. They are not simply arm's-length, one-off supply or distribution contracts executed through the external market. Rather, the alliance uses the firm's internal hierarchy just as FDI does but without the initial capital cost.

> *Nonequity strategic alliances play a crucial role in the export success of Indian software firms. More Indian firms had foreign alliances, and had more of them than Chinese software firms. Indian firms with more alliances also showed faster sales revenue growth.*

Software firms can have domestic alliances as well as foreign alliances, but foreign alliances potentially offer advantages for export performance. More Indian software firms had nonequity strategic alliances (69 percent) than Chinese software firms (42 percent). The most dramatic discrepancy between the two countries' firms, however, was in their foreign alliances. As table 6.6 shows, Indian software firms were more than five times more likely to have foreign nonequity alliances than their Chinese counterparts. In fact, most Indian firms with alliances had foreign alliances, whereas Chinese firms with alliances all had domestic alliances but

Table 6.6   Types of International Links

Finding: *Domestic alliances were more prevalent among Chinese firms, both in frequency and numbers, but this difference is not statistically significant.*

Finding: *Many more Indian software firms had foreign nonequity strategic alliances than did Chinese software firms, and this difference is statistically significant. Among Indian firms, those with more alliances grew faster than those with fewer alliances.*

Nonequity strategic alliances	China	India
Firms with nonequity strategic alliances (%)	42.4	68.6
Firms with foreign nonequity strategic alliances (%)	11.9	60.2
Firms with domestic nonequity strategic alliances (%)	42.4	31.3
Number of alliances among firms with alliances (mean)	10.7	10.1
Number of foreign alliances among firms with alliances (mean)	*4.9*	*6.8*
Number of domestic alliances among firms with alliances (mean)	5.8	3.3
Effect of each additional foreign alliance on revenue growth	No effect	+6%

Finding: *More Indian than Chinese software firms had some foreign ownership, but the average foreign equity stake in Indian firms was less because foreign portfolio investment was more prevalent in Indian firms while wholly owned foreign subsidiaries were more common in Chinese firms. Chinese software firms with greater foreign ownership grew faster, but Indian firms did not.*

Foreign ownership	China	India
Some foreign ownership (percentage of firms)[a]	32	58
< 25% foreign ownership	2	20
≥ 25% foreign ownership	30	30
100% foreign ownership	22	10
Foreign ownership stake, average over all firms	*29%*	*23%*
Contribution of 10% greater foreign ownership stake to sales revenue growth	19%	No effect

Finding: *More Indian software firms reported a role played by nonresidents than did Chinese firms, and the importance of the role was greater, but only in access to markets; this difference is not statistically significant for the two countries' firms in a multivariate analysis. Indian firms that reported more importance of nonresidents' roles were more profitable, but Chinese firms that reported more importance of nonresidents' role were faster growing.*

Role of nonresidents	China	India
Firms in which nonresidents have had a role (%)	23.3	48.3
Importance of nonresidents' role (sum of four scales where 0 = no role and 5 = very important role)	2.8	6.1

Type of role played by nonresidents in firms in which they have a role (where 1 = no benefit and 5 = very important benefit)		
Access to markets	2.9	3.9
Access to management practices	3.8	3.4
Access to technology	3.2	3.2
Access to capital	2.5	2.8
Contribution of 10% greater role importance of nonresidents to the firm's revenue growth	25% faster	No effect
Contribution of 10% greater role importance of nonresidents to the firm's profit margin	No effect	2% larger

Source: IFC survey.

Note: The variables in italics are statistically significant, differentiating between Chinese and Indian software firms in a multivariate analysis.

a. International standard clarification of foreign investment: < 25% foreign ownership is portfolio investment; ≥ 25% foreign ownership with foreign management interest is FDI; and 100% foreign ownership is wholly owned subsidiary.

few had foreign alliances. The purposes of the Indian firms' alliances ranged from installation of a foreign firm's software platform at a customer's site to coequal software design and customer problem solving (Siddharthan and Nollen 2004). The difference in the use of nonequity strategic alliances is a statistically significant difference between Indian and Chinese software firms in a multivariate analysis.

Nonequity alliances are more prevalent among software services firms than among software products firms, without regard to country: in the combined sample, 66 percent of services firms and 51 percent of products firms had alliances. It is not the firm's services versus products business that matters, but rather the firm's location (country): both Indian software services and products firms had more nonequity strategic alliances than their Chinese counterparts.

Among the Indian and Chinese firms that had alliances, the mean number of alliances was about equal. The difference was in the foreign or domestic character of the alliances. Not only did more Indian firms have foreign nonequity alliances, but the Indian firms with these alliances had more of them (6.8 on average) than Chinese software firms (4.9 on average). In contrast, Chinese firms with alliances had more domestic alliances (5.8 on average) than did Indian firms (3.3 on average).

The contribution these alliances make to sales revenue growth of the firms demonstrates the importance of foreign nonequity strategic alliances for Indian firms (see box 6.2). Each additional alliance contributed 2 percentage points to an Indian firm's growth rate, which amounted to a 6 percent increase. Firms with more alliances can grow faster than firms with fewer alliances because the firms learn how to benefit from their alliances, thus increasing their success, especially in expanding access to export markets (Contractor, Hsu, and Kundu 2005).

Foreign Ownership

Foreign ownership was important to Chinese software firms, a statistically significant difference from Indian firms and a contributor to their short-term growth.

Given the tradition of private enterprise established in colonial times and maintained in the Nehruvian socialist era (see chapter 3), home-country ownership predominates in the Indian software industry. Although MNCs stimulated the development of the industry, it grew mostly from indigenous startups (like Infosys Technologies) and entry of established firms in other businesses into software (for example, Wipro). Even in the late 2000s, foreign ownership of software operations in India is relatively infrequent (table 6.7). Only 8 of the 25 largest software firms in India in 2004 were subsidiaries or joint ventures with a foreign company; among the top 100 firms, 25 were foreign-owned; and in 2002, foreign-owned firms' share in revenue of the Indian-located software industry was estimated to be 26.6 percent (Desai 2005).

Foreign investment in the Indian software industry is increasing, but the dollar magnitudes are small, in part because of the low capital requirements of software services production. Many of the foreign operations established in India are cap-

---

Box 6.2 Tata Consultancy Services: A Hard Alliance as a Springboard to Software Success

The Tata Group, one of India's largest privately owned industrial conglomerates, has interests ranging from steel to tea to power to auto manufacturing to hotels. Tata Consultancy Services (TCS), one of the largest companies in the group, was formed in 1968 as an internal management consulting group for the Tata companies. Initially, TCS's main responsibility was to manage punch card operations and act as an IT service bureau, but it soon began to serve customers beyond the Tata Group. Import restrictions on hardware, however, made it difficult for the company to grow. To obtain permission to import hardware, TCS needed to export software. Therefore, in 1973 it entered into an agreement with the American hardware manufacturer Burroughs. According to the agreement, Burroughs would find software work for TCS in the United States, and in return TCS would be Burroughs' sales agent in India. This agreement led to the acquisition of software clients in the U.S. market, starting with the Detroit Police Department in 1974, mainly linked to Burroughs hardware. The alliance was less successful in selling hardware in India because of continuing import restrictions. (By 1978, TCS had only sold seven computers.) When IBM withdrew from the Indian market in 1977, Burroughs formed a joint venture with the Tata Group to manufacture comput-

ers in India. The Burroughs sales agency was combined with this new company as Tata Burroughs, which later became Tata Infotech (absorbed into TCS in 2005). TCS continued as a pure software company and switched its focus to developing software, including packaged products, for IBM hardware as well as providing software services. The track record established with Burroughs helped TCS win business on its own in the United States, and over time it moved up the value chain from simple programming to more complex project management.

TCS also expanded the scale of its projects, giving it an enduring competitive advantage over newer, smaller firms. Because large projects tend to be mission critical, reputation and quality count for more than low price. As a result of telecommunications bottlenecks, most of TCS's work was done onshore at the client's location until the late 1980s. In 1988, TCS established a development center in Chennai to undertake offshore work. By 1992, TCS was the largest Indian software company and the largest software exporter. By 1998, 40 percent of its work was done offshore. In 2004, TCS issued an IPO in India and the United States; it had 41,000 employees in 210 offices in 33 countries.

Source: Kennedy 2001.

---

tive cost centers that produce software for the parent company but neither export to third-party customers nor sell to the domestic market (for example, Philips Innovation Campus of Philips Electronics). Foreign-owned operations range from BPO call center enterprises that do not produce software on one end of the spectrum to research laboratories (belonging to IBM and Microsoft, for example) on the other.

Foreign ownership encompassing foreign management interest or control is more prevalent among Chinese than among Indian software firms. China's attraction as a destination for FDI applies to the software industry as well as to the country's economy generally (see box 6.3). More than half of the top 10 packaged software firms in China were foreign owned in 2005 (table 6.8), and in 2001, the number was 8 out of 10 (Saxenian and Quan 2005).

Table 6.7   Ownership of the 25 Largest Indian Software Companies in 2004

Company	Country of ownership
Tata Consulting Services	India
Infosys Technologies	India
Wipro	India
IBM India	United States
Satyam Computer Services	India
HCL Technologies	India
Patni Computer Systems	India
Cognizant Technology Solutions	United States
Oracle India	United States
Microsoft India	United States
I-Flex Solutions	India (acquired by U.S. company in 2005)
Mahindra British Telecom (Tech Mahindra)	India-UK joint venture
Tata Infotech	India (merged into TCS in 2005)
SAP India	Germany
Polaris Software Lab	India
CMC	India
Perot Systems TSI	United States
Computer Associates India	United States
Hexaware Technologies	India
Larsen &Toubro Infotech	India
Siemens Information Systems	Germany
iGate Global Solutions	India
Mastek Limited	India
CMS Computers	India
NIIT Technologies	India

4 of the top 10 software companies are foreign owned (40%).

8 of the top 25 software companies are foreign owned (32%).

16 of the top 50 software companies are foreign owned (32%).

25 of the top 100 software companies are foreign owned (25%).

Source: Dataquest 2005.

Note: Companies are ranked in order of total revenue, not just software revenue. Companies are included in the list if at least 25 percent of their revenue is earned from production of software services or products. Predominantly excluded are hardware companies (for example, Hewlett Packard, Intel, Cisco, Samsung, Moser Baer) and software distributors (for example, Redington India, Ingram Micro).

One-third of all software firms in China are wholly or partly foreign owned, both in the IFC survey sample and as reported by others (Saxenian 2005), and 22 percent of Chinese software firms are 100 percent foreign owned compared with 10 percent of Indian software firms that are wholly foreign-owned in the IFC sample (table 6.6). As chapter 3 reports, FDI inflows have been an important vehicle

Box 6.3 HiSoft: A Wholly Foreign-Owned Enterprise in China

HiSoft Technology Co. Ltd., a wholly foreign-owned enterprise based in Dalian, China, provides software application development, maintenance, IT operations, and outsourced engineering. HiSoft is owned by a Cayman Islands–based vehicle, HiSoft International, which is in turn owned by several foreign enterprises: JAFCO Asia, Intel Capital, Granite Global Ventures, and the International Finance Corporation. (There was an interim period of ownership by an enterprise established by Dalian Maritime University and China Hualu Group.)

HiSoft has offices in China, Japan, and the United States and serves customers worldwide, including Unisys, Fujitsu, IBM's Japanese affiliate, and Nomura Research Institution. Its clients are assured of high-quality products and services: HiSoft was the first Chinese software company to pass the CMM

Level 5 Assessment at the organizational level and the first global development center for General Electric in China. The company also is becoming a certified independent software vendor for IBM.

One underlying factor for HiSoft's growth was its emphasis on the higher–value added segment of the software business. While most of its competitors focus on lower-level design and production outsourcing, HiSoft emphasizes a comprehensive end-to-end delivery platform. To do so, the company concentrates on designing system specifications, outlining them, and providing design solutions.

HiSoft has a joint venture with JBCC, which is owned by IBM Japan. The company has received numerous awards, one of which was inclusion in the 2004 Deloitte Asia Pacific Top 500 Fastest Growing Technology Companies list.

Table 6.8 Ownership of the 10 Largest Chinese Packaged Software Companies, 2005

Company	Country of ownership
Microsoft	United States
IBM	United States
Oracle	United States
BEA	China
UFIDA (UF Soft)	China
SAP	Germany
Kingdee	China
Sun	United States
Sybase	United States
BMC	China

6 of the top 10 packaged software companies are foreign owned (60%).

In 2000, 8 of the top 10 packaged software companies were foreign owned (80%).

Source: Analysys International 2005.

for technology transfer in China. Although the frequency with which Indian firms reported some foreign ownership is actually higher (58 percent in the survey), this figure reflects foreign portfolio investment without management interest or control, a situation that occurs frequently in India but hardly at all in China (Commander 2005).

In the multivariate analysis, the higher foreign ownership stakes of Chinese software firms were statistically significant. In addition, Chinese firms with greater foreign ownership stakes were faster growing, whereas foreign ownership did not contribute to the growth of Indian software firms.

Why Did Foreign Ownership Not Drive Chinese Export Success?

Although the prevalence of FDI in the Chinese software industry differs from that in the Indian software industry, and the inflow of FDI contributed to Chinese software firms' growth, it did not result in an export orientation. In India, foreign nonequity alliances rather than FDI were important to firms' growth and export success. Why did the foreign influence matter in one case but not the other?

The first of four related arguments is that although FDI inflows into China were exceedingly large for several years, they were not so large in the 1980s, the formative years of the software industry (when Indian body shopping got under way). FDI in China reached $10 billion for the first time just in 1991.

Second, in the years since 1991, the absolute magnitude of FDI into the Chinese software industry has not been nearly so great as might be expected when reckoning the country's overall attractiveness for FDI. Most of the FDI in China was in manufacturing industries and other industries in the secondary sector, not in the services sector and therefore not into software services and products. Among the Chinese firms in the IFC survey, 30 percent were foreign owned and managed (these are firms whose shares were more than 25 percent foreign owned)—a higher percentage than Indian firms but not absolutely large.

Third, most of the FDI in China did not come from the United States, but from other Asian countries. Therefore, their foreign ownership did not particularly influence Chinese firms to export software to the United States, the main software services export market. In addition, a sizable portion of the FDI coming into China was "round-tripping,"[8] especially to and from Hong Kong, China, and did not represent true business and economic forces (table 6.9).

Fourth, much of the direct investment in the IT industry from the United States or other Western sources was motivated by the desire to serve the Chinese domestic market. China probably had a comparative advantage in the production of hardware (compared with software production in the United States), but in turn this made it less likely that China had a comparative advantage in software—the reverse of the situation in India.

A fifth and different type of circumstance might explain why the Chinese software industry did not develop an export orientation in software services to the

Table 6.9   Cumulative FDI Inflows into China, 1998–2004

From the United States	Into manufacturing and other secondary sector industries, from all countries	Into services sector, from all countries	Into services excluding real estate services, from all countries
$33.6 billion	$247.6 billion	$86.6 billion	$48.0 billion
9.9% of total	72.8% of total	25.4% of total	14.1% of total

Source: China Statistics Bureau Annual Report, compiled by Zhen Wu.

United States in particular. U.S.-China political and economic relationships until the 1990s carried limitations on access to computing hardware by Chinese firms and foreign-invested firms in China. Chinese software employees were thus unable to learn about this equipment. The result was reduced contact and familiarity with U.S. software export markets.

The U.S.-imposed export controls against China were tightened after the Tiananmen Square incident in 1989, which occurred near the beginning of the growth of software services outsourcing. Even conventional equipment for scientific computing (such as the HP9000 and HP7200) was barred until 1993. The hardware limitations meant that Chinese software engineers could not use advanced computers to create software programs, and they were not familiar with the equipment on which their software programs would run at a foreign client's place of business. Even if advanced computing hardware had not been necessary for software writing or running, the export controls indirectly reduced U.S.-China international business relationships in the IT sector.

Indian software firms also faced limitations on importing advanced computing equipment, but change in technology and business models permitted software to be written independently of the hardware on which it was to run.

Overseas Residents

The connection with the home country made by a country's citizens who live overseas is a third international link. One of the most common explanations for the growth of the Indian software industry is the role played by nonresident Indians (NRIs). For example, the export success of Indian software firms has been attributed to the role of NRIs who made the United States a source of demand to substitute for the lack of demand from India (Kapur 2001). Yet none of the very largest Indian software firms had any significant NRI relationship, and another observer claims that "the role of the Indian diaspora in the 1990s was in no way pivotal" (Pandy and others 2004, p. 18).

The role of overseas Chinese in the Chinese software industry, whose growth was achieved mainly by domestic rather than export sales, is not at issue.

The potential for a role to be played by a nation's diaspora, referring generally to the dispersal of a country's or ethnic group's population to other lands, is substantial. About 3 percent of the world's population lives outside its country of origin, and India's and China's large populations permit many emigrants.

Indians, who are English speaking if they are educated, are drawn disproportionately to the United States with its large English-speaking labor market. The Indians who migrate tend to be technically educated professionals. Among all NRIs in the United States, two-thirds had university degrees and 40 percent had a graduate or professional degree, many of which were in engineering and computer science fields.[9] During 1964–86, 59 percent of all Indian Institute of Technology-Madras graduates in computer science migrated abroad (Kumar 2002). In 1998 alone, 30,000 Indian professionals went to the United States, and in 1999–2000, 42.3 percent of H1-B visa applicants were from India (compared with 9.8 percent from China). Because of the area's engineering bias, NRIs are heavily represented in IT-intensive Silicon Valley. More than 200,000 Indians worked there in the late 1990s. In addition to the Indians who migrated to the United States, additional numbers of Indians studied there—34,000 students in 1998. Two-thirds of Indian students studying in the United States were enrolled in science and engineering courses.

China's emigrant population exceeds that of India (estimated at 20 million Chinese living abroad). However, the Chinese diaspora was more small-business oriented than professional, less concentrated in high technology corridors, and more devoted to businesses in Asia. The Chinese emigrant population was less suited geographically and occupationally to contribute to the growth of the Chinese software industry.

Mechanisms for overseas residents to assist home-country industry. In principle, members of a diaspora should be able to assist the development of an industry in their home country. Especially for a new industry in a developing country, a key role can be played in providing access to markets. Firms in a new industry in a developing country are not likely to have the benefit of formal institutions that facilitate their export growth (for example, industry associations and government agencies). In a new industry, especially a service industry, potential customers harbor uncertainties about exactly what the service provider's output will be and whether the service provider is reputable and will deliver the output in full and on time. For Indian firms in particular, a negative country-of-origin reputation had to be overcome.

Informal networks of managers can substitute for formal institutions for the purposes of reaching potential customers, obtaining finance, and transferring technology. For Indian software firms, access to export customers was more important than access to either finance or technology. NRIs in the United States could identify potential export customers and vouch for the capability of Indian software service providers. In some cases, an NRI-owned firm in Silicon Valley was the export customer. NRIs were located in the right geographical regions in ample numbers with the right educations and occupations. They were a bridge between the U.S. export market and the India-based software services provider. Such bridges were needed because of the decoupling of India from global markets as a result of Nehruvian economic policies.

In addition to access to markets, NRIs could provide access to management and finance. Those who returned to India after the economic reforms of 1991 brought with them the software project management skills they had acquired in the United States. They could serve as conduits for management know-how. NRIs served as "tolerant mentors of early Indian software development companies" and "brand ambassadors" (Pandey and others 2004, 11). Some NRIs, having accumulated wealth in the United States, could finance new startup businesses in India.

Do NRIs matter in practice? In actual practice, the extent to which NRIs were responsible for the export growth of the Indian software industry was, as late as 2001, yet to be documented (Kumar 2001). One piece of evidence is that among the NRIs in Silicon Valley, 80 percent relayed information about business opportunities to people in India and 67 percent helped to arrange business contracts or served as advisers (Saxenian 2002). Over 10 percent of firms reported that emigrants or their firms were customers of Indian firms. Although 25 percent of firms had retained links with workers that had gone abroad, there was little evidence of emigrants investing in the Indian firms (Commander and others 2004). A network of Indian IT professionals called The Indus Entrepreneurs (TiE), started in 1992 in Silicon Valley, is an example of mentoring by successful entrepreneurs for new managers (Kapur 2001).

Although the Indian government officially considers any Indian who lives outside India for 183 days or more to be an NRI, this analysis of the IFC survey data refers more restrictively to someone who was born and reared in India but who as an adult lives and works outside India, not temporarily; an NRI who subsequently returns to India to live and work is still considered an NRI for the purposes of examining NRI influence on the growth of the Indian software industry.

The evidence from the IFC survey gives a mixed picture, casting doubt on the NRI role.

NRIs were important to the growth of Indian software firm exports in the early years of the industry, first for access to export markets and second for management of export business once obtained. But the role of NRIs is no longer critically important, is not a statistically significant difference between the two countries' software firms, and does not currently explain differences among Indian software firms' short-term growth.

NRIs played a role in 48 percent of Indian software companies, either as a founder or investor (24.6 percent) or top manager (23.7 percent). (See box 6.4 for an example of a company founded by an NRI.) Surveyed companies indicated that the most important benefit of NRI involvement was access to markets through

Box 6.4   NRI Founds Software Companies

Some NRIs who immigrated to the United States during their business careers founded companies in the United States, established operations in India, and exported software services back to the United States. The Indian internet services provider, Rediff, gives an example, from which this report is excerpted.

Sashi Chimala is no ordinary entrepreneur. He is not only a "Jack of all trades," but—strangely enough—master of all. Even as a young boy Chimala dreamt of becoming an entrepreneur. And become he did. Chimala founded not one, not two, but many companies, and they are in diverse fields like software to coffee to cricket.

He is one of the founding members of Covansys; founder of Indigo Technologies (which was later acquired in a two-way deal between SSI and NASDAQ); of Qwiky's Coffee, a pioneering retail venture in Asia; and of CricTV.com, the first social video network for cricket. In this interview with Contributing Editor Shobha Warrier, he travels through his ventures, needless to say all quite successful.

"It may sound very corny, but my inspiration was Mahatma Gandhi. I always dreamt of becoming an entrepreneur. This may have grown from my obsession with being independent. Both financial independence and independence of thought mean a lot to me. As creativity is the core component of entrepreneurship, I want to tell you about my cartooning days. I started drawing cartoons, which appeared in almost all Telugu publications, as a schoolboy in Andhra Pradesh. The money I earned went towards my education. By now, I must have drawn around 5,000 cartoons.

After completing engineering at Kakinada in Andhra Pradesh, I went to Bombay (now Mumbai) for my postgraduation.

Then in 1979, I went to the United States. I was a programmer at the Tatas. The story of Indian IT outsourcing actually started around that time. . . . I was in the second batch and the 60th person to go to the U.S. Those days were difficult because the Americans wouldn't understand our accent. We were treated as "aliens"! The word alien was an official term to describe an immigrant. Your green card says "permanent alien" even when we are all

human beings and not residents of outer space! Anyway, it was the beginning of Indians making it big in the U.S. . . . As an entrepreneur, I saw better chances in the U.S. than in India in those days. If you have a good idea, nothing limits you as an entrepreneur in the U.S. You don't have to come from a rich family to create a big company; you only need to have a great idea.

In 1987 I helped Raj Vattikutti to start a company called Complete Business Solutions (later renamed as Covansys). . . . On the one hand, it was easy since we were among the very few Indian companies, and, on the other, it was difficult because we were trying to prove to the world that Indians were good entrepreneurs. In a couple of years the message was out that ours was a good company. . . .

I always wanted to start a company that was into products as almost everyone else was focusing on services. In 1992, I founded Indigo Technologies in Cupertino, California. We built an audacious product to automate stock exchanges. Tandem Computers, the de facto providers of stock exchanges and banks, liked our product, and they helped us sell it in Taiwan. NASDAQ was already their customer and they introduced us to them. The chief technical officer of NASDAQ went on record saying our product was ten times more saleable than what they had at that time. . . . We eventually sold our company when NASDAQ formed a company called IndigoMarkets, which used our software.

After living in the U.S. for 20 years, I came back to India because of Indigo Technologies. Tandem became Compaq Computer and took equity in our company, so we had to consolidate all our operations and business. Since we had quite a big team in India, it was suggested that I run the company from here as its chief executive officer. And it was quite a homecoming. I came back to a hugely different India—a new India—in 1998. The new India has tasted the fruits of enterprise. It will never go back to the old ways.

Source: www.rediff.com/money/2007/jul/03 bspec.htm.

connections with U.S. companies that were potential customers and to management practices and technologies; access to capital was deemed less important. Chinese software firms were less likely to report a role for overseas Chinese (23 percent), but for those companies for which overseas Chinese did play a role, it was no less important than for Indian firms (see table 6.6).

In the multivariate analysis with other potential differences accounted for, the role of nonresidents was not a statistically significant difference between Indian and Chinese software firms. Although this finding appears contrary to conventional wisdom, it is caused by the relatively inconsequential role played by nonresidents: managers' reports from the two countries were not very different, and the importance of the role played (when they had a role) was only midway between "no benefit" and "very important." In the simple comparison, the sole exception was a more important role in market access for Indian software firms.

Even though nonresidents did not statistically distinguish Indian from Chinese software companies, they did contribute to firm performance. Indian companies in which NRIs had a role reported gross profits of 21.9 percent of revenue, compared with 15.1 percent if NRIs did not play a role, after other profitability determinants were accounted for. Overseas Chinese added to Chinese software firms' current revenue growth.

A more fine-grained analysis shows that the role of NRIs was unevenly distributed. Some firms made less use of the NRI network than others. Software firms located in clusters (such as Bangalore, Mumbai, Delhi-Gurgaon-Noida) relied less on the network of NRIs than did firms located outside the clusters—and most Indian software firms were located in one of a few geographic clusters (Nanda and Khanna 2007). Firms whose top manager lived abroad before the founding of the firm in India relied more on a network of NRIs than firms whose top manager had not lived abroad—and about half of top managers from larger firms had not lived abroad (Nanda and Khanna 2007).

Notes

1. "Capability Maturity Model® Integration (CMMI) is a process improvement approach that provides organizations with the essential elements of effective processes. It can be used to guide process improvement across a project, a division, or an entire organization. CMMI helps integrate traditionally separate organizational functions, set process improvement goals and priorities, provide guidance for quality processes, and provide a point of reference for appraising current processes" (from www.sei.cmu.edu, accessed March 30, 2006).

2. Capability Maturity Model, the predecessor to CMMI.

3. These culture dimensions have been used in many scholarly and practitioner studies in the social sciences literature, following Hofstede.

4. While China also has a low score on uncertainty avoidance, it is generally regarded in the literature as invalid and that the fifth culture dimension added later—long-term orientation—should be used; China diverges the most from the average of other countries on

this dimension, but we do not see strong links between more or less long-term orientation and the type of workplace that is conducive to software production; thus it is not taken up here.

5. A high context culture is one in which meaning is obtained in part from the context of the situation, with less reliance on written and verbal communication than in low-context cultures (Hall 1976); it is typical of East Asian countries in contrast to most Western countries that are characterized as low-context cultures. Similarly, diffuse cultures value relationships and appear to be less immediately open than specific cultures.

6. Nanda and Khanna (2007) report on several company experiences in both countries amid their historical and cultural backgrounds.

7. One might wonder about the Indian tendency to question instructions revealed in the IFC survey in view of the Indian national cultural feature of power distance that is above the world average (but slightly below the Chinese figure). The frequency of questioning instructions is not absolutely very large—less than half the Indian firms report this behavior—but it is large compared with the Chinese frequency. In addition, power distance will be much lower among young professionals and managers in an internationally oriented new industry than would be for the nation at large. Finally, India also scores high on individualism, and that is conducive to speaking out, which is consistent with questioning authority.

8. Round-tripping refers to FDI made in mainland China from Hong Kong, China to take advantage of Chinese government policies that favored foreign investment when the original FDI in Hong Kong, China came from mainland China itself.

9. The data reported in this section are from Kapur (2001) unless noted otherwise.

Chapter 7

The Effects of the Business Environment and Competition on Software Industries in China and India

The business environment—government policies, infrastructure, and institutions—contributes to the success or failure of a country's industries. This chapter examines the effects of these factors on the software industries in China and India, based on the IFC survey data. World Bank Investment Climate Assessments (ICA) data from the two countries are also used. Although the ICA findings were focused more on manufacturing than on services, and thus used more extensively in the chapters on the hardware industries, some of those findings are also applicable to software firms.

Market competitiveness, as measured by ease of entry, pricing power, and market concentration, also influences the international strength of an industry. This chapter examines home-country competitiveness and how it may have affected the export success of the software industries in China and India. The chapter also takes up what contributions, if any, English-language proficiency and work on the Y2K problem[1] made to the success of software-services exporting in India and China.

Government Policies and Regulations

A commonly cited belief holds that the Indian software industry thrived because the central government stayed out of it. The opposite is true. The Indian government was engaged with the software industry in several ways, partly by exempting software firms from regulations—thus, the notion of staying out of it—but also by direct and positive promotion. Software firms did not face the same constraints on flexibility of labor use that applied to manufacturing companies; they were not subject to the detailed planning and licensing regulations imposed on the industrial sector; and they did not have to deal with government inspections to the same degree that manufacturing companies did and were therefore freed from many of the costs of government regulation. Still, surveyed companies reported spending over 10 percent of their management time on government regulation. Informal payments, however, were significantly lower than for manufacturing companies (0.74 percent of revenue compared with 1.33 percent of revenue, respectively). Examples of direct and positive government promotion are identified and quantified below.

In China, it is widely believed that the government strongly influenced the software industry; this analysis supports that belief. The Chinese government's support of science and technology may partially explain why many software firms originated in the state or state-supported sectors, or were allied with universities and received research subsidies (Tschang and Xue 2005). In some cases, the Chinese government used its influence to help create software firms. Of the 30 firms interviewed by Tschang and Xue (2005), four came out of the Chinese Academy of Sciences, seven originated in universities, and three had government origins. In fact, 9 of the largest 13 firms had government or university origins. Moreover, many of the founders of the software firms were permitted to maintain their university appointments and apply the results of their academic research and development (R&D) in their companies. Successful firms tended to have capital support from government-linked venture capital firms (see box 7.1 for a case study example).

The Chinese government's commitment to the success of the software industry is evident in the State Council's Document Number 18, "Notice of Certain Policies to Promote the Software and Integrated Circuit Industry Development." This document identifies information technology (IT) industries in general as critical to the development of China's other industries, and China's 10th Five-Year Plan (2001–05) identified software as a critical, or "pillar," industry essential to economic progress and national security, hence deserving of government promotion, along with more established industries such as computer manufacturing, telecommunications, laser technology, and aerospace.

China also used government procurement at national, regional, and local levels as another tool to support domestic industries. Government procurement represented about 14 percent of the overall software market revenue in 2002 (IFC 2005), much of it for systems integration work, but also for packaged software. The government also maintained a list of software enterprises that could receive preferential treatment; by the end of 2002, 106 enterprises were on the list. The government used procurement policies to support specific firms in the software business deemed to be in the national interest, including Red Flag's Linux, Chinese Academy of Science's Hopen, and Beijing University's Jade Bird and its database program (intended to rival Oracle's).

Box 7.1   SUPCON: Technology and Management Support from the Chinese Government

The automation business is an attractive segment of the Chinese IT sector for firms with technical manufacturing ability. Chinese domestic automation companies have become major competitors of multinational companies such as GE, Honeywell, and Siemens. One of these Chinese competitors, SUPCON Group (for "super control"), was established in 1993. Its products are widely used in chemicals, oil refining, petrochemicals, metallurgy, and electric power processing operations, and in public projects, such as intelligent traffic, water treatment, and education.

Many Chinese IT firms have university or research institute origins—Lenovo from the Chinese Academy of Science, Neusoft from Northeastern University, and SUPCON from Zhejiang University. All of these companies benefited from the Chinese 863 Program, begun in 1986 to stimulate and guide innovation in universities and research institutes. The program focuses on eight major fields related to economic core competences and national security, of which the IT sector is the most important. It also has a fund to support research teams to enable them to commercialize their research results. Using 863 Program support and university facilities, SUPCON began life in a little laboratory at Zhejiang University, then effectively translated its research results into feasible and profitable IT industry applied technologies and production.

SUPCON's main software product, Distributed Control System (DCS), is a central software control package combined with software embedded in a hardware controller. SUPCON's success mainly came from its lower price and its provision of products of equal or higher quality compared with those of foreign companies.

Relying on the National Laboratory of Industrial Technology at the Institute of Advanced Process Control, SUPCON took advantage of Zhejiang University's research abilities and technology consciousness. Its ownership structure is unusual: Zhejiang University owns 40 percent, the central government 10 percent, and managers 50 percent. This ownership configuration gives SUPCON both cost and technical advantages. SUPCON does not pay royalties for the use of technology patented by the university or pay the government for its development portion of R&D support (that is, translating new technology into production). Compared with other high tech companies, SUPCON also benefits from highly skilled employees at relatively low wages because 80 percent of the workforce comes from Zhejiang University and 90 percent of the senior executives have joint appointments at the university.

SUPCON has made great contributions to upgrading conventional industrial operations, improving the level of automation technology in China, and enhancing product quality and manufacturing efficiency. After a decade of hard work, SUPCON's revenue grew from $40,000 to $400 million and its assets grew from $20,000 to $100 million. Its average annual rate of revenue growth is 50 percent.

Sources: www.soft6.com/news/detail.asp?id= 14785; www.supcon.com/supcon/jsp/index.jsp; www.863.org.cn/863_105/indust/index.html; Zhen Wu personal interview.

Set against government promotion of the software industry is a long list of regulatory issues in China that reduce the effectiveness of the incentives its policies offer. A multitude of agencies regulate parts of the industry, and competing regulators vie for a larger say in the future of new lines of business. Lack of transparency in the regulatory decision-making process remains a concern for industry players and complicates business planning. Ongoing reform, however, is gradually leading to a more transparent regulatory environment. As part of these changes, China's regulatory agencies are moving from an economic planning function to acting more as independent regulators.

Growth-Promoting Policies

The analysis of IFC survey data indicates specific impacts of government policies that either promoted or hindered the growth of software companies. Managers in the surveyed firms reported the perceived effects of these policies.

> *Government policies intended to promote the growth of software firms had only a moderate impact, and the overall impact on firms in China was not greater than the overall impact on firms in India.*

Three sets of policies have statistical significance in the multivariate analysis of Indian and Chinese software firms. Provision of infrastructure and liberalization of import policies had stronger growth-promoting impacts for Indian than for Chinese software firms. Of course, these different impacts could be reflecting the inferior starting position of the Indian industry. The Indian government's provision of infrastructure does not indicate an advantage for Indian firms; it implies at best an equalizing of the infrastructure gap between China and India. Even so, the strength of the impacts for Indian firms, measured by the mean scale scores of 3.8 and 3.5 (out of a maximum of 5.0) for provision of infrastructure and liberalization of import policies, respectively, is not that great. Marketing support, which takes the form of both government procurement and directives to state-owned enterprises to use software from Chinese-owned companies (Saxenian and Quan 2005), was more beneficial to Chinese firms (table 7.1).

The impacts of provision of infrastructure, liberalization of import policies, and support for marketing were about the same for software services firms and software products firms, with one exception: Chinese software products firms were notably unenthusiastic about liberalized import policies, which follows from their largely domestic business.

Chinese software firm managers viewed the impact of government support of R&D more positively than did Indian managers, but Indian managers reported their government's education policies had a greater impact than did Chinese managers. Both of these differences were statistically significant in a simple comparison but neither survived a multivariate test. Similarly, Chinese managers found a less-positive impact than did Indian managers from government liberalization of foreign direct investment policies. As with import policies, the domestic-market focus of Chinese software firms led to less enthusiasm for more foreign firm participation.

Most software companies benefited from corporate income tax concessions (90 percent of Chinese firms and 81 percent of Indian firms); Indian and Chinese firms do not differ significantly in this respect. Within the Indian software indus-

Table 7.1   Impact of Government Policies on Firm Growth
(scale: 1 = no impact, 5 = great impact)

Finding: *Most Indian and Chinese software firms got government tax concessions, and managers reported the impact on firm growth was substantial. Policies with substantial positive impact that differed with statistical significance between the two countries in a multivariate analysis were (1) provision of infrastructure and liberalization of import policies that had greater impact on Indian firms and (2) marketing support that had more impact on Chinese firms.*

Policies that encourage growth	China	India
Tax concessions	3.6	4.0
Infrastructure provision	*3.0*	*3.8*
Marketing support	*3.7*	*2.6*
R&D support	3.6	2.8
Education policies	2.3	3.4
Liberalization of import policies	*1.4*	*3.5*
Foreign direct investment policies	1.9	3.4

Finding: *The growth of Indian software firms was hindered by U.S. government visa policies restricting travel, and by domestic government bureaucracy, both of which hindered Chinese firms less in a multivariate analysis.*

Policies that hinder growth	China	India
Taxes—corporate income, excise, and sales	3.6	3.6
Infrastructure quality and quantity	3.2	3.9
Travel and visa restrictions	*2.5*	*3.9*
Bureaucracy and paperwork requirements	*2.5*	*3.6*
Efficiency of government services (low)	2.5	3.4
Import tariffs and import restrictions (high)	2.0	3.2

Source: IFC survey.
Note: Policies in italics show a statistically significant difference between Indian and Chinese firms in a multivariate analysis.

try, however, software services firms reported greater benefit than did software products firms.

Growth-Hindering Policies

Both Indian and Chinese software managers reported, on average, modest negative impacts of government policies on their firms' growth; the overall negative impact on firms was greater in India than in China.

The mean overall impact of government policies that hindered firm growth was reported to be 3.4 by Indian managers and 2.6 by Chinese managers (where 1 = no impact and 5 = great impact). For every government policy investigated, Indian managers perceived stronger adverse impacts than did their Chinese counterparts; some of these differences were significant in a multivariate analysis while others were not (see table 7.1). This reflects either a real difference in the magnitude of impacts or a cultural difference in reporting perceptions. For Indian managers, however, negative impacts were slightly stronger than positive impacts, whereas among Chinese managers the reverse was true, although these differences are not significant.

The government policies that are expected to hinder the growth of software firms did show these adverse impacts in the analysis of the IFC survey data. Indian software managers were adversely affected by government bureaucracy and paperwork requirements, more so than their Chinese counterparts, and this difference is significant in a multivariate analysis. Indian managers were also adversely affected by travel and visa restrictions resulting from U.S. government policies, which affected Indians much more than Chinese because of the dominance of exports in Indian businesses. Indian managers more than Chinese managers complained about poor infrastructure and inefficient government services, but the differences were significant only in simple comparisons. High import tariffs and other import restrictions also had a greater negative impact for Indian than Chinese software managers in a simple comparison (but not in a multivariate analysis), probably because of the greater reliance of Indian software firms on imported inputs, whereas Chinese software firms, with a stronger and lower-cost domestic hardware industry, were more self-sufficient. Government tax policies had an equal impact on both Chinese and Indian software firms.

Infrastructure and Institutions

Infrastructure and institutions affect the ability of firms in an industry to grow and complete. Their impacts on Chinese and Indian software firms are analyzed in this section.

Infrastructure

Infrastructure requirements for software production are modest. The critical requirements are a reliable but modest electrical power supply; urban transportation to bring staff to work; and broadband telecommunications connectivity for receiving inputs and delivering outputs, especially internationally. Software production does not depend on other physical infrastructure, such as road or rail transportation and ports.

Comparisons of physical infrastructure in China and India uniformly favor China (table 7.2). The deficiencies in Indian physical infrastructure are well known. Unreliable electric power supply from the public grid is a continuing problem for all of Indian industry. By many measures, Indian telecommunications connectivity is far below the levels achieved in China. One reason for the past dominance of bodyshopping was to avoid reliance on Indian infrastructure (A. Desai 2003). In 1990, more than 95 percent of software exports were on-site. This number had declined to 45 percent by 2003 as telecommunications infrastructure improved (A. Desai 2003; Kapur 2002).

Table 7.2   Infrastructure Impact on Growth
(1 = no problem, 5 = major problem)

Finding: *Both electric power cuts and public transportation failures were more serious problems for Indian than for Chinese software companies, but telecommunications infrastructure problems were not significantly different between the two countries. Most software firms in both countries were located in special parks or zones.*

Infrastructure	China	India
Electric power		
Power cuts: seriousness of problem	*1.9*	*3.1*
Have own electric power facilities (percentage yes)	*23*	*87*
Transportation		
Public transport failures	1.6	2.6
Telecommunications		
Unavailable telephone service	1.8	2.1
Unavailable internet broadband service	2.2	2.5
STPs, SEZs, or export processing zones (percentage of firms in survey located in these places)[a]	83	88

Source: IFC survey.
Note: Variables in italics show a statistically significant difference between Chinese and Indian firms in a multivariate analysis.
a. SEZ = Special Economic Zone (China). STP = Software Technology Park (India).

Electrical power was a more serious problem for Indian software firms than for Chinese firms, and many more Indian firms had their own power generation facilities. These differences are statistically significant in a multivariate analysis of the two countries' firms. Public transportation failures affected Indian software firms more than Chinese in a simple comparison.

Managers at Indian software firms in the IFC survey reported that electric power cuts or surges from the public grid were, on average, closer to a "major problem," while their Chinese counterparts reported results closer to "no problem." Accordingly, most Indian firms (87 percent) had their own electric power supply facilities while only 23 percent of Chinese firms did. These results were true whether the firms were software services or software products firms, and were statistically significant in a multivariate analysis of the two countries' firms.

Public transportation problems were less serious for Chinese software companies than for Indian companies in a simple comparison (though not in a multivariate analysis), probably because many Indian software companies were located away from the center of major urban areas in software technology parks, to which public buses and trains did not run. Almost half of all Indian software firms in the

---

Box 7.2 Wipro: From Edible Oils to Hardware to Software

In 1945, Hasham Premji founded Western India Vegetable Products (Wipro) to make vegetable oil and soaps. In 1966, when his son was still at Stanford University, Hasham died. The 21-year-old Azam Premji returned to India to manage the company. After modernizing the vegetable oils business, he diversified into soaps and hydraulic power systems in the 1970s. In 1979, when IBM withdrew from India, Wipro Infotech was launched, using licensed technology from the United States to build mini-computers. The hardware business did well in a market protected from imported hardware and grew 70 percent to 80 percent a year from 1988 to 1995. After 1995, India's branded hardware business stalled, as imports of computers were liberalized and competition from unbranded PCs increased.

Meanwhile, Wipro had turned to developing software. Beginning in 1984, Wipro sought to develop branded software packages for its mini-computers. Although that effort was unsuccessful, the company began writing software for IBM computers in 1987. Following the lead of TCS (see box 6.2), Wipro supplied IT staff to work on-site in the United States and Europe. As bandwidth in India and client comfort levels increased, more of this work was brought back to India, and as the hardware business declined, staff transferred to the software business. In 1998, the two businesses were combined. In 1998, Wipro Infotech became the world's first software services company to obtain the Capability Maturity Model (CMM) Level 5 rating from the Software Engineering Institute. By 2000, Wipro's turnover was $530 million annually, of which 80 percent came from its IT businesses. Wipro's software production is located in software technology parks in Bangalore, Hyderabad, Chennai, New Delhi, and Pune.

Wipro benefited from tax breaks to the software industry. Wipro Infotech's effective tax rate is around 14 percent compared with the Indian average of 38.5 percent.

Source: Paine, Knoop, and Raju 2001.

---

survey provided transportation services. India's road network is deficient, with higher costs and slower service compared with China.

The evolution of the Indian company Wipro from a hardware manufacturer to a major software house illustrates the role of STPs and tax concessions in supporting growth (box 7.2).

Institutions

Institutions—legal, financial, regulatory, educational—are necessary for the efficient functioning of markets (table 7.3); when they are well developed a firm's growth is facilitated. India's legal institutions, which follow the British model, are especially important to the functioning of markets in general and are better regarded than China's. Indian judicial processes are respected for fairness although criticized for long delays.

Financial institutions are also important for the growth of firms generally; Indian financial institutions, banks, stock markets, and sources of venture capital are all well developed. However, the Indian regulatory burden on firms is widely criticized. The analysis investigated several of the effects of these institutions.

Table 7.3   Similarities in Perceptions of Chinese and Indian Institutions

Finding: *None of the features of the institutional environment perceived by the firms' managers was statistically significantly different between China and India.*

Indicator	China	India
Legal: Judicial system effectiveness in enforcing contractual and property rights (5 = fully effective, 1 = not at all effective)		
Mean	3.5	3.5
Median	4.0	4.0
Regulatory: Management time spent dealing with government regulations (percentage of time)		
Mean	8.9	10.6
Median	10.0	10.0
Labor: Desired employment level compared with actual (percentage of existing workforce)		
Mean	106.2	106.8
Median	100.0	100.0
Customs: Customs clearance time (average number of days)		
Imports	9.0	9.9
Exports	7.3	6.3
Corruption: Informal payments to public officials to get things done (percentage of revenue for a typical firm)		
Mean	0.8	0.7
Median	0	0.01

Source: IFC survey.

None of the features of the institutional environment deemed important for the software industry shows a statistically significant difference between China and India as reported by the firms' managers, except for education.

Despite the claimed superiority of Indian institutions, the lack of differences in their effects in China and India as perceived by managers is probably due to the relatively small impact of the institutions investigated by this analysis on the software industry.

The Indian and Chinese judicial systems were reported to be equally effective in enforcing companies' contractual and property rights. The similar judgments of managers apply whether the firms in question were software services or software products firms. For software in China and India, the protection of intellectual property rights in the home country has not been critical if only because the amount of proprietary intellectual property created has been small.

The need for financial capital in the software industry is not great. The well-regarded Indian financial services sector, which includes debt, equity, and venture capital financing, was not decisively important to Indian software firms. Somewhat more than one-third of the Indian firms had debt capital and a similar proportion had equity capital. While fewer Chinese software firms had either of these two forms of finance, the difference between the two countries' firms was not statistically significant (see the section on capital in chapter 5).

Educational institutions are another critical element of the business environment, and software firms depend on them as the source of technically prepared professional labor. India's educational system, which established high-quality technical institutes in the late 1960s, and the government's thrust toward science-based research are both regarded as important for the success of the Indian software industry. Chapter 5 showed that both entry-level educational qualifications and the share of professional employment in the firm were statistically significant differences between Indian and Chinese software firms.

Restrictive Indian labor laws did not yield a disadvantage for Indian software firms compared with their Chinese counterparts. The median firm in both countries was at its desired employment level (the mean desired level was above the actual for both countries' firms, at about 106 percent). Restrictive Indian labor laws that made it very difficult to reduce the number of employees did not adversely affect software firms noticeably because most of these firms were fast growing and did not face threats of layoffs. Most software firms were small, and many were exempt from the provisions of Indian labor laws. Managers also found ways to get around the more onerous provisions of these laws.

The regulatory burden and bureaucratic maze software firms faced was no different for Indian and Chinese firms and no different for software services versus software products firms. The time that managers spent dealing with government regulations was the same for firms in each country at about 10 percent of their time. This time burden was smaller than that reported by managers in other industries, where the figure was nearly 15 percent of their time (World Bank 2004b).

The problems, if any, that firms faced with delays in customs clearances were about the same for both Indian and Chinese software firms, with an average of 9–10 days for imports to clear customs, and 6–7 days for exports to clear customs.

If corruption is indicated in part by the need for firms to make informal payments to public officials to get things done (with regard to customs, taxes, licenses, regulatory approvals), then there was no difference between the perception that Indian and Chinese software managers had about payments that were required. The figures that managers gave were low—the median was zero and the mean less than 1 percent of revenue.

Market Competitiveness

Firms are stronger internationally if the markets in which they participate are more competitive. This analysis examined market-level variables characteristic of the product market that software firms face and the industry in which they compete.

Indian software firms faced more competitive markets than did Chinese software firms, partly but not wholly because most Indian firms were software services firms facing export markets, whereas Chinese firms were software products firms facing domestic markets.

Three common indicators of market competitiveness are ease of entry, pricing power, and market concentration. The easier it is to enter a market, the more competitive it is. The less willingly customers accept price increases, the less pricing power the firm has and the more competitive the market. On both these indicators, Indian firm managers reported that they faced more competitive markets— easier entry and less ability to raise prices.[1] The market competitiveness difference also holds for software services firms (taking Chinese and Indian firms together), which faced more competitive markets than did software products firms (table 7.4). For software products firms, ease of entry was no different for Indian than for Chinese firms.

The market concentration of an industry can be estimated by the market share accounted for by the few largest firms and by the size distribution of firms. Software industries in both China and India consist of many small firms (see chapter 4). In 2004, India had more than 3,000 software firms with an average firm size of 175 employees. In 2001, China had more than 5,000 firms with an average firm size of 25 employees. While scale economies in software services production are not important and entry into the industry is quite easy, many Chinese software firms may still be too small to be effective in international markets. The Indian software industry is more concentrated: the largest 25 Indian software firms had about two-thirds of the industry's sales revenue in 2002, whereas it took 70 firms to account for half of the Chinese software industry's sales revenue. This comparison, however, does not accurately reflect competitiveness among Indian software

Table 7.4   Software Market Competitiveness

Indicator	China	India	Services	Products
Ease of entry into the industry (1 = very easy, 5 = very hard)	*3.7*	*3.0*	*2.9*	*3.7*
Pricing power with customers (1 = do not accept, 5 = accept willingly)	*3.2*	*2.5*	*2.5*	*3.0*
Threat from imports (1 = no threat, 5 = big threat)	*4.3*	*2.0*	*2.2*	*3.5*
Threat from foreign firms producing in home market (1 = no threat, 5 = big threat)	3.9	3.0	3.2	3.5
Gross margins compared with other industries in the home country (1 = lower, 5 = higher)	3.2	3.6	3.7	3.2

Source: IFC survey.
Note: The variables in italics are statistically significant, differentiating between Chinese and Indian software firms in a multivariate analysis.

firms because they also compete with software firms from other countries for export business. Even so, the four-firm concentration ratio in Indian software was still only 22 percent in 2003 (below the U.S. industry average concentration ratio of 36 percent). Athreye (2005) also concludes that the Indian software industry is competitive, with substantial volatility in market shares among leading firms over time. India's market economy tradition may also contribute to greater rivalry among firms, and the Indian software industry's greater representation in international markets may result in more demanding customers.

Competition arises from foreign sources as well as from local firms. Firms that are less threatened by imports or less threatened by foreign firms that produce in their domestic industry are stronger international competitors, as long as the lack of threat does not come from government protection in the form of restrictions on either imports or FDI. For software, whether in India or China, both trade and investment are relatively free of these restrictions.

From the reports of the surveyed managers, Indian firms were less threatened by imports and less threatened by foreign firms operating in their home country than were Chinese firms. It is also true that software services firms overall (taking China and India together) are less trade- and investment-threatened than software products firms overall. But the India-China difference remains: both Indian software services and products firms are less threatened by foreign competition than their Chinese counterparts.

All of these results taken together imply that Indian software firms operate in more competitive markets than do Chinese software firms, partly because they are predominantly services producers, but also because Indian software firms are themselves more competitive in international markets.

Other Contributing Factors

Two factors—English-language proficiency and the Y2K problem—have often been cited as explanations for India's software services advantage in the world market. This section examines the validity of these explanations.

English-Language Proficiency

One of the first reasons offered to explain why India is a major software exporter and China is not is that the English language is spoken by all educated Indians but not by all educated Chinese. Because many services, including software services, are more language dependent than is manufacturing, India has an advantage over many other countries. The largest markets for software exports by far are the English language–speaking United States and the United Kingdom (62 percent of Indian software exports went to the United States and Canada). The three largest software services exporters are English-speaking countries: India, Canada, and Ireland (see table 1.3). The Philippines and South Africa, however, which also have educated English-speaking professionals, are farther down the list of software exporters and not much different in rank than the Russian Federation, which is not an English-speaking country and does not have large numbers of English-speaking professionals. Furthermore, the second and third largest markets, Japan and Germany, are not English-language countries.

Although some studies of the strengths and weaknesses of the Indian software industry cite English language as an important factor (Aggarwal and Pandey 2004), others do not claim it to be critical (NASSCOM 2004).

India's English-language capability was a contributing factor to its firms' export success, but it was not a decisive factor and is not a sufficient explanation. A lack of English-speaking software engineers did not hamper Chinese exporting, but English-language deficiency coupled with project management weakness among managers did.

Writing lines of code and testing software, which are entry-level software services tasks, and which constituted by far the largest share of Indian software services exports, did not require great skill with the English language. Many Chinese university graduates familiarized themselves with the English language during their studies, and while they could not be termed English speakers, their capability was sufficient to do coding and testing. The vocabulary and grammar of English-language software code was simpler and easier to grasp than the spoken and written language. Chinese software managers themselves in interviews conducted for the IFC survey were quite clear about the way in which the English language affected Chinese software growth, especially exports. It does not take English proficiency to write lines of code, and there are ample and growing numbers of Chinese software engineers who can do that; lack of English proficiency was not a constraint.

The number of technically educated university graduates is large in China as it is in India, and the supply of these graduates in China appears to have increased at least as fast as the demand for them. The supply of labor qualified to write and test English-language software code appears to have been sufficient in China.

The English language capability of Chinese software managers was a limiting factor in Chinese software export performance, but it was coincidental with limited project management capability among these managers. Greater English-language capability without greater project management capability probably would not have resulted in greater Chinese software export growth.

The number of qualified and experienced English-speaking software project managers in China was insufficient to develop a rapidly growing and large export business. Fluency in written and spoken English was necessary not only to obtain software outsourcing business from the United States, the United Kingdom, and other foreign customers, but also to manage the client relationship. The ability of Chinese software managers to negotiate contracts, provide follow-up customer service, and obtain export business was limited because the number of managers able to work in English comfortably was insufficient. However, it was not only English language that was necessary; it was also skill in enterprise-level solution architecture, design, and implementation of projects. One without the other was ineffective.

The lack of project management skill derived from three sources. One was the emphasis on traditional engineering fields in universities. A second was the discomfort stemming from national cultural traits that many Chinese managers would feel in open and collaborative environments that characterize progressive, outward-looking software companies. A third source was the relative youth of Chinese software managers (younger than Indian managers) and their associated lack of experience, especially in a market economy, which contributed to the weaker project management skills of Chinese compared with Indian software managers. Export business demanded those skills.

The English-language proficiency of Indian engineers had another effect: the common language reduced barriers to adoption of U.S. software products for use in India. These products can be imported without adaptation, thus reducing incentives for software engineers in India to develop products rather than services and further facilitates software services, because suppliers and customers use common software products.

Y2K

In the late 1990s, fear ran rampant over concerns about the possible failure of computer systems at the stroke of midnight on December 31, 1999, when the calendar changed to "year 2000" (hence the shortcut, Y2K). The basis for this fear was the way in which code had been written thus far (that is, only the last two digits were used to designate years). This fear of worldwide system failures gave rise to a temporary surge in software conversion work. Some claim the Y2K problem was a serendipitous piece of good luck for Indian software firms and is therefore partly responsible for the growth of the Indian software industry.

Indian software firms were indeed well placed to take advantage of Y2K work. Indian programmers were familiar with obsolete code that had been developed and used many years before; Y2K conversion was labor intensive and at the low end of software development, where India was especially labor abundant; Indian software professionals were low cost for foreign clients; links from Western clients to Indian software firms had already been established via body shopping; and by the late 1990s, it was possible to do this work inexpensively offshore in India using international telecommunications links. While software firms in other countries could also perform Y2K conversion work, they did not have the combination of first-mover advantage and low labor costs that the Indian firms had.

It is easy, however, to overstate the importance of Y2K to the growth of the Indian software industry. According to figures reported by NASSCOM and *Dataquest*, Indian software firms earned 16.5 percent of their export revenue from Y2K-related work in 1998/99 and 12.0 percent in 1999/2000 (Kumar 2001). These shares are significant but not dominant. Furthermore, the growth rate of Indian software export revenue was actually higher after Y2K than before: up 57 percent in 2000/01 over 1999/2000 versus up 52 percent in 1999/2000 versus 1998/99. Y2K was at best a modest demand booster for Indian software firms at the time. The more important role played by Y2K was the increase in exposure to new export customers and the spreading of a reputation for quality work completed on time and within budget. The latter advantage would become especially valuable for the future of the industry.

Note

1. It is hazardous to draw conclusions from perceptions compared across countries with different cultures and business systems. "Easy" and "hard" can have different meanings to different managers. That the data come from reasonably homogeneous firms reduces the hazard somewhat, and there is objective validation for some of the observed differences in perceptions.

Chapter 8

Summary of Factors behind the Success of China's and India's Software Industries

This chapter summarizes the findings of the analysis reported in chapters 4 through 7 and incorporates information from previous chapters to answer two questions:

- Why did the Indian software industry grow so fast as an export-oriented industry?
- Why did the equally fast-growing Chinese software industry thrive in its domestic market but not compete as an export business?

Reasons for India's Export Success

Labor

India's export success was more a matter of skill than low cost. India had an absolute advantage and probably a comparative advantage in software services production that explains Indian firms' export success in Western markets but does not explain why the Indian industry was export oriented while the Chinese industry was not.

Both China and India had large pools of technically educated labor. Chinese labor wages were not significantly different from Indian wages. Chinese labor productivity was higher than Indian productivity industry-wide although probably not in software services firms, and unit labor costs did not differ between the two countries. Therefore, India's abundant and cheap labor does not explain India's export success relative to China.

Indian software firms had two labor advantages over their Chinese counterparts. First, they employed proportionally more professionals than Chinese firms, and Indian software professionals had higher educational qualifications than did their Chinese counterparts. Second, those Indian software firms that had higher labor productivity grew faster than those with lower productivity, whereas labor productivity did not affect growth in Chinese software firms.

The inference from these findings is that Indian software firms had better managers and more skilled workforces than Chinese software firms without incurring higher labor costs.

Management

The characteristics of Indian firm managers were one of India's leading advantages. Top managers can lead a firm's growth and development in several ways. Indian software managers were able to use their experience to accelerate growth. They appeared to use inputs more productively than Chinese managers. They achieved quality certifications when Chinese managers did not, and they created successful organizational cultures.

Quality certifications, one of the most important features of Indian software firms, stem from management action. Many Indian software firms obtained Capability Maturity Model Integration (CMMI) software quality certifications, which assured export customers that the supplier could deliver the contracted service on time, in full, and within budget. More Indian software firms than Chinese software firms had CMMI quality certifications, and Indian firms had more certifications and at higher levels. Furthermore, both Indian and Chinese firms with quality certifications had faster revenue growth than firms without them; this favored the Indian software industry.

Indian managers took advantage of the national cultural traits exhibited in their workforce that fit well with the software industry's requirements for creativity and initiative. The analysis of the IFC survey data shows that the interaction between the entrepreneurial orientation of the firm and the independence of action of its professional employees was a statistically significant difference between Indian and Chinese software firms. Entrepreneurial orientation alone was not sufficient—Chinese professionals were no less entrepreneurial than Indian professionals—rather, it was the combination of entrepreneurship with the questioning habit of Indian professionals that mattered. Management decisions extended further, most notably into the choice to forge strategic alliances with foreign firms. Finally, Indian software managers had more years of experience than Chinese software firm managers, and firms with more experienced managers grew faster.

Technology

India's technology lag was not a major hindrance to success. Indian software firms lagged behind their Chinese counterparts in technology inputs and outputs, but that situation did not hamper the Indian industry's growth. Fewer Indian than Chinese software firms had research and development (R&D) expenditures, and those that did spent less on R&D than did their Chinese counterparts. This result is due only in part to the greater concentration of software services firms over products firms in India (software products firms are more likely to have R&D expenditures than software services firms). In addition, Indian software firms introduced fewer new products than did Chinese software firms. Until very recently, however, the software business was not an especially high technology business. Software services firms especially did not compete on the basis of advanced technology. Moreover, the export business consisted mostly of customized software services, much of which involved low-end, entry-level work for which neither R&D nor new product introductions were important. As software firms move toward more high–value added work, the technology level increases.

International links

Alliances were among the most important of Indian advantages. The links firms established with foreign companies may be the most important explanation for Indian software industry export success. Many more Indian software firms had nonequity strategic alliances, especially marketing alliances, than did Chinese software firms; Indian firms had more of such alliances; and among Indian firms but not Chinese firms, a larger number of alliances contributed to faster revenue growth. Links with foreign companies generated exposure to best practices in the industry, and facilitated more rapid adoption of successful corporate cultures.

The role of nonresident Indians (NRIs), another frequently mentioned advantage for Indian software firms, is not as important as it once was. The role of NRIs and overseas Chinese (for example, in providing access to markets and best practices in management) made only a modest contribution to export success. The roles and importance of these nonresidents were not different for Indian firms compared with Chinese firms.

Foreign ownership of software firms located in India most often is in the form of portfolio investment, whereas foreign ownership of Chinese software firms tends to be in the form of direct investment. Foreign ownership did not contribute to the growth of Indian software firms but it did to Chinese software firms. The potential for foreign owners to provide access to foreign markets was not important for Indian software firms—nonequity strategic alliances did this—but it did contribute to the growth of Chinese firms that did not have other alliances.

Government policies

India's export growth was partly due to active government promotion, not just to governmental benign neglect. The software industry, a services industry that emerged only a few years before the Indian "license raj" was dismantled, did benefit from less government regulation than the longer-established hardware manufacturing industry. The government actively promoted the software industry in three principal ways:

• Government policies helped software companies overcome the major infrastructure weaknesses they faced in India—unreliable electric power and lack of international telecommunications—by creating software technology parks with satellite telecommunications links. The government also allowed companies to build their own power and telecommunications facilities, which added a modest amount to the cost of software services and products.

- Other government policies facilitated imports of equipment that software companies needed and drastically reduced tariffs on the import of computers and components.
- The government gave incentives for exporting software by applying specific income tax concessions to software exports. (Chinese software companies also received income tax concessions from the government, but the Chinese tax concessions were not so directly linked to exports.)

Not all government influences on the Indian software industry were positive. More Indian software firm managers than Chinese managers considered government bureaucracy and inefficiency burdensome. These subjectively reported differences may be due to a greater tendency among Indians to voice disagreement.

Infrastructure

Indian firms found ways to work around infrastructure weaknesses. The most important infrastructure component needed for software production is reliable electric power, and Indian firms suffered from much more serious electric power problems than did their Chinese counterparts. In fact, China's infrastructure superiority over India's was a benefit to Chinese industry. Indian firms mitigated this disadvantage, however, by installing their own generators to supply electric power. Also, most Indian firms are located in software technology parks that provide a more stable power supply but still depend on the public grid.

Institutions

The role of institutions was not significant in either Indian or Chinese firms. Indian legal and financial institutions are reputed to be quite good, yet Indian firms claimed that restrictive labor laws and government regulations were burdensome. According to the managers surveyed, however, none of these institutional features mattered for Indian or Chinese software firms. This result could be due to the relatively small intersection these institutions have with the software industry.

Market competitiveness

India had an edge over China in market competitiveness. Firms are stronger internationally if the markets in which they participate are more competitive. Indian software firms faced more competitive markets than did Chinese software firms: they had less pricing power with customers, and market entry was easier. The greater prevalence of services rather than products businesses of Indian firms may partly, but not wholly, explain this greater competitiveness. Indian software firms were also less threatened than Chinese by the potential of having foreign companies operate in their home market. Indian software firms were not competing against foreign multinational firms operating in India to nearly the same extent as Chinese software firms were in Chinese. Few of the largest software firms operating in India were foreign, and those that were there were usually captive cost centers that "exported" software services only to their parent companies abroad.

Influence of the English language

English-language proficiency was important but not sufficient to explain India's export success. That English is spoken by all educated Indians but not by all educated Chinese is an oft-cited reason for India's success at becoming a major software exporter while China has not. The largest market for software exports by far is the English language–speaking United States. Other English-speaking countries are not major software services exporters, however, and other countries that are not English speaking are exporters. English language among programmers is adequate in China, but managers' inability to conduct business in English was a handicap.

Y2K

This worldwide crisis-prevention effort was an unexpected opportunity for Indian software developers. Chance or luck often plays a part in favoring or complicating an industry's growth. The Y2K problem gave rise to a temporary surge in software conversion work and was, it is claimed, a stroke of luck for Indian software firms. The evidence shows that Y2K was at best a modest demand booster for Indian software firms. Y2K revenue never was a large share of Indian firms' total revenue, and revenue growth actually was faster after Y2K than before. The more important role played by Y2K was to increase Indian software companies' exposure to new export customers and to spread their reputation for quality work completed on time and within budget.

The Chinese Software Industry Success Story

The Chinese software industry grew equally as fast as the Indian software industry and is as large, if not larger. The Chinese industry's growth, however, came mainly from domestic sales. The success factors for the Chinese software industry are, with one exception, different from those that underpin the Indian software industry.

The Chinese domestic market

Rapid expansion of software-using industries boosted domestic growth. The Chinese software industry grew rapidly by serving the domestic market. Software demand is largely a derived demand that depends on the growth of the businesses that use software as well as on retail consumer demand. The Chinese economy overall grew rapidly for many years—the average annual real GDP growth rate was 9.6 percent over the span from 1979, when economic reform first began, to 2004—a period that embraces the entire development of the software industry (Economist

Intelligence Unit 2006). But the Chinese software industry grew more than three times faster than the overall economy, in part because demand for software increased faster than overall demand.

The most software-intensive industries in China are telecommunications, financial services, education, government, and energy. These industries were also faster growing than the Chinese economy overall.[1] For example, the telecommunications industry showed a 25 percent growth rate in 2005. Furthermore, the very large Chinese hardware industry is itself a heavy user of software that is bundled with hardware. Among the 10 largest Chinese software firms, 6 are also hardware firms (such as Huawei). The hardware industry grew almost as fast as the software industry and is much larger, thus contributing sizable increments to software industry growth.

English language and local practices
The need for adaptation to local conditions provided a ready market for domestic software firms. As educated Indians' English-language proficiency contributed to their firms' export performance, the lack of English proficiency among Chinese businesspeople contributed to the growth of the domestic Chinese software industry. Most businesses did not find it useful to import software products or services written in English, so local firms needed to produce local-language software. To be sure, the existence of English-language software platforms and applications aided Chinese firms in producing local-language products with similar functionality, but the market demand was still met by Chinese software firms. Additionally, domestic market demand encompassed not only customized software services, but also standardized packaged products.

Even if Chinese software customers could use software products written in English, such products probably were unsuited for direct, off-the-shelf use because of differences in business practices ranging from accounting to human resources management. These differences in business practices were sometimes quite wide because of substantial underlying differences in both regulation and national culture.

International links
Foreign direct investment facilitated output of software products. Chinese software firms developed most of their international links through foreign direct investment. More than one-third of Chinese software firms were wholly or partly foreign owned. In particular, packaged software products firms that produced mainly for the Chinese domestic market had extensive foreign ownership. Foreign investment brings capital and technology, both of which are more necessary for software products than for software services.

Resources
Ample supplies aided industry growth. Chinese software firms had the necessary resources to meet rapidly growing domestic market demand, including a sizable

labor pool, adequate productivity, and low wages—not better than the same factors in India, but adequate. They also had technology, both from foreign investment and from their own R&D. Almost all Chinese software firms spent money on R&D, even if for adaptive rather than innovative purposes; many of them also introduced new products and applied for Chinese patents. Software firms enjoyed reliable infrastructure, could produce software to grow with the market, and were not resource constrained.

Government

Active promotion aided software firms but not exporters to the same degree. Chinese government at both the central and local levels promoted the software industry. The government did so directly and actively by creating Special Economic Zones where technology companies were favored in a variety of ways even if they were not exporters. For example, the government offered income tax concessions (such as no income tax for three years and half the usual tax rate for the next two years). Governments provided marketing support by means of their procurement policies, which often included encouraging state-owned enterprises to use Chinese software vendors and foreign-owned software companies to use Chinese suppliers. Governments provided competitively awarded grants to software firms as well as cheap loans. And in the early days of the industry, governments created software firms as spin-offs from research institutes and universities.

Governments also supported the software industry (along with many other industries) indirectly by permitting foreign direct investment and doing so early in the industry's life.

Note

1. These claims are supported in part by statistics on the share of information technology revenue that is accounted for by various sectors (IDC 2006) and by the expert opinions of Chinese IT consultants who were interviewed for this study.

Part III
Hardware

Chapter 9

Hardware Industry Performance in China and India: An Introduction

The global computing hardware industry has grown rapidly, driven by technological change that led to the widespread use of computers and related hardware in more-advanced economies. Much of the industry's growth occurred as China and India were reforming their economic policies; today's prevailing business environment and production conditions in those countries have mitigated the influence of past regimes (see chapter 3). Under these changed conditions, China attained prominence in the hardware industry. The Chinese industry, including its exports, is huge and growing rapidly. India's hardware industry, until very recently, was small and growing much more slowly. To understand the differences in the performance of the hardware industries in the two countries, two questions are asked:

- What are the specific production and business environment conditions that propelled the Chinese hardware industry into its world-leading position?
- Why did the Indian hardware industry fail until recent years to keep pace?

Before responding to these questions, however, it is important to describe the context for analyzing the key features of the hardware industries in the two countries.

Overview of the Hardware Industries in China and India

This section describes the key features of Chinese and Indian hardware firms: size, growth, types of products, and export and domestic sales. The comparison of Chinese and Indian hardware industries is complicated by differences in data coverage and availability. For example, Chinese statistics refer to sales revenue for information technology (IT) and electronics products whereas official statistics for India

The empirical analysis of the survey data in chapters 10 through 12 was conducted jointly with Professor N. S. Siddharthan of the Delhi University Institute of Economic Growth until 2007 and the Madras School of Economics since 2007, whose contributions the authors acknowledge with gratitude.

refer to production of electronics products. Both countries' data include computers and peripherals and their components, telecommunications equipment, and industrial electronics products, but this analysis excludes consumer electronics from both countries' data.

Industry Size

One immediately apparent difference is that the Chinese hardware industry is massively bigger than the Indian industry. China's IT and electronics manufacturing industry appears to be more than 40 times larger than India's, and the gap has grown over time. The estimated sales revenue for China's IT and electronics products industry reached approximately $320 billion in 2004, while the Indian industry's production value was just $7.5 billion in 2004/05 (table 9.1 and figure 9.1). By 2006, the Chinese industry had increased dramatically—to $579 billion—while the Indian industry had grown to $9.9 billion.

Employment in the Chinese electronics and telecom equipment industries in 2002 was estimated to exceed 1,865,000 persons, and 4,560 firms had annual revenue over $600,000. By 2004, the employment figure had risen to 3,794,500 (National Bureau of Statistics of China 2003, 2005).

Worldwide, the hardware industry in 2004 was estimated to have a market value of $965 billion to $1,164 billion, depending on the source of the data. Computers, peripherals, and their components accounted for one-third to one-half of the market, and telecom equipment accounted for another one-quarter to one-third. The other subindustry included in the worldwide market is semiconductors.

Industry Growth

The large size and rapid growth of China's IT and electronics products industry are related in part to the rapid growth of the Chinese economy overall. The growth of export-oriented industries, which include China's IT and electronics manufacturing industry, is in turn related to the inputs available to it and to the productivity of those inputs.

In general, a nation's economic growth depends on the use of additional inputs or increases in the productivity of inputs. For China and India, increases in capital accounted for one-third of each nation's growth in aggregate output during the 1980–99 period, and input productivity accounted for the remaining two-thirds. However, China's much faster rate of economic growth was attributed to much larger absolute gains in input productivity and capital accumulation, both of which increased more than twice as fast in China as in India (Bosworth and Collins 2003). Improvements in education over the same period played a much smaller role (table 9.2). Productivity improvements may reflect access to better technology or a better business environment that enables inputs to be combined more efficiently to produce more output. In general terms, China was able to be more productive with the labor force and capital it had. The empirical analysis that follows takes into consideration these aggregate findings.

Table 5.1 Size of Hardware Industry in China, India, and Worldwide

India ($ millions)	1990/91	1991/92	1992/93	1993/94	1994/95	1995/96	1996/97	1997/98	1998/99	1999/2000	2000/01	2001/02	2002/03	2003/04	2004/05	2005/06	2006/07
Electronics production value	2,617	2,487	2,514	2,775	3,193	3,348	3,503	3,658	3,812	3,902	4,191	4,202	4,994	6,366	7,554	8,807	9,870
Computers	361	320	318	334	401	—	—	—	546	577	744	744	860	1,510	2,018	2,393	2,759
Components	670	675	713	783	910	—	—	—	1,128	1,200	1,204	1,195	1,367	1,200	2,018	1,964	1,921
Industrial electronics	617	545	525	541	617	—	—	—	784	866	875	943	1,036	1,344	1,766	1,975	2,208
Telecom equipment	718	747	826	1,003	1,080	—	—	—	1,045	924	985	943	1,235	1,690	1,055	1,670	2,185
Strategic	251	200	132	114	185	—	—	—	309	335	383	377	496	622	700	677	1,060
Exports	—	—	—	—	—	—	—	—	427	323	1,048	1,250	1,240	1,330	2,007	2,173	2,539

China ($ billions)	1998	1999	2000	2001	2002	2003	2004	2005	2006
Information and electronic products sales revenue	40.7	51.9	70.0	94.5	169.1	227.1	320.0	464.5	579.3
Exports	26.9	39.0	55.1	65.0	92.0	142.0	207.5	—	—

Worldwide ($ millions)	1998	1999	2000	2001	2002	2003*	2004
Total market value	—	—	947,300	861,000	849,100	890,600	965,200
Computer hardware	—	—	308,000	299,600	308,000	320,500	338,500
Computer storage and peripherals	—	—	107,400	110,200	104,600	113,000	116,900
Semiconductors	—	—	210,700	145,300	147,300	166,400	210,600
Telecom equipment	—	—	321,200	305,900	289,200	290,700	299,000

Sources: China: China Information Industry, Annual Report, various years, via www.chinaunicom.com.cn.
India: Indian Department of Information Technology, Annual Reports 2002/03, 2003/04, 2004/05, 2006/07 via www.mit.gov.in for 1997/98 to 2004/05; Indian Department of Electronics via Indian Electrical & Electronics Manufacturer's Association (www.ieema.org) for calendar years 1990–94.
Worldwide: Datamonitor Industry Market Research reports on each of the sectors shown, 2005 (various dates). Other sources give other figures.
Note: — = Not available.

For India data, industrial sector includes embedded control systems, networking and communication technologies, dedicated electronics hardware; strategic sector includes satellite communication, navigation surveillance, underwater electronics, infra-red detection, GPS tracking systems. Consumer electronics excluded ($3,856 billion in 2004/05).
Worldwide total market value is the sum of the four industries. Computer hardware includes personal computers, servers, mainframes, workstations, and peripherals.
Computer storage and peripherals includes data storage components, motherboards, audio and video cards, monitors, keyboards, printers, other components and peripherals.
Communications equipment includes telephones, switchboards, exchanges, routers, local area networks, and wide area networks.
Compiled by Stanley Nollen with assistance from Zhen Wu, Qi Lei, and Diliwar Bajouri

Figure 9.1   Hardware Market Size, 1991–2006

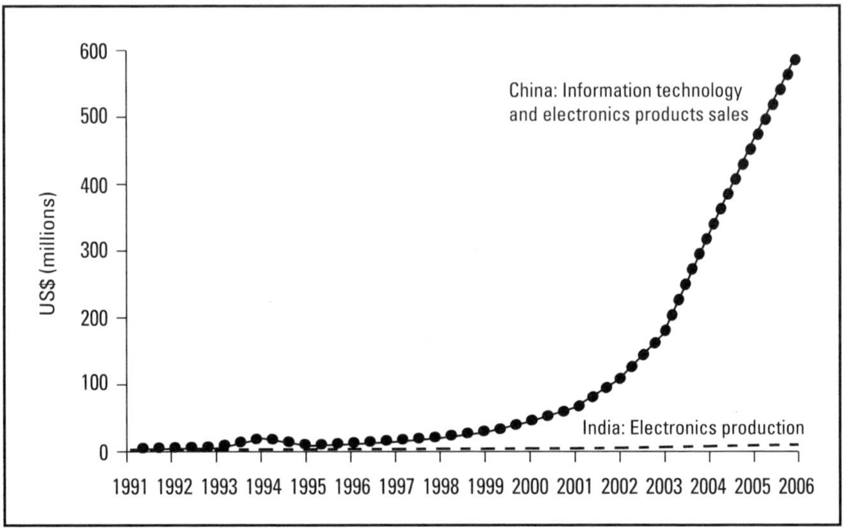

Source: Table 9.1.
Note: 1993–94 comparison for China is biased by change data definition and coverage.

Table 9.2   Contributions to Growth of Output, 1980–99

	China	India
Annual percentage growth rate		
Output	9.75	5.73
Output per worker	7.85	3.60
Source of annual growth rate of output per worker		
Percentage points		
Factor productivity	4.71	2.05
Physical capital	2.63	1.18
Education	0.36	0.33
Percent of total		
Factor productivity	60	57
Physical capital	33	33

Source: Bosworth and Collins 2003.

The Chinese hardware industry grew much faster than the Indian hardware industry, especially in the mid-2000s, and at same pace as the Chinese software industry, if not faster. The Chinese electronics industry compound annual growth rate was 38 percent per year over the 1991–2004 period and 44 percent per year during 1995–2004 (see figure 9.1). In the three years ending in 2004, the Chinese hardware industry's revenues more than tripled.

The compound annual growth rate (CAGR) of Indian electronics production was between 4 percent and 8 percent, depending on the period—only 4.4 percent from 1990/91 to 2001/02, but 7.9 percent from 1990/91 to 2004/05. The two-year growth rate from 2002/03 to 2004/05 was 22 percent, and the annual growth rate in 2005/06 and 2006/07 was in the 12 percent to 15 percent range; these figures are much larger than previous years' but still far slower than the Chinese industry's pace. Among all hardware subindustries, computer output by the Indian industry increased the fastest.

The growth rate of the worldwide hardware industry was 6.3 percent over the 1998–2004 period. This rather slow growth rate reflects the absolute decline in the market in both 2001 and in 2002 and a quite slow recovery since then.

Types of Products

The main product lines in the Chinese hardware industry were computers and telecom equipment, accounting for two-thirds of total sales revenue, and components, which accounted for another third of overall industry sales revenue in 2002, the year for which the IFC survey data apply. As table 9.3 shows, in India, the breakout of the hardware industry includes an industrial electronics category, which renders the comparison to China's industry inexact. These proportions have changed somewhat since 1990, with computers and components gaining in share of total production in India. Table 9.3 also shows the percentage of sales revenue by product and process type for the firms in the International Finance Corporation (IFC) survey.

Worldwide, computers and telecom equipment constituted the largest shares of hardware sales revenue—$339 billion in 2004 or 35 percent of the total market accounted for by computers and $299 billion or 31 percent of the total market accounted for by telecom equipment (see table 1.5). The proportions of world revenues have remained stable through 2007 for these two subindustries and for peripherals and semiconductors, the other subindustries presented in the data.

Industry Exports

Production combines different inputs, often from several countries. If an industry serves a global market, domestic demand is one determinant of the growth of the industry and export demand is the other. If the home country offers comparative production cost advantages, that country's industry's growth will exceed the overall growth in global demand at the expense of industry growth in other nations. These cost advantages accrue to factors of production that are less mobile among nations, because factors that are more mobile will tend to cross national boundaries to join less mobile factors of production (see chapter 2). Therefore, factors of production, especially labor, have to be analyzed for each country.

Hardware manufacturing involves industries with different properties. Some subindustries, such as telecom equipment manufacturing, are oriented primarily

**Table 9.3   Proportion of Hardware Market by Type of Hardware
Product and Process, 2002**
(percent)

	All firms	
Product or process	China	India
Computers	—	20
Telecom equipment	—	27
Computers and telecom equipment	67	47
Components	33	30
Industrial electronics	—	23
	IFC survey firms	
	China	India
Type of product		
Computers and peripherals	33	67
Telecom equipment	26	14
Industrial electronics	41	19
Type of process		
Component manufacturing	59	27
Assembly of finished products	61	75
Other (not specified)	13	16

Sources: Table 9.1 in this chapter; IFC survey.
Note: — = Not available. The sum of the "Type of process" figures exceeds 100 percent
because some firms do both component manufacturing and finished product assembly.

to domestic markets because of low value-to-weight ratios that make transportation expensive and exporting less cost-effective. Others, such as manufacturers of industrial electronic components, may have a greater export orientation because the products have high value-to-weight ratios and are less susceptible to infrastructure weaknesses that raise transportation costs.

More than 60 percent of all Chinese hardware sales revenue comes from exports. For India, production for export is much smaller, ranging between 20 percent and 30 percent since 2000/01 and standing at 25 percent in 2006/07. Previously, Indian export intensity was even less, as low as 10 percent (table 9.1 and figure 9.2).

Table 9.4 shows the export intensity of firms in the IFC survey. In both countries, the firms in the sample are somewhat less export oriented than the aggregate for the industries.

Basis for Analysis

To answer the questions posed at the outset of this chapter, differences in the performance of the Chinese and Indian hardware industries are analyzed in chapters

Figure 9.2   Domestic and Export Hardware Markets

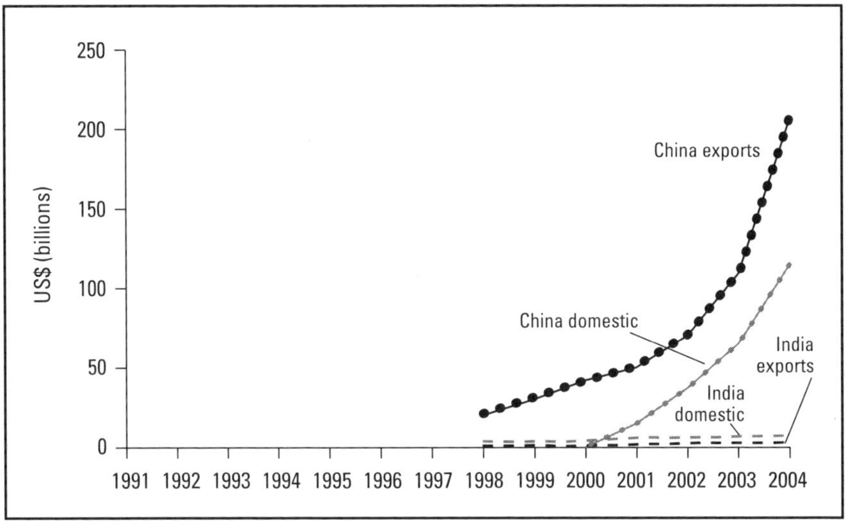

Source: Table 9.1.

Table 9.4   Export Intensity of Firms in the IFC Survey

Export orientation	China	India
Percentage of firms with 10% or more of revenue from exports	36	23
Percentage of firms with 50% or more of revenue from exports	24	14
Export intensity of firms with exports (percentage of revenue from exports)		
Mean	58	30
Median	40	8
Export intensity of all firms, including those with no exports (percentage)	23	16

Source: IFC survey.

10 through 13. The methods and primary source of data (IFC survey) used in this analysis are described in chapter 1.

The task of the analysis is to explain differences between the hardware industries in China and India that relate to the differential growth and development of the two countries' industries. The organization follows the framework set forth in chapter 2: chapter 10 takes up factors of production, chapter 11 examines production processes, and the business environment and market competitiveness are the subjects of chapter 12. Chapter 13 concludes with a brief summary of the findings.

The firm is the unit of analysis for the survey data, and variables (for example, labor wages, quality certifications, research and development spending, and electric power supply) refer to the firm. To the extent that firms in the survey represent their industries, the averages, medians, and frequencies refer to the industries, and simple comparisons that are significant can represent differences between the two countries' industries. The multivariate analysis of the firm-level data is constructed so that the interfirm differences obtained also represent differences between the two countries' industries. To consider the effects of the investment climate on the firms in an industry, the analysis uses country-level information, such as government policies, which are usually industry specific.

To serve domestic or international demand, hardware industry growth requires the combination of two relatively mobile factors of production (capital, both equipment and finance, and technology) with two relatively immobile factors (infrastructure and labor) within the context of a country's public policy and regulatory framework. Comparison of the differences in the availability of these factors of production and the adequacy of the policy and regulatory framework can help explain the divergent growth patterns of Chinese and Indian hardware manufacturing.

Chapter 10

The Influence of Factors of Production on the Hardware Industries in China and India

Labor, capital—both physical and financial—and land are examined in this chapter for the effects country differences have on the electronics hardware manufacturing industries in China and India.

Labor Force

China's labor force, including the labor force employed in manufacturing, is the largest in the world. Nevertheless, despite China's growing prominence as the workshop of the world, only about 11 percent of the workforce is in manufacturing. Both in absolute and relative terms, manufacturing employment declined in the last decade. A similar share of total employment in India is engaged in manufacturing (table 10.1).

China

The large size of the Chinese labor force did not by itself automatically confer advantages to manufacturing employers. Government actions facilitated adjustment to employers' needs. Over the years of economic reforms, mismatches between job opportunities and the workers to fill them were subjects of government policies intended to make labor markets more flexible. Local governments slowly eased the well-known obstacle to migration, the household registration system (*hukou*). Until recently, *hukou* and its associated discrimination against migrants was the most visible obstacle to rural-urban and urban-urban labor flows. Unregistered migrants were denied jobs that were formally or informally reserved for local urban residents and faced discriminatory pricing for education and other public services. Since 2001, several local governments have enacted important initiatives to ensure that treatment of migrants is on par with that of local residents. Since mid-2002, the central government has publicly encouraged these initiatives. The

**Table 10.1   Labor Force and Manufacturing Employment in China
and India**

China	1983	1993	2000
People in labor force (millions)	548.0	682.3	738.9
Workforce in manufacturing			
Percentage of total	11.9	13.6	10.9
Millions	65.1	93.0	80.4

India	1983	1993/94	1999/2000
People in labor force (millions)	312.9	376.0	408.8
Workforce in manufacturing			
Percentage total	11.0	10.9	11.2
Millions	29.3	35.9	40.5

Source: World Bank 2006b; Naughton 2007.

ban on hiring migrants for certain urban industries and jobs was officially lifted. Migrants with jobs were becoming entitled to local residence permits and to basic public services; collecting extra school fees from migrant children, as had been done previously, was made illegal.

More indirect obstacles to migration remained. In rural areas, land use rights were weak, making it difficult for households either to maintain or monetize their land use rights when migrating. In urban areas, despite rapid residential development, low-income housing needed by most of the relocating labor force was scarce. Labor mobility was also complicated by remaining problems in the provision and portability of social benefits. As a result, Chinese industry was not able to benefit fully from its large pool of labor because of remaining barriers to migration from labor-surplus regions in the west to labor-shortage coastal regions, where manufacturing and services activity were concentrated.

In China, it has always been difficult to adjust the urban labor force in the context of business restructuring. Local governments typically stipulated that no more than 10 percent of the labor force could be laid off in privatizations, for instance (Garnaut and others 2005). Enterprises had more flexibility to adjust migrant labor. However, in the early years of the 2000s, there was a trend toward stronger rights for migrant workers (Tenev and Chaudry 2004), thus reducing flexibility for employers. Furthermore, labor shortages have been reported in the coastal areas, especially in Guangzhou, because rising agricultural prices have been keeping more farmers in the fields, reducing the flow of migrant workers looking for jobs in the booming industrial centers along the coast.

India

As in China, India's large labor force and large numbers of engineering and science graduates (large in absolute terms, although small relative to the population

Table 10.2   Labor Flexibility Indicators

	China	India
Difficulty of hiring index	11	33
Rigidity of hours index	40	20
Difficulty of firing index	40	90
Rigidity of employment index	30	48
Firing costs (number of weeks)	90	79

Source: World Bank 2004b.
Note: Indexes are on a scale of 0 to 100 and represent expert opinion on the category concerned, where 100 = most difficult or rigid and 0 = easiest or most flexible.

as a whole) provided the necessary supply conditions for labor-intensive manufacturing and services as well as the skilled labor required for more complex manufacturing. Nevertheless, only 11 percent of the workforce was in manufacturing during the 1980s and 1990s (table 10.1), and illiteracy was a barrier to participation in the formal employment sector for over 40 percent of the population.

The efficient use of India's labor force was impeded by restrictions on the hiring and firing of workers by medium and large firms (table 10.2). India's complex labor market legislation includes some 47 different labor laws and 157 regulations at both state and national levels. The government set the minimum wage and regulated wage increases across 19 industries (Zagha 1998). This protected formal sector workers but deterred the creation of formal jobs. Among the most onerous laws is the 1947 Industrial Disputes Act, which requires firms with more than 100 workers to obtain state permission for plant closure and labor retrenchment— permission that is rarely granted. These provisions made labor rationalization in registered firms very difficult, discouraged hiring in the formal sector, and were especially onerous for labor-intensive sectors. As a result, the formal labor force was less than 14 percent of the total labor force as of 2000 (Tendulkar 2003).

One consequence of applying restrictive labor laws to firms with more than 100 employees is that firm size remains artificially small. The Indian manufacturing sector overall shows a dualistic structure, with a bimodal distribution of large formal sector firms and small informal sector firms, with a "missing middle" of smaller formal sector firms (World Bank 2006a). A second consequence is that firms are overstaffed. In the World Bank Investment Climate Assessment, Indian manufacturing firms reported having 17 percent more workers than they wanted and identified labor laws and regulations as the main reason why they could not adjust to the preferred level (World Bank 2004b).

However, only some Indian managers of firms in the International Finance Corporation (IFC) survey saw labor regulation as a serious constraint. Most Indian hardware firms reported neither over- nor underemployment. Disaggregating by firm size, the analysis found that only firms with more than 100 employees showed any pattern of overemployment, with 17 percent of these

Figure 10.1 Labor Regulation as a Bottleneck to Business Growth

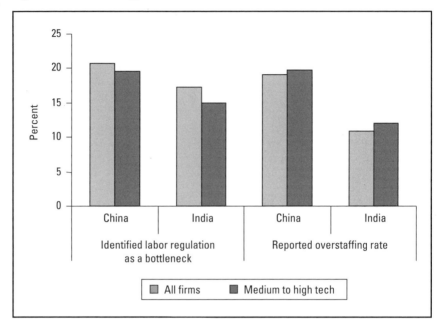

Source: World Bank 2004b.

firms reporting that their optimal workforce would be 95 percent or less of their current workforce.

Indian states with more restrictive labor regulations have smaller manufacturing sectors, according to one study (Besley and Burgess 2004). Another survey of plant-level data in 40 major cities found that rigid labor laws and inadequate power supply resulted in lower manufacturing productivity (Lall and Mengistae 2005).

According to the World Bank's investment climate surveys, more manufacturing firms in China than in India report labor regulations as a bottleneck to growth and also report overstaffing (figure 10.1), despite the greater difficulty with firing staff reported in India. One interpretation of these data is that Indian firms have found ways to work around the restrictions on firing workers, including treating labor as more of a fixed asset, substituting capital or not adjusting the workforce in response to demand variations, using contract labor not subject to firing restrictions, and contracting work to companies too small to be subject to firing restrictions (World Bank 2006a).

Labor Skill and Cost

Labor is an important factor of production for information technology (IT) hardware, although hardware is less labor intensive and less skill intensive than soft-

Table 10.3   Educational Attainment of the Workforce in China and India
(percent)

Country and educational level

China	1983	1993	2000
No formal schooling	34.5	15.8	9.0
Primary school	30.8	43.5	32.9
Middle school	33.8	38.6	53.5
Tertiary (above grade 12)	1.0	2.1	4.7

India	1983	1993/94	1999/2000
Illiterate	56	48	43
Primary school	24	24	23
Middle school	10	12	14
Graduate school	7	12	14
Postgraduate	3	5	6

Sources: World Bank 2006b; Naughton 2007.

ware. In the firms in the IFC sample, labor costs ranged from 15 percent to 20 percent of total costs, depending on the year. Do Chinese hardware firms have a labor advantage over Indian hardware firms in skill, education, wages, or productivity? The answer appears to be "no," according to quantitative measures based on data provided by the firms in the IFC survey.

Education and Occupation

The analysis first considers the educational attainment of the workforces in China and India from which hardware firms can draw employees. Shown as proportions of the total workforce, the differences between China and India are striking: the Chinese workforce possesses more literacy and more primary and secondary education; only in the postgraduate ranks does the study find the thin stratum of workers in India who are more highly educated than those in China (table 10.3). Of course, the absolute numbers of workers with sufficient education to be skilled employees are abundant in both countries.

Hardware manufacturing uses professionals, skilled workers, and unskilled labor—especially the latter—for assembly of components into finished products. Labor, unskilled labor in particular, has limited international mobility. Therefore, indigenous labor skill and its cost, determined by education, wages, and productivity, are potentially important determinants of differential hardware industry performance among different countries.

Neither the skill mix of Chinese hardware firm workforces nor the educational qualifications of their workers was better than in Indian hardware firms.

Table 10.4   Labor Force Composition and Education

Finding: *Chinese firms used fewer skilled workers and more unskilled workers in a simple comparison, but this is partly due to differences in the product mix of Chinese and Indian firms. The intensity of use of either professionals or skilled or unskilled workers is not a statistically significant difference between Chinese and Indian hardware firms in a multivariate analysis.*

Composition of labor force (median share of total employment, percent)	China	India
Professionals	18	23
Skilled workers	21	29
Unskilled workers	29	15

Finding: *The higher educational qualifications required for new entry-level professional employees by some Indian hardware firms is a statistically significant difference between Indian firms and Chinese firms, even when other differences are accounted for, but entry-level qualifications for skilled workers did not differ between the two countries.*

Entry-level required educational qualification	Share of firms (average percent)	
	China	India
Postgraduate degree (≥17 years)		
Professional employees	2	35
Skilled workers	2	4
Undergraduate degree or diploma (13–16 years)		
Professional employees	91	65
Skilled workers	74	73
Secondary school (12 years)		
Professional employees	5	0
Skilled workers	21	20
Education and experience of managers		
Managers with postgraduate degree (average percent of all managers in the firm)	22	39
Managers with work experience abroad (average percent)	2	4
Years of experience of top manager in this industry (average)	21	18

Source: IFC survey.

Professionals do not dominate the workforces of hardware firms, unlike in software firms, and the intensity of usage of professionals differs little between Chinese and Indian firms. More Indian hardware firms required postgraduate qualifications for professionals than did Chinese firms, but almost all Chinese firms required an undergraduate degree or diploma. These multivariate differences between the two countries are statistically significant, but they apply to a relatively small share of the workforce: 23 percent for Indian firms and 18 percent for Chinese firms (table 10.4).

Chinese hardware firms used somewhat fewer skilled workers and somewhat more unskilled workers than Indian firms, but the difference in numbers of un-skilled workers is partly due to the difference in the product mix among firms. China has more industrial electronics firms, which are heavy users of unskilled labor, than computer or peripherals manufacturing firms. Hardware firms in both countries usually required an undergraduate degree or diploma as an entry-level qualification for skilled workers.

The managers of hardware firms in China and India appeared on balance to be roughly equivalent in their skills. More Indian hardware firm managers had post-graduate degrees than did their Chinese counterparts, but Chinese top managers had somewhat lengthier experience in the hardware industry; these are statistically significant simple comparisons.

Productivity and Cost

Chinese hardware firms did not have a labor productivity advantage, and they did have a labor wage disadvantage; therefore, they had higher unit labor costs than Indian hardware firms.

Higher unit labor costs in Chinese hardware firms compared with Indian firms could be overcome by the greater labor flexibility that Chinese managers had and by the superior depth and breadth of the Chinese manufacturing base.

Labor productivity, measured as output per worker per year in the surveyed firms, was lower in China than in India, at $30,509 per worker per year at the median for Chinese firms versus $46,900 for Indian firms. Value added by labor was also lower in China than in India (table 10.5). This difference, however, was largely due to the fact that more Chinese than Indian firms in the sample were in the industrial electronics and telecom products businesses than in the computers and peripherals businesses. Labor productivity is higher in computers and peripherals firms (a median of $60,612) than it is in industrial electronics and telecom equipment firms ($26,250). When the data were disaggregated into the two hardware subindustries, the Chinese and India firms had similar labor productivity and value added figures within each one of the two subindustries. The analysis concludes that there is no material difference in the labor productivity performance of Chinese and Indian hardware firms in similar lines of business.

Labor productivity is important to hardware firms insofar as firms with higher labor productivity showed faster one-year sales revenue growth in a multivariate analysis that included both Chinese and Indian firms and that controlled for the physical capital to labor ratio in the firms.

Wages paid to entry-level employees were higher in Chinese hardware firms than in their Indian counterparts; this held true for all classes of employees from

Table 10.5 Labor Productivity
(all measures are $US per worker)

Finding: *Chinese hardware firms had lower labor productivity than Indian hardware firms in a simple comparison, but this difference is partly due to different product mixes in these countries and is not a statistically significant difference between the countries' firms when other variables are accounted for. Firms with higher labor productivity grew faster.*

Labor productivity measures	China	India
Value of output	30,509	46,900
Value added by labor	2,453	5,385

	Computers and peripherals, both countries	Industrial electronics and telecom equipment, both countries
Value of output	60,612	26,250
Value added by labor	4,345	2,775

	China		India	
	Computers and peripherals	Industrial electronics and telecom equipment	Computers and peripherals	Industrial electronics and telecom equipment
Value of output	56,984	19,200	63,031	26,722
Value added by labor	7,442	2,514	6,813	5,212

Effect of 10% increase in labor productivity on sales revenue growth	+ 3 to 4 percentage points

Source: IFC survey,
Note: Sample size for Indian industrial electronics and telecom equipment subindustry is small, n = 16.

professionals to unskilled workers. Benefit payments were also higher in Chinese firms. The higher wages paid to professionals was a statistically significant difference between Chinese and Indian firms when accounting for other variables. Table 10.6 shows the value of the starting wage and benefits for employees in Chinese and Indian hardware firms, from which the sizable gap between the two countries can be seen, as well as the wage gap and the benefits differences between workers in the two countries. For skilled workers, the wage gap was about the same in absolute terms as it was for professionals but greater in relative terms, to China's disadvantage. For unskilled workers, benefits added another 15 percent to the starting wage in Chinese firms as compared with 10 percent in India, partly because Chinese employers provide housing. The combination of higher wages but not higher labor productivity could be the result of greater state ownership of hardware firms in China than in India (discussed below).

The median labor cost per worker firmwide (table 10.6) captures both the effects of wage rates and occupational distribution. Even though Chinese hardware firms employed relatively more unskilled workers while Indian firms employed

Table 10.6   Wages and Benefits and Labor Cost per Worker, 2003

Finding: *Wages and benefits were higher in Chinese than Indian hardware firms, and the difference in wages for professionals in the two countries' firms is statistically significant.*

Entry-level wages and benefits	China	India
Professionals		
Wages ($/month)	240	137
Benefits (% of wages)	20	15
Skilled workers		
Wages ($/month)	180	84
Benefits (% of wages)	19	13.5
Unskilled workers		
Wages ($/month)	96	53
Benefits (% of wages)	15	10
Labor cost per worker (median $/year in 2002)	China	India
All firms	4,288	2,735
Computers and peripherals firms	8,836	2,272
Industrial electronics and telecom equipment firms	3,744	2,939

Sources: IFC survey.

more skilled workers and professionals, the higher wages paid to each occupation in Chinese firms resulted in a higher median labor cost per worker. This difference did not depend on the firm's line of business.

There are significant and persistent wage differences in China across localities and ownership categories. State-owned enterprises (SOEs), for example, offer premium wages compared with other employers: in pay alone, state sector workers earn more than workers in urban collectives. When adjusted for benefits, compensation for state sector workers is the highest among low-skill workers and second highest (after foreign and mixed-funded enterprises) among skilled workers. On average, however, labor productivity in SOEs is lower than in private, mixed, and foreign ownership enterprises. Thus, the premium wages paid in the state sector contrasts with the sector's relative weaker performance. Significant wage differentials also exist across geographic areas: wage differentials between coastal areas and the interior have been growing.

What matters to the competitiveness of a firm's product is not only labor productivity and labor wages, but unit labor cost (and, of course, the cost of other factors of production, some of which are discussed below). For Chinese hardware firms, the combination of higher wages and equivalent productivity left them at an apparent labor cost disadvantage compared with Indian hardware firms (table 10.7). Higher Chinese unit labor cost applied both to firms whose main line of

Table 10.7   Unit Labor Costs

Finding: *Unit labor costs were significantly higher in Chinese than in Indian hardware firms.*		
Unit labor cost ($ labor cost per $ output)	**China**	**India**
All firms, median	0.18	0.07
Computers and peripherals firms	0.14	0.06
Industrial electronics and telecom equipment firms	0.18	0.07
All firms, average	0.22	0.09
Computers and peripherals firms	0.23	0.09
Industrial electronics and telecom equipment firms	0.21	0.10

Source: IFC survey.

Figure 10.2   Hardware Firm Labor Costs per Employee, 1999–2002

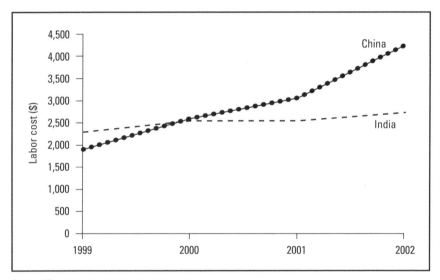

Source: IFC survey.

business was computers and peripherals and to firms whose main line of business was industrial electronics or telecom equipment.

Higher labor costs in China are a recent development. In the IFC sample of firms, Chinese labor costs per employee per year increased from $1,910 in 1999 to $4,288 in 2002, a much faster increase than in India (figure 10.2).

These findings about China's apparent disadvantage compared with India based on narrow measures of labor productivity, labor wages, and unit labor cost, while true, do not necessarily result in a competitive disadvantage for Chinese hardware firms. Other features of the Chinese business environment, such as labor flexibility (discussed above) and supply chains, come into play to the advantage of Chinese hardware firms.

Supply Chains

The depth and breadth of the manufacturing base is another positive feature of the Chinese hardware manufacturing environment (see chapter 2 for the theoretical basis for this argument). China has developed supply chains that allow local labor forces to be better used than is the case in India. A deep equipment-manufacturing sector allows hardware firms to source many inputs locally. China is able to use a higher proportion of local labor, including both direct labor and labor embedded in plant and equipment and components, than other countries in which firms have to import a higher proportion of their plant and equipment and components.

China's labor advantage over India in hardware production, therefore, does not come from wages or productivity at the firm level. Instead, its low total cost of production comes from the depth and breadth of its manufacturing base and its developed supply chains through which low labor cost is leveraged. Few countries are large enough to develop and maintain such a deep and diversified manufacturing base. India has the potential, but has not yet been able to do so. Only after the relaxation of both industrial and import licensing in India (see chapter 3) was hardware manufacturing fully free to develop, but at a later date than the emergence of the industry in other low-cost Asian locations—such as China.

Capital and Finance

Hardware production requires plant and equipment; therefore, physical capital is an important factor of production. Capital intensity varies, being most intensive for manufacturing of components and least intensive for assembly operations. Many hardware manufacturing firms in China and India are assembly operations. The cost and availability of capital thus have variable effects on the competitiveness of the hardware industry. In the survey data, Chinese and Indian hardware firms had similar capital intensities, and differences in capital intensities across firms did not contribute to the firms' growth when other growth determinants were taken into account (table 10.8).

Costs of Capital

The cost of capital depends on both the cost of capital goods and the cost of financing their acquisition. In general, equipment and machinery are tradable, so prices do not vary greatly between countries. However, high weight-to-value capital goods such as buildings and heavy, simple equipment and machinery (lifting equipment, for instance) are less tradable, and differences in construction and

Table 10.8 Physical and Financial Capital

Finding: *Capital intensity was not significantly different between China and India.*

Physical capital	China	India
Capital-labor ratio ($ fixed assets per employee)		
Mean	17,776	21,930
Median	6,667	8,325

Finding: *Fewer Chinese hardware firms had bank loans than Indian firms in a simple comparison, and few hardware firms in either country had equity or venture capital finance.*

Financial capital	China	India
Have bank loans (% yes)	42	71
Have equity or venture capital finance (% yes)	18	14

Source: IFC survey.

equipment costs for factories can affect manufacturing competitiveness. The advantage of low-cost labor can contribute to lower construction and equipment costs to the extent that low-cost labor is used to build or manufacture it.[1]

The availability and cost of financing should be important for the growth of capital-intensive industries in the long term. Even though financial capital is a highly mobile factor of production, capital controls and market-entry barriers mean that a nation's domestic financial services industry can be important to its economic development (see chapter 2). Manufacturing is better able to use debt to finance its growth than are other industries because cash flows for debt service tend to be stable and predictable, and a large proportion of the firm's assets (land and capital goods) can be pledged as collateral. In the IFC survey, most Indian firms used debt finance, but fewer than half of Chinese firms did so. Few firms in either country mobilized external equity (table 10.8).

Sources of Capital

Firms can finance investment domestically or from abroad using bank lending, venture capital, or other forms of equity investment.

China. China's national savings rate is high relative to that of other countries.[2] Between 1978 and 1995, for example, the national savings rate averaged 37 percent in contrast to the international average of about 21 percent. In principle, the balance between savings and investment is available as net financial investment. Based on financial assets data, estimates are that this balance has been approximately 14 percent of GDP in recent years in China (Kuijs 2005).

Combined savings by enterprises and the government accounted for most of the difference in the savings rate between China and other countries (table 10.9). Government savings are remarkably high compared with those of other countries

Table 10.9   Multicountry Comparison of Savings Rates

	China (2003)	United States	France	Japan	Korea, Republic of	Mexico (2001)	India
Domestic savings rate (% GDP 2002, except China and Mexico)	42.5	14.3	20.7	25.5	31.0	20.8	29.0
Difference: China vs. others	—	28.2	21.8	17.0	11.5	21.7	13.5
Source of differences (percentage points)							
Household savings	—	11.8	5.8	8.4	12.1	8.6	–5.4
Enterprise savings	—	8.6	9.4	–0.5	4.1	. 8.3	14.1
Government savings	—	7.9	6.7	9.2	–4.7	4.8	4.8

Sources: China National Bureau of Statistics (national accounts) via OECD National Accounts; Kuijs (2005); authors' calculations.
Note: — = not available.

and are much higher than suggested by the fiscal data reported in the headlines; for example, government savings reached 7.5 percent of GDP in 2004. Household savings were 16 percent of GDP in 2004.

Enterprise savings are also significant in China. Nonfinancial enterprises' own savings from retained earnings increased from approximately 12.5 percent of GDP in 1996 to almost 15.0 percent in 2001 and an estimated 18.0 percent in 2003. In 2004, enterprise savings were approximately as large as household savings. Structural factors driving this trend include the increasing profitability resulting from restructuring in the SOE sector and the increased share of private enterprises in the economy.

Foreign direct investment (FDI) has been a main source of capital in China, mostly from neighboring countries and economies, including Hong Kong, China; Macao, China; Singapore; and Taiwan, China (Shang-Jin Wei 1999). Foreign firms are a significant presence in the hardware industry in China (see the section in chapter 12 on international links). Foreign portfolio flows are, by contrast, very low. The government maintained strict capital controls on portfolio investment until the mid-2000s. The overall inflow of foreign savings has been growing rapidly, and is the highest among developing countries.

Savings are only available for private investment to the extent that they are intermediated through the financial system into debt and equity products, or mobilized directly by the enterprise (in the form of retained earnings, interenterprise investments, or FDI). In China, debt from domestic banks and debt and equity from FDI have been the main sources of financing for the manufacturing sector. Gross bank borrowing by enterprises was 14 percent of GDP in 2002, and FDI was 3.4 percent of GDP in 2002.

China's domestic savings were mainly intermediated by the banking sector. Over 90 percent of households' net financial investment was in bank savings deposits. China's large financial sector was overreliant on banks. In 2005, financial assets represented 220 percent of GDP. About 95 percent of all financial assets were in the banking sector. Nevertheless, borrowing from banks was difficult for private enterprises, and many Chinese hardware companies in the IFC sample were privately owned. Among firms in the survey, only 42 percent had taken out bank loans (table 10.8).

Bank borrowing for Chinese hardware companies has been eased for companies located within China's Special Economic Zones (SEZs), where banks were encouraged to provide loans to new enterprises located within the SEZs, and enterprises oriented to the export market received preference for loans of foreign exchange. Loans within the SEZs were treated as development loans divided into fixed and circulating capital. Banks within the districts where SEZs were located could withhold a certain proportion of their profits to set up loan risk funds and Sino-foreign-funded risk investment companies for the more uncertain ventures. Local governments in China also assisted with funding by lobbying the state-owned banks, offering guarantees for enterprises that were seeking loans, or creating innovation funds to lend directly to enterprises.

The low rate of bank borrowing by Chinese hardware firms can be offset by finance from retained earnings and capital transfers from the government. However, in the sample, only 18 percent of Chinese hardware firms had equity or venture capital. Among Chinese enterprises economy-wide, more than one-half of investment was financed by retained earnings. External financing declined in the mid-1990s to about 30 percent of enterprise investment, reflecting the underdevelopment of private equity markets and venture capital. Securities firms, asset exchanges, and trust and investment companies played a limited role in facilitating private equity financing. Until recently, numerous legal obstacles hindered the development of the venture capital industry in China. The Company Law of 1993 permitted no more than 50 percent of capitalization to be invested in subsidiaries or other legal entities; the concept of callable capital was not explicitly recognized; and the ability of companies to structure investments using a range of securities, such as preferred stock, was limited.

The low use of venture capital is illustrated by its geographical concentration: almost two-thirds of Chinese venture capital firms are located in Beijing, Shanghai, or Shenzhen. Most venture capital firms invested in companies at different stages of development, but only 6 percent of Chinese and 11 percent of foreign firms considered providing seed capital.

The limited external equity mainly comes from the government, SOEs, or foreign investors. Government entities established more than half of the Chinese venture capital firms, and state-owned industrial or financial companies established one-third of such companies, although foreign venture capital has increased in recent years. Large SOEs are among the most active domestic investors in smaller firms, and many of the early leaders in China's hardware industry trace their origins back to SOEs (for example, Lenovo, TCL, ZTE, and Bird) or state-backed firms. Although technically a private firm, China's largest handset maker,

Huawei, which has its roots in the Chinese military, also benefited from government support. In 2004, foreign venture capitalists invested $1.269 billion in 253 mainland China or mainland-related companies, according to the research firm Zero2IPO.

India. Although lower than China's, India's domestic savings rate of 29 percent was also above the international average of 21 percent (table 10.9). Household savings were higher in India than in China but were offset by lower government and enterprise savings. Chronic fiscal deficits in India of over 6 percent of the budget for the central government, and similar levels for state governments, absorbed much of the domestic savings, crowding out private investment and raising the cost of capital (figure 10.3). Losses from SOEs reduced net savings by the private enterprise sector.

Unlike China, India was, until the economic reforms that began in 1991, reluctant to allow inflows of FDI. Restrictions were placed on which sectors could be open to FDI, and limits were placed on maximum shareholding by foreign investors (with limits ranging between 0, 26 percent, 49 percent, 74 percent, and 100 percent, depending on the industry).

Since the 1991 economic reforms, FDI inflows to India amounted on average to only around $3 billion to $5 billion annually (but increased substantially beginning in 2006), compared with $40 billion annually to China. As a share of GDP, FDI in India stood at less than 1 percent in 2002/03, compared with 4 percent in China and between 2 percent and 3 percent in many emerging-market countries. Portfolio capital inflows increased from $2 billion per year in 2001/02 to $9 billion per year in 2004/05 but were again highly concentrated in top-tier companies that met investor requirements for liquidity and corporate governance (table 10.10).

India's financial intermediation has been far below that in China. The role of banks is small and the government has twice nationalized the leading banks in the country, leading to state dominance and lack of competition and innovation in banking services. The share of financial assets in GDP in India is about 93 percent, compared with 220 percent in China.

However, because of crowding out by the public sector, the ratio of private credit to GDP in India was 37 percent of GDP in 2004, compared with 141 percent in China. In 2005, more than 40 percent of banking system resources were invested in government securities, well above the statutory reserve requirement of 25 percent. Real interest rates have been higher than in China (figure 10.3), meaning that returns on capital tend to be higher in India than elsewhere,[3] but the growth of capital-intensive manufacturing has been slower.

The government has controlled the allocation of credit in various ways, according to its explicit and implicit priorities. Priorities have included allocation of credit to the rural sector and to small-scale industries, both seen as important for poverty reduction. As a new sector characterized by medium and large enterprises without direct connection to the rural economy, the hardware sector did

Figure 10.3   Real Interest Rates and Fiscal Deficits, China and India

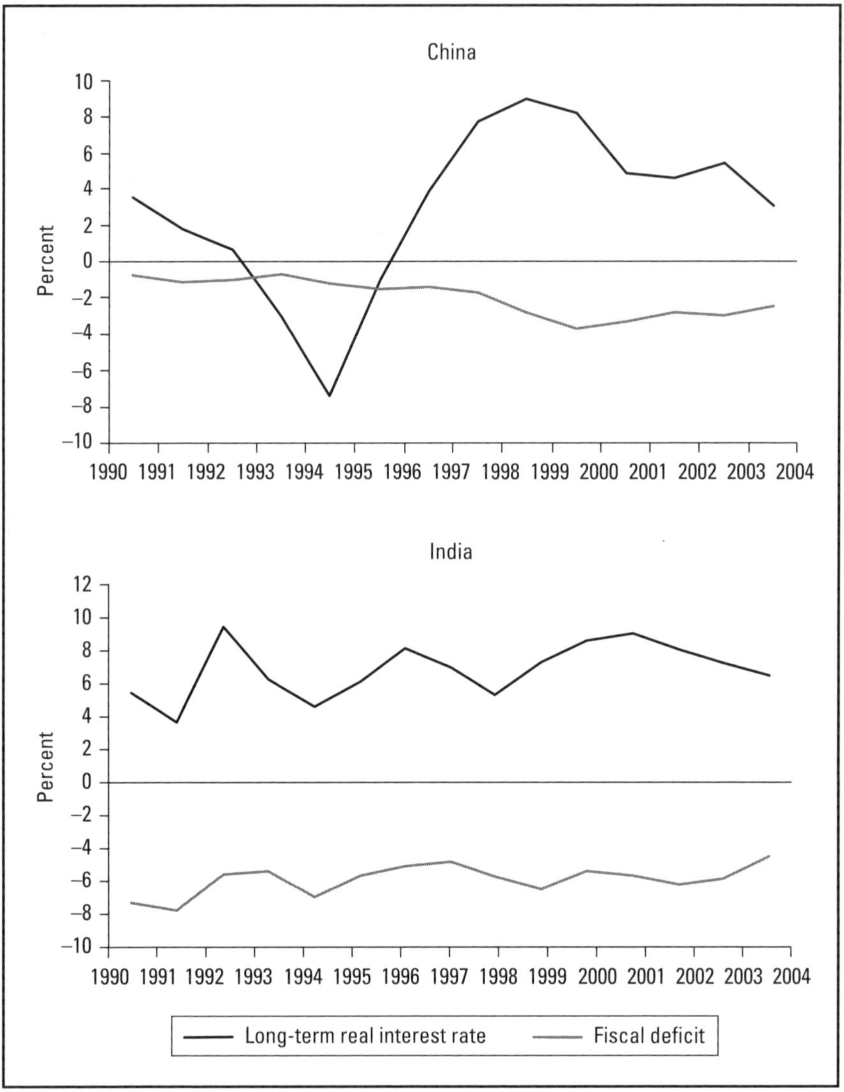

Sources: Reserve Bank of India (RBI) and World Bank data.

not benefit from government allocation of credit. Public sector banks continue to dominate India's banking system, thus providing one channel for government influence. As of March 2004, public sector banks accounted for 75.0 percent of the assets of commercial banks and 52.4 percent of those of financial institutions. Reserve requirements and directed lending constitute other channels of government influence. The combination of these influences has led banks to concentrate their

Table 10.10 Capital Inflows into China and India from Balance of Payments Data, 2004

($ billions)

	China	India
Trade balance	59.0	−33.7
Net services and other income	−13.2	10.4
Net transfers	22.9	20.8
Current account balance	68.7	−2.5
Net inward FDI	53.1	3.7
Net inward portfolio investment	19.7	9.3
Net other inward capital flows	37.9	15.0
Capital account balance	110.7	28.0
Errors and omissions	27.1	0.6
Overall balance	206.5	26.1

Source: International Monetary Fund, International Financial Statistics, balance of payments data.

assets in government paper and in blue chip lending to counterbalance a weak portfolio of mandatory lending to small-scale industries and the rural sector. The combination of high real interest rates in India and a government-influenced bias toward allocating capital to established, creditworthy companies and not to startups and riskier companies favored lending to large manufacturing corporations but not to early-stage manufacturing or services companies in new IT industries. Some of the Indian hardware firms in the survey that did not have bank loans cited high interest rates as the reason. Capital scarcity, however, did not lead companies to forgo bank borrowing. Instead, it seems to have led to payment of high interest costs, thus eroding competitiveness.

Indian equity markets are comparable to those in many developed markets in market capitalization and number of listed companies. Established in 1875, the Bombay Stock Exchange is the oldest in Asia. In 2004, Standard & Poor's ranked India 18th in both market capitalization and total value traded and second in number of securities listed. India had four times as many listed companies as China, but trading was concentrated in a few securities: in 2004, for example, the top 10 most actively traded securities accounted for over 40 percent of turnover and market capitalization. Only one-quarter of listed equities were actively traded, and one-third were traded for fewer than 100 days a year, partly because of the low public float of many equities. On average, sponsors of Indian companies held around 60 percent of the total shares and the Indian public around 16 percent. Nonresident Indians and overseas corporate bodies held about 8 percent, and the public float (holdings by foreign institutional investors, mutual funds, and other domestic institutions) was only about 16 percent.

India has a relatively well-developed venture capital industry. Only 14 percent of the Indian hardware firms in the sample, however, had financing from external equity or venture capital, indicating continued reliance for financing on internal sources within family-held groups.

A comparison of World Bank investment climate survey data for China and India shows that India's financial system is better than China's at allocating capital to private enterprises. In these surveys, Chinese firms, especially small firms, reported greater difficulty in accessing bank loans (Huang 2006). Although China's financial system has been more effective at channeling financial resources to enterprise investment, these resources have gone mostly to SOEs.

While Chinese and Indian hardware firms did not differ in their capital intensity, their sources of finance did differ: the Chinese industry benefited from FDI, while Indian firms used bank lending but at high prices. Use of equity or venture capital finance was secondary in both countries.

Land Use

Hardware firms require more land than do software firms, and the location of plants may have a significant impact on industry growth and quality (see chapter 2). Hardware manufacturers can gain access to a larger and better qualified labor pool and a better supply of components by locating near other hardware manufacturers. China's early creation of SEZs and the concomitant clustering of hardware firms gave China's hardware manufacturers an advantage. Hardware requires specialized manufacturing of various components combined with assembly operations. Clustering of component manufacturers and assemblers offered logistical advantages, and helped overcome constraints imposed by land and by excessive regulation if the region in which firms clustered benefited from special government treatment. In China, for example, the creation of SEZs eased the problem of acquiring land for factories. Such clustering created a type of economy of scale for the industry that was unavailable to individual enterprises because it enabled companies to share the external benefits of each other's operations. India's late start in creating the policy framework for hardware manufacturing delayed the creation of manufacturing clusters.

Clusters have proven to be powerful engines of growth in the hardware industry globally by improving the labor pool, shortening supply chains, and enabling the sharing of common infrastructure. Productivity gaps between manufacturing plants in different cities in India have been partly explained by differences in labor regulations and severity of power shortages and partly by differences in clustering economies (Lall and Mengistae 2005).

The Chinese hardware firms in the IFC survey reported greater benefits from clustering than did the Indian firms, and this is a statistically significant difference between the two countries' firms after other variables are accounted for, as was also true for software firms (table 10.11). This result offers empirical evidence of the role of clustering in the growth of the Chinese hardware industry (see also box 10.1).

Table 10.11   Importance of Geographic Location

Finding: *Chinese hardware firms benefited more from the talent pool and knowledge-sharing effects of clustering than did Indian firms, and this difference is statistically significant.*

Clustering: Importance of firm's geographical location	China	India
Knowledge sharing among employees	3.8	3.4
Availability of talent pool (average of 5-point scales; higher score means more importance)	4.3	3.7

Source: IFC survey.

Box 10.1   EVOC Intelligent Technology: Access to Flexible Labor and Advanced Technology

EVOC Intelligent Technology Co. (EVOC) is a leading Chinese supplier of embedded intelligent platform products used in telecom, transportation, Internet, video frequency control, data monitoring, and military and industrial equipment. A principal team member from the marketing department of Advantech, a Taiwan, China–based computer hardware supplier, established EVOC in 1993 as a technically oriented manufacturing company. Both EVOC's revenue growth and profitability have been remarkable since: revenue of Chinese renminbi (RMB) 152.5 million in 2001 ($18.5 million), RMB 202.6 million in 2003 ($24.5 million), and a record RMB 723.3 million in 2006 ($88.2 million)—a 376 percent increase in five years. The gross margin grew from RMB 65.0 million ($7.9 million) to RMB 92.4 million ($11.2 million), and net profit grew 31 percent from RMB 39.3 million ($4.7 million) to RMB 51.6 million ($6.2 million) in this period.

What accounts for EVOC's performance? Familiarity with China's marketing channels and customer demand, which enabled it to get orders at its startup, was one factor. The fast-growing Chinese domestic market enabled EVOC's revenue to grow rapidly. EVOC's success, however, came primarily from the flexibility to manage labor within the electronics industry cluster in the Shenzhen SEZ. The location, combined with low-cost manufacturing equipment and flexible manu-

facturing capability, enables EVOC to fulfill small orders at low cost.

Throughout its life, EVOC has focused on advanced technology research, high-level quality management, and flexible manufacturing capabilities. EVOC was the first company to achieve ISO[a] 9000 quality certification in China, and it has nearly 1,000 patents and copyrights. The company strives to lead its competitors in the application of intelligent technology for rapid growth industries.

In 2001, EVOC's successful initial public offering in Hong Kong, China provided enough funding to support the company's further development. EVOC is the only Hong Kong, China–listed company that has a large production and research and development capability on the mainland.

In 2004, the Chinese Social Sciences Academy ranked EVOC ninth in its Hong Kong, China H Unit enterprise competitiveness index rankings tables. In addition, the State Science and Technology Ministry awarded the firm the "State Torch Plan Key High-Tech Enterprise."

Sources: Contributed by Zhen Wu, based on www.advantech.com.cn/, http://finance.news.tom.com/1535/1310/2005512-227638.html.

a. ISO = International Organization for Standardization, a network of international standards institutes; ISO 9000 is a family of standards for quality management systems.

Notes

1. For example, in a typical foundry operation, the cost of buildings will be about 10 percent and that of facilities will be about 30 percent of total capital expenditures. In China, the building and facilities will cost about half what they would cost in the United States because of lower labor costs.

2. Data in this section are from National Bureau of Statistics of China (various years); China Statistical Yearbook (www.stats.gov.cn/tjsj/ndsj/2007/indexeh.htm); and Kuijs 2005.

3. In 2005, *Businessweek* calculated an average return on investment capital for listed Indian companies of 16.7 percent, versus 12.8 percent in China.

Chapter 11

The Influence of Management on the Hardware Industries in China and India

Managers assert their influence on the firm through the skills they bring to the job and by the decisions they make on behalf of the firm. Among management features that are important to the hardware industry are the management of quality, the relationship to national culture, the use of technology, and the forging of international business relationships.

Management

Management determines, in part, the production process. Management skill in doing so can be measured in part by objective skill indicators such as experience. It can also be indicated by outcomes that could be important to a hardware firm's growth and development such as the achievement of quality certifications manager's experience, and the match between the way the workforce is managed and the country's national culture.

Experience

The longer top managers' experience in the industry, the more knowledge they are potentially able to possess and the more skillful they can be. After some threshold length of experience, however, it is possible that incremental knowledge gains are small and that changes in the industry render knowledge from prior experience either useless or actually damaging if it hampers adjustment to new conditions. The IFC sample of hardware firms found that Chinese managers have somewhat more industry experience than Indian managers. This difference is significant in a simple comparison but not when accounting for other firm-level differences. The effect of length of experience on hardware firm growth is negative, given other growth determinants. Without distinguishing between Chinese and Indian hardware firms,

Table 11.1   Experience of Top Managers

Finding: *Chinese hardware firm managers had slightly more experience than did Indian managers, but longer experience had adverse effects on the sales growth of firms.*

Experience	China	India
Average years of experience in the hardware business	20.8	17.7
Contribution of one more year of experience to revenue growth	–8%	

Source: IFC survey.

firms whose top managers had one additional year of industry experience had 8 percent slower sales growth (table 11.1).

Although the Chinese hardware industry is more export oriented than the Indian industry, few managers or professionals in the survey had either studied abroad or worked abroad. For both Chinese and Indian hardware firms, the figures are between 2 percent and 7 percent and not systematically or significantly higher in China than in India.

Chinese hardware firms differed significantly from Indian hardware firms in two aspects of management that favored their competitiveness: Chinese firms were more likely to have quality certifications (but gained less in sales growth from having more of them than did Indian hardware firms), and they had more-compliant employees who fit better with the hardware production process.

Quality Certifications

Possession of International Organization for Standardization (ISO) quality certification assures a firm's customers, especially its export customers, that the hardware firm follows the same product specifications as other firms in the industry, uses technologically up-to-date manufacturing and testing methods, and complies with regulations (www.iso.org). Possession of ISO 9000 certification, in particular, signals that the firm has a system for managing quality.

More Chinese hardware firms (86 percent) in the IFC sample had ISO quality certificates than did Indian hardware firms (71 percent). In addition, Chinese hardware firms with ISO certificates had, on average, 1.4 of them while Indian firms had 1.0 (table 11.2).

Management within National Culture

Hardware manufacturing, unlike software services production, is best accomplished in an environment of order, structure, and discipline. Production, especially the assembly operations that characterize many of these two countries' hardware firms, is routinized, and each worker must fit into the overall flow of output. Hofstede's (1991) analysis of national culture and management style (see chapter 6) suggests that Chinese national culture is unusual in its low degree of individualism (the single greatest cultural-dimension difference between China and India) and in

Table 11.2 Quality Certifications

Finding: *More Chinese hardware firms had ISO quality certifications than did Indian hardware firms, which was a statistically significant difference between them, even when accounting for other differences.*		
Finding: *Indian hardware firms with more ISO quality certifications showed much faster revenue growth; for Chinese firms, the gain from more quality certifications was smaller.*		

Indicator	China	India
Share of hardware firms with ISO quality certification (percent)	*86*	*71*
Average number of ISO certifications (for those with certification)	1.4	1.0
Effect on revenue growth of having ISO certification	+5%	doubled

Source: IFC survey.
Note: The variables in italics are statistically significant, differentiating between Chinese and Indian software firms in a multivariate analysis.

its high score on the long-term orientation dimension. These cultural traits suggest that Chinese employees may be more likely to put the interests of the group ahead of their individual interests, that long-term commitments may be more highly valued, and that a strong work ethic may be prevalent. Accordingly, to the extent that dominant national cultural traits influence corporate culture, hardware manufacturing is more likely to find a suitable corporate culture in Chinese firms than in Indian firms, the opposite of the contention for software production.

According to the results from the surveyed firms, professional employees in Chinese hardware firms exhibit less independence of action than do their counterparts in Indian firms. Chinese managers reported that only 3 percent of their workers need to be convinced to follow instructions without questioning when they do not fully agree with them, whereas Indian managers reported 37 percent need convincing. This is a statistically significant difference between the two countries' firms, even when accounting for other possible differentiating variables, suggesting that the predominant national culture in China may favor the hardware industry just as the predominant national culture in India may have favored the software industry (table 11.3).

Entrepreneurship

The analysis of management practices in software firms addressed the entrepreneurial orientation of firms as perceived by their top managers and found no difference between Chinese and Indian firms (chapter 6). The results for software firms indicated that the interaction of entrepreneurial orientation with independence of action was the factor favoring Indian software firms, not entrepreneurial orientation alone. Entrepreneurial orientation was not expected to be as important in hardware firms as in software firms. The hardware industries in both countries are more mature than the software industries, the average age of the firms is greater, and the firms are typically larger—much larger in China, as measured by both employment and sales revenue, and larger in India in sales revenue although not in employment (see chapter 1).

Table 11.3 Independence of Action

Finding: *Chinese hardware professionals did not exhibit as much independence of action as did Indian hardware professionals; this is a statistically significant difference between Chinese and Indian hardware firms, even after accounting for other differences.*

Independence of action	China	India
Percentage of managers who say professional employees have to be convinced to follow instructions when they do not fully agree	*3*	*37*

Source: IFC survey.
Note: The variables in italics are statistically significant, differentiating between Chinese and Indian software firms in a multivariate analysis.

An analysis of entrepreneurial orientation similar to that done for software firms could not be conducted among hardware firms because it was not possible to construct such a variable from the survey questions asked: the concept of entrepreneurial orientation was not identified, could not be measured, or did not exist as such in the minds of these managers. (Technically, the factor analysis of the five questionnaire items failed statistically to extract a common or underlying dimension and therefore no scale that could be termed "entrepreneurial orientation" existed among these hardware firms, unlike the case for software firms. Because the questionnaire items were standard and have been used frequently in prior survey research, the conclusion is that the failure to extract a scale was not due to faulty questionnaire items or managers' responses but rather due to the weakness of the concept for these firms in this industry.)

This finding does not mean that entrepreneurship was irrelevant to the performance of Chinese or Indian hardware firms. It does mean that it was not sufficiently prominent in the minds of top managers to be capable of either explaining differences between the two countries' hardware firms or contributing measurably to their performance.

Technology

Hardware manufacturing is a high technology industry, and the firms in it should perform better if they are more technologically engaged. To the extent that hardware production comprises simple assembly operations rather than more complex component manufacturing, however, technology should be somewhat less important.

National Technology Features

China as a nation has an advantage over India in its production of homegrown technology, measured by research and development (R&D) spending (1.09 percent of GDP in China compared with 0.78 percent of GDP in India; Dahlman and Utz 2005); by the number of researchers engaged in R&D (742,700 in China and 95,428 in India in 1997–2001); and by U.S. patents granted. China also imports and exports more technology than India in the form of royalties and license fees paid and received (table 11.4). Nevertheless, both China and India are far behind

Table 11.4 Technology Output

Indicator	China	India
Royalties and license fees paid, 2002 ($ million)	3,114	350
Royalties and license fees received, 2002 ($ million)	133	12
Number of scientific and technical journal articles, 1999	11,675	9,217
Number of U.S. patents granted, 2003	424	355

Source: Dahlman and Utz 2005.

Organisation for Economic Co-operation and Development (OECD) countries in their commitment of resources to R&D. For example, OECD countries spend, on average, 3 percent of GDP on R&D.

China's science and technology infrastructure is stronger in basic research than in technology diffusion, although efforts have been made in the latter direction. Engineering research centers were launched in 1991 to demonstrate technology, and productivity centers were launched in 1993 to disseminate technology information and provide consulting, training, innovation, and marketing support to small and medium enterprises. Both types of centers, however, depend to a great extent on self-financing. In search of revenues, these centers often deviated from their main tasks.

Many Chinese researchers have set up enterprises affiliated with universities. These institutions are investing massively in new research fields, increasing student intake, promoting science parks, and expanding cooperation with foreign partners. China's elite universities, such as Peking University and Qinghua University, are leading the way and becoming major actors in the knowledge economy. Each has spun off more than 60 companies, some of which are major companies on China's stock exchanges and even internationally.

China has made progress in making the research activities of government institutes and universities more economically relevant. A deliberate policy of rushing innovations to market and improving the commercialization of research activities may have affected long-term research capabilities (Dahlman and Aubert 2001). Recently, the share of R&D performed by enterprises has increased at the expense of R&D by government institutes. Several national programs to boost applied and technical research have been funded over the two decades since 1990. Some of them, such as Program 863, the Torch Plan, and the Program of Key Technology Projects and Programs, have a major focus on information technology (IT), telecommunications, and electrical engineering. Stimulated by government incentives such as allowing researchers to keep at least 50 percent of the earnings from commercializing technologies, new companies have spun off from universities and government institutes.

Major progress has been made in stimulating R&D at the enterprise level. In addition to the strong role played by some large state companies, new, smaller enterprises are emerging as important sources of R&D. In 1998, state-owned enterprises were still responsible for approximately 55 percent of all science and technology

---

Box 11.1   Technology Transfer through FDI: Suzhou

The city of Suzhou, in Jiangsu province, attracted more than $20 billion in FDI in the 1990s. Foreign-funded enterprises in the city have benefited from imports of more advanced technology through their foreign investors and have produced internationally competitive products. A World Bank survey found, however, that technology diffusion to other domestic firms has been limited. Among more than 7,000 foreign-funded enterprises, fewer than 100 have signed contracts with domestic firms to share technology. Contracting out by foreign-funded enterprises has remained mainly within the vicinity of Suzhou and has focused on low-

tech inputs, such as raw materials and simple parts and components. Surveyed foreign-funded companies indicated that the main obstacle to greater technology diffusion was a shortage of qualified technical staff and skilled workers in domestic companies. About one-third of the surveyed firms have been conducting significant R&D, but few have had any technical cooperation with domestic firms or research institutions and universities. None of the surveyed companies has had any direct contact with enterprises or institutions located in central or western China.

Source: World Bank 2002.

---

spending by the enterprise sector, but the role of private concerns, small and medium enterprises, and foreign-invested firms is increasing. Returnees with education and experience from leading technological centers in the United States and Europe have established many of these new private companies.

The transfer of technology through foreign direct investment (FDI) has been a major factor behind China's success. A survey conducted for the World Bank showed that technology transfer through FDI in the city of Suzhou was massive (see box 11.1). Studies of Japanese investments in Northeast China reached similar conclusions (Young and Lan 1997).

In general, studies have found that the spillover of industrial and civilian technology developed domestically or transferred through FDI has not spread inland from the coast (Steinfeld 2004). Similarly, creation of domestic technology has been concentrated in eastern China, and its diffusion has been geographically constrained. Partly as a result, total factor productivity growth and new product sales differ sharply across regions. Local protectionism, localized shortages of skilled labor, and weaknesses in technology-oriented policies have hindered broader technology diffusion. China's poor technical regulations and standards in the areas of product quality, work safety, and environmental protection are major obstacles to proper diffusion of modern technology and know-how (Dahlman and Aubert 2001).

India's long period of import restrictions coupled with U.S. restrictions on high tech exports hampered the development of technology-intensive activities and reduced the incentive to adopt cutting-edge technologies to improve production efficiency. In the years since economic reforms began in the 1990s, each 10 percent reduction in India's import tariffs has been estimated to increase total factor productivity by 0.5 percent (Topalova 2004). However, import restrictions encouraged domestic innovation, including the development of an indigenous supercomputer (first developed in the 1950s and continuously updated since). For hardware manufacturing, the result was that Indian firms were best able to compete in low tech assembly operations, mainly producing IBM personal computer (PC) "clones" until technology restrictions were eased in the 1990s.

R&D Inputs by Firms

Simple comparisons among the firms of technology inputs and outputs showed Chinese hardware firms with an advantage over their Indian counterparts (table 11.5). Chinese hardware firms spent more on R&D partly because a greater proportion of Chinese hardware firms made R&D expenditures. Even comparing only firms that reported R&D expenditures revealed that Chinese firms still spent more (8 percent versus 6 percent for the median firm). This important factor is a statistically significant difference between the two countries' firms even after accounting for other potential differentiators. See boxes 11.2 and 11.3 for examples of Chinese and Indian successes based on R&D.

Chinese hardware firms exceeded Indian firms both in technology inputs and outputs, and the result may be a small competitive advantage for Chinese firms compared with Indian hardware firms.

Patents, Royalties, and New Product Outputs

R&D spending is a technology input while patents and royalties or technology fees paid to the firm are technology outputs. Many more Chinese than Indian hard-

Table 11.5   Technology Inputs and Outputs

Finding: *Chinese hardware firms spent more on R&D than Indian hardware firms, and this is a statistically significant difference between them, partly because more Chinese firms made R&D expenditures.*

Technology input: R&D spending	China	India
Firms with R&D expenditure (percentage)	81	70
R&D costs as percentage of total costs (all surveyed firms, median)	*6.0*	*2.8*
R&D costs as percentage of total costs (firms with R&D expenditures, median)	8.0	6.0

Finding: *Chinese hardware firms were more likely to file for patents than Indian hardware firms, which is a statistically significant difference between the two countries' firms; slightly more Chinese hardware firms also earned royalties or technology fees from abroad.*

Technology outputs	China	India
Firms with new product introductions (percentage)	30	24
New product introductions in the past year (average of firms with new product introductions)	10.5	6.4
Firms with patent filings in 3 years before survey (percentage)	*45*	*8*
Firms with royalties and technology fees earned abroad in 3 years before survey (percentage)	8	2

Source: IFC survey.

Note: Variables in italics are statistically significant differentiators between Chinese and Indian hardware firms when many other features of the firms were accounted for in a multivariate analysis.

Box 11.2 Huawei Technologies: International Leadership through Advanced Technology and Chinese Government Support

Huawei Technologies Co. (Huawei) is an aggressive high tech company in the Chinese IT sector that provides next-generation telecom networks for operators around the world. Huawei's products and solutions include wireless and network products, terminals, and applications software. Because of its ability to innovate, its international management style, and its aggressive marketing strategy, Huawei developed from a small, privately owned company into a leading international telecom products supplier in just 18 years.

Huawei's initial success was due in part to the booming telecom industry in China, but also to its advantageous location. With headquarters in the Shenzhen Special Economic Zone near Hong Kong, China, Huawei benefited from Shenzhen's cluster of IT firms and the associated advantage of a large labor pool. Compared with other provinces, Shenzhen's SEZ had a flexible labor policy, which attracted numerous graduates from the whole nation. In addition, many foreign-owned electronics plants support Huawei's supply chain, from chips to printed circuit boards.

Although the number of private telecom equipment firms increased dramatically, they suffered the disadvantage of being without mainstream financing. Credit for buyers is essential, but Huawei was not able to get support from a Chinese state-owned bank because of its private ownership. Huawei, therefore, was unable to bid for important contracts. Huawei's technological ability attracted the attention of Zhu Rongi, the Chinese premier in 1992. Subsequently, Huawei received several benefits from the government, including purchaser credit and mainstream marketing permits. With this government financial and marketing support, Huawei began its international expansion in 1994. For many years, Huawei engaged leading consultancies, such as IBM, Hay Group, and PwC, to carry out management transformations so that the firm could keep abreast of international trends. As a result, the firm adopted a totally American management model in its business processes, organizational structure, financial management, quality control, customer satisfaction, and human resources. The human resources system, for example, includes employee stock options as part of an incentive plan. In 2005, 58 percent of Huawei's $8.2 billion came from international markets.

Huawei has a very large R&D effort with R&D centers in Bangalore, Silicon Valley, Dallas, Stockholm, and Moscow in addition to locations in Beijing, Shanghai, Nanjing, Shenzhen, Hangzhou, and Chengdu. Nearly half of Huawei's 44,000 employees are engaged in R&D in some way. The firm invests 10 percent or more of its annual revenue into R&D and uses 10 percent of that investment for basic research so that the firm can stay at the forefront of new technologies. By the end of June 2006, Huawei had filed over 14,000 patent applications with 2,000 approved by foreign patent offices. By the end of 2005, it held 5 percent (69 patents) of the world's Universal Mobile Telecommunications System patents.

Sources: Zhen Wu, based on interviews with three Huawei managers; www.huawei.com/cn/about/AboutIndex.do; http://column.chinabyte.com/ccclub/303/2100303.shtml.

---

ware firms filed for patents—45 percent compared with 8 percent—and somewhat more earned royalties or technology fees from abroad, although these numbers are small for both countries. These results for the hardware firms in the IFC survey are consistent with aggregate comparisons of both technology inputs and outputs for China and India as a whole.

New product introductions, another technology output, were not statistically significantly different between Chinese and Indian hardware firms.

Box 11.3   Moser Baer: An Exception to the Rules

Based in New Delhi, Moser Baer manufactures and markets optical storage media, including recordable compact discs (CD-Rs) and rewritable compact discs (CD-RWs). The company has become the fourth largest, and perhaps the lowest cost, manufacturer of CD-Rs in the world, with a 10 percent market share. Moser Baer sells its products to 9 out of the top 12 original equipment manufacturer (OEM) brand customers in the world and to blue chip customers in 82 countries, a strong indicator of the company's product quality and service level.

How did an Indian manufacturing company achieve this record during times when most Indian manufacturing firms were not export competitive? The first reason among several relates to technology and quality. Moser Baer is an ISO 9002 company and adheres to standards specified by the American National Standards Institute as well as Ecma International (a Geneva-based standards organization). Its technology matches the best in the world. Since its founding in 1983, Moser Baer has focused on R&D, has set industry benchmarks, and is among the lowest-cost optical media manufacturers in the world. Even while pursuing growth, the company consciously focused on moving up the technology value chain.

Product marketing is a second feature of Moser Baer's business success. The company has a complete line of optical storage media products and typically is first to market with new products. When a product is mature or starts declining, Moser Baer is ready with the next one. When floppy disks went out, the company moved to CDs; when CDs were in the mature phase, it moved to DVDs, which are now in the growth phase. When DVDs reach maturity, Moser Baer will be ready with the next product.

Attaining this success was not always easy. Deepak Puri, chairman and managing director of Moser Baer, faced a series of setbacks in the 40 years of his business life but kept trying to succeed and to find solutions to problems. If he had difficulties at the Indian ports, he set up his own supply chain. If he had problems with power shortages, he built his own supply. After two unsuccessful attempts in manufacturing businesses, Puri spotted the opportunity in data storage. He went to California to meet with Xidex, then the largest manufacturer of data storage media in the world. India was not known as a manufacturing or technology location at that time. Xidex formed a partnership with Puri, however, and Moser Baer started with a clear strategy: to operate in product markets with high technology and capital entry barriers.

Another feature of Moser Baer's success is international links—not only the original alliance but also continuing support from international organizations, including the IFC, which has made substantial equity investments in Moser Baer over the years.

Sources: Zhen Wu, based on www.microsoft.com/asia/case/casedetail.asp?casestudyid=15195; www.rediff.com/money/2006/aug/22mc.htm; and www.moserbaer.com/aboutmoserbaer_ overview_history.asp.

The differences favoring Chinese firms might give them a competitive advantage, but not a major one. R&D spending and patent filings are statistically significant differences between Chinese and Indian firms when other variables are considered. However, much of the R&D spending was adaptive rather than innovative, most Chinese hardware firms filed for patents in China (80 percent) and not in the United States or other foreign markets, and less than half the new products introduced were new to the market. None of these indicators of technology activity contributed to the revenue growth of Chinese (or Indian) hardware firms.

Intellectual Property

China's record for protection of intellectual property (IP) rights is not good. The World Economic Forum ranked China 60th on quality of contracts and law and 47th on technology transfer conditions out of 104 countries. India's rankings were much better (World Economic Forum 2004). China's hardware industry thrives despite this apparent disadvantage, which may be explained by the practice on the part of foreign firms of locating the least technologically advanced operations in China or by spreading the more technologically sensitive work across several locations in China.

Chinese and Indian hardware firms gain access to technology in markedly different ways. India has some advantages over China because of its stronger IP protection and its access to technology through personal networks but probably not enough of an advantage to outweigh China's advantages of greater domestic resources spent on R&D and greater access to imported technology through FDI. The difference in FDI flows, therefore, plays a key role in explaining not just availability of capital, but also of technology. FDI is a technology transfer mechanism.

When asked about compliance with IP rights laws, however, managers of Chinese hardware firms actually gave more positive replies than their Indian counterparts. According to these managers, in a simple comparison, significantly more competitors' products did not comply with IP rights laws in India than in China. The figures are substantial: medians of 25 percent noncompliance for India and 15 percent for China. Comparisons such as these are fragile, however, both because of differences in the laws in each country and in the perceptions across cultures of what constitutes compliance.

International Links

Three different types of international links may contribute to the performance of hardware firms: foreign ownership (already mentioned as a source of capital and technology inputs); nonequity strategic alliances that do not provide capital but can be entered into to obtain technology, production capability, market access, or state-of-the-art management practices; and links with overseas residents who might provide startup finance, management skill, or access to foreign markets and technology.

Foreign Ownership

Where natural or artificial barriers separate the domestic from the international market, domestic demand conditions become important to an industry's growth and development. If the domestic market in China offers prospects for business success that are better than prospects in other countries, the Chinese market will attract foreign capital. China is one of the largest and fastest-growing markets in the world and is relatively protected by a low cost structure and by cultural, language, and policy barriers. In such circumstances, the domestic market will attract mobile factors of production to serve it, which has been an important driver of FDI flowing into China.

That FDI in Chinese manufacturing is extensive is a well-known fact. Foreign owners are of two types: U.S. and European multinational corporations (MNCs) and businesses based in Taiwan, China; Hong Kong, China; or Macao, China. The first group was attracted to the Chinese domestic market, while the second group was attracted mainly by tax concessions and lower labor costs on the mainland, which were used to create export platforms. Beginning in the early 1990s, Taiwanese computer companies, working with leading U.S. computer OEMs, played an important role in integrating China into global production networks. Taiwanese suppliers sourced about one-third of their export orders from production lines in China, and Taiwanese factories in China shipped approximately 40 percent of China's electronics exports by the turn of the 20th century (Ernst 2005).

The U.S. and European OEMs, such as Cisco, Compaq, Hewlett-Packard, Intel, Motorola, Nokia, Philips, Siemens, and Sun Microsystems, also have large investments in China. Foreign firms in the IT sector are among the largest foreign investors in China and the largest exporters from China (box 11.4). For example, Motorola's investment in China exceeded $3 billion in 2003 and Motorola is also China's fourth largest exporter, selling over $3 billion of its production from China in overseas markets in 2003. Nokia exported more than $2 billion in 2003, ranking 10th among China's largest foreign investors. In addition to Motorola and Nokia, China's top 20 exporters in 2003 included Dell, Intel, a company invested in by IBM, and five Taiwanese IT companies (IFC 2004).

As more companies invested in the Chinese market and an industrial ecology developed, the domestic market began to generate additional demand, which in turn attracted additional mobile factors of production. If a domestic market— such as the Indian market in the past—does not offer sufficient growth potential to attract mobile factors of production, it will have difficulty developing a critical mass of industry to support production for the world market. India's domestic market, heavily protected by government intervention and relatively small with low purchasing power from consumers, offered relatively little attraction for foreign or domestic investors until India's economic growth rate picked up in the early 2000s.

India's government also maintained controls on inward FDI until recently. These controls discouraged international manufacturers who were looking for offshore production bases. Until 1991, explicit regulations capped foreign equity stakes at 40 percent, when permitted at all, and the investment climate was generally perceived as difficult for all investors and especially hostile to foreign investors. These factors severely limited FDI.[1] Beginning in 1991, reforms loosened FDI restrictions; as a result FDI flows into India increased substantially although they remain small compared with those in China (box 11.5).

Box 11.4   Siemens: A Foreign-Owned Company's Success in China

Siemens, one of the world's largest electrical and electronics companies, is among the most well-known and respected foreign companies in China. All of Siemens' fields of business—information and communications, automation and control, power, medical, transportation, lighting, and household appliances—are active in China. When Siemens established its first joint venture in 1989 in China, the company had a total of 200 employees in China. In 15 years, the number exceeded 36,000, making Siemens one of the largest employers among foreign companies in China.

The major economic policy shift that began in China in 1978 paved the way for the dramatic transformation of the country and its opening up to foreign trade and investment. To Siemens, these new political and economic developments signaled new opportunities and fresh attitudes toward cooperation. The company's fast-moving reaction to the opening up and modernization policies established the foundation for long-term cooperation between Siemens and China, aimed at modernizing China's machine-tool, electrical engineering, and electronics industries.

Siemens Ltd, China, the first holding company formed by a foreign company in China, was founded in Beijing in 1994. This enterprise soon became the corporate headquarters for Siemens in China, focusing on management, integration, and promotion of business activities. Siemens had established a broad local manufacturing base comprising more than 40 companies in all areas of business, covering the fields of private networks, mobile phone networks and terminals, transmission equipment, factory automation, power plant control systems, medium-voltage switchgear, and electronic control gear.

A local presence in the provinces allowed Siemens to be near its customers to respond quickly and effectively to their needs and gain reliable knowledge about local market conditions and potential projects. An important part of cooperation between China and Siemens was technology transfer. Siemens, together with Beijing Municipality, opened the Beijing Technology Exchange Training Center to train Chinese partners and customers in advanced automation technologies.

Local procurement and management training both exemplify Siemens' approach to doing business. Developing China into a major procurement base for Siemens' local and global operations created opportunities for local suppliers. Siemens worked with local suppliers to prepare them to meet the company's high standards for quality and reliability, thereby transferring modern management know-how to its partner companies. After a decade's effort, localization rates in some of Siemens' business areas in China reached 75 percent. Of about 2,000 managers working for Siemens in China, more than 90 percent are local Chinese. As of 2007 Siemens has established more than 70 operating companies and 55 regional offices in China. Siemens annually sources in China materials worth over Y1.6 billion ($2.2 billion) and this volume is growing substantially. At the end of 2005, the total long-term investment exceeded Y10.6 billion and sales reached RMB 44.3 billion ($55 billion).

Source: Zhen Wu, based on www.siemens.com/index.jsp?sdc_p=l9oumc34dnsfp and http://tech.sina.com.cn/other/2004-06-20/1739377842.shtml.

The average share of hardware firm ownership accounted for by foreign firms in the IFC sample was 33 percent in Chinese firms compared with only 15 percent in Indian firms (table 11.6). The average foreign equity stakes of the two countries conceal a clear difference in the pattern of foreign ownership of hardware firms. As table 11.6 shows, more hardware firms in China are wholly owned foreign sub-

Box 11.5 HCL Perot in India: From Import-Protected Hardware to Software

In 1974, the Indian government changed the rules on FDI, reducing the maximum foreign share in joint ventures from 51 percent to 40 percent. Some foreign investors complied, but others, including IBM, sold their joint venture stakes instead. As a result, India had no foreign manufacturer of computers just as PCs were taking off. Moreover, high tariffs and restrictions on imports made it difficult to import PCs. This encouraged domestic companies to start up the manufacture of IBM PC clones. One such company was Hindustan Computers Limited (HCL), which began manufacturing PCs in the early 1980s.

As with other domestic manufacturers, HCL's greatest challenge was getting access to fast-changing technologies. Because of lack of access, the company's PCs were technologically inferior to imports, and only found a place in the market because of import restrictions. To obtain access to technology, HCL became a contract manufacturer for Hewlett-Packard, making PCs and servers for the Indian market. Its products were more costly than imported products, however, as a result of inflexible labor laws that led to low

productivity, and poor infrastructure that created delays in the supply chain, power interruptions, and high power costs. Once imports of computers were liberalized in the early 1990s, margins declined rapidly, and the company was unable to compete with imported hardware.

HCL Technologies was formed from HCL as a software company in 1991, and in 1996 HCL Technologies formed a joint venture with Perot Systems of the United States. HCL Infosystems retained the hardware business. HCL Perot was able to hire talented engineers and obtained Capability Maturity Model Level 5 certification in 2000. The company offered software design services to U.S., U.K., and Irish banks, taking advantage of lower labor costs. Unlike its foray into hardware, its growth in the services market was not hindered by labor regulations or other government restrictions. In December 2003, HCL Technologies sold its share of the joint venture to Perot Systems, which continues to operate as a software development company in India.

Source: IFC and Booz Allen Hamilton 2003.

sidiaries, while fewer firms in China have small amounts of portfolio investment—none in the IFC sample with foreign ownership have less than a 25 percent foreign stake compared with 16 percent in the India sample. (These are univariate comparisons; the greater Chinese foreign ownership is not a significant differentiator from Indian hardware firms in a multivariate analysis.)

Chinese hardware firms with more foreign ownership did not, however, show faster short-term sales revenue growth, whereas foreign ownership did make a small contribution to Indian hardware firm growth after accounting for other potential growth determinants. The Chinese hardware industry is more mature than the Indian industry and has a longer history with foreign ownership. In contrast, the Indian hardware industry is a more recent recipient of foreign investment and only in the early 2000s began to show substantial growth.

Nonequity Strategic Alliances

Nonequity strategic alliances are long-term relationships between firms with specific purposes that require close cooperation and knowledge sharing with mutual benefit but without ownership stakes of one firm in the other. (See chapter 6 for

Table 11.6   Foreign Ownership

Finding: *Foreign ownership was greater among Chinese than Indian hardware firms, on average, in a simple comparison; more Chinese firms were wholly foreign owned; more Indian firms had portfolio investment. Foreign ownership did not contribute to the recent short-term revenue growth of Chinese hardware firms, but it gave a small boost to Indian hardware firms.*

	China	India
Some foreign ownership (percentage of firms)[a]	39	37
< 25% foreign ownership	0	16
≥ 25% but < 100% foreign ownership	16	12
100% foreign ownership	23	8
Foreign ownership stake (average percentage over all firms)	33	15
Contribution of 10% greater foreign ownership stake to sales revenue growth	No effect	+2.6%

Source: IFC survey.
a. < 25% foreign ownership is portfolio investment; ≥25% foreign ownership is direct investment; 100% foreign ownership is wholly owned subsidiary.

additional details.) Alliances can be formed with domestic firms as well as with foreign firms, although the interest of this analysis is mainly with the latter.

Chinese and Indian hardware firms were roughly equal users of nonequity strategic alliances overall, but foreign alliances, especially marketing alliances, were more frequent among Indian firms, and domestic alliances were more frequent among Chinese firms. Alliances were less important overall for hardware firms than for software firms.

The difference in use of alliances between Chinese and Indian hardware firms was small overall except that Chinese firms made more use of domestic alliances than Indian firms, and Indian firms made somewhat more use of foreign alliances. (This comparison considers both the number of firms that had such alliances and the number of the alliances that were active.) In India, noninvestment forms of commercial links abroad, such as strategic alliances, were somewhat more important than FDI and acted as a partial substitute for FDI—some of the advantages of FDI such as market access or technology transfer could be gained from a nonequity strategic alliance. In the China sample from the IFC survey, 44 percent of the firms had domestic alliances, but only 22 percent had foreign alliances. In the India sample, the proportions were reversed: 23 percent had domestic alliances and 33 percent had foreign alliances. Among firms that had alliances, the number of alliances was not significantly different but was reported as slightly higher for Indian firms (table 11.7). These simple comparisons were not a statistically significant difference between the two countries' firms in a multivariate analysis, and there was no effect on the firm's short-term revenue growth when accounting for other growth determinants. Whether the hardware firm was a computer or periph-

Table 11.7 Nonequity Strategic Alliances

Finding: *There were no significant differences in the use of nonequity strategic alliances between Chinese and Indian hardware firms, and there was no effect of these alliances on firm growth. Domestic alliances were more prevalent than foreign alliances among Chinese firms.*

	China	India
Firms with nonequity strategic alliances (percentage)	50.0	41.7
Firms with foreign nonequity strategic alliances (percentage)	22.1	33.3
Firms with domestic nonequity strategic alliances (percentage)	44.2	22.9
Number of alliances (average, among firms with alliances)	10.1	12.1
Number of foreign alliances	4.6	5.4
Number of domestic alliances	5.5	6.8
Number of marketing alliances (average among all firms)	1.4	2.4

Source: IFC survey.

erals firm on the one hand, or an industrial electronics or telecommunications firm on the other hand, did not influence the use of nonequity strategic alliances. Marketing alliances with domestic firms were the most frequent type of alliance among Chinese firms and also the most common type of alliance with foreign firms among Indian hardware firms. Growth among Indian hardware firms that was promoted by foreign ownership might also have been reinforced by the use of nonequity alliances, although this effect could not be demonstrated in the multivariate growth analysis. Both technology alliances and production alliances were less frequently used, although they were used more by Chinese than Indian hardware firms.

Overseas Residents

Overseas residents did not often play a role in the performance of either Chinese or Indian hardware firms.

A country's professionals living abroad—overseas Chinese and nonresident Indians—is a potential advantage to the home country's firms. Overseas residents can provide marketing links from their home country to their country of residence, which would be especially important for export business. They also can serve as sources of investment capital and contribute management skills or technological know-how. The Indian diaspora is amply represented in Silicon Valley. The ready availability of engineering and management skills among the Indian diaspora is thought to give Indian firms an advantage in the United States and other world markets. The concentration of technological innovation in Silicon Valley and other technology centers in the United States gives value to personal connections to those locations.

Table 11.8 Role of Overseas Residents

Finding: *The role of overseas residents was roughly the same for Chinese and Indian hardware companies—both infrequent and small.*

	China	India
Firms in which overseas residents have had a role (percentage)	22.7	17.7
Importance of overseas residents' role (sum of four scales where 0 = no role and 5 = very important role)	2.7	2.3
Type of role played in firms when overseas residents have a role (1 = no benefit and 5 = very important benefit)		
Access to markets	3.0	3.1
Access to management practices	3.4	3.2
Access to technology	2.9	3.0
Access to capital	2.5	3.2

Source: IFC survey.

The role played by overseas residents is usually associated with software exporting firms, especially Indian firms, rather than hardware firms. As would be expected, managers of Indian hardware firms reported a role for nonresident Indians with much less frequency than did managers of Indian software firms. Only 19 percent of Indian hardware managers reported any such role, and when they did report a role, it was judged to be of only middling importance, whether that role was access to markets, capital, technology, or management practices. For hardware firms, Chinese and Indian firms did not differ, either in frequency of a role or in importance of the role of nonresidents when there was one (table 11.8).

Note

1. Wei (2000) shows that corruption and red tape have been significant deterrents to FDI in India and China.

Chapter 12

The Effects of Business Environment and Competition on Chinese and Indian Hardware Industries

Governments play a role in creating and enhancing or detracting from the business environment in which firms operate. Policy and regulation can help or hinder industry growth and influence market competitiveness.

Government and the Business Environment

The environment within which businesses operate can be either growth promoting or growth hindering. The environment consists of the nation's infrastructure and institutions and a diverse range of government policies that regulate the conduct of firms and the functioning of markets, the quality and efficiency of public services, and specific incentives targeted to particular industries. This chapter considers the direct influences of government on the business environment, both positive and negative, first for the Chinese and Indian economies overall and then for the Chinese and Indian hardware firms in the IFC survey as perceived by their top managers.

Hindrances to Growth in the Business Environment
Several aspects of the business environments in China and India have been assessed by the World Bank's Doing Business surveys and compared with the same indicators for Organisation for Economic Co-operation and Development (OECD) countries. China and India both are notably worse than OECD averages for most of the indicators. Out of 155 countries in 2005, China ranked 108th in the overall ease of doing business and India ranked 138th (table 12.1). Both China and India score especially poorly on aspects of starting a business and closing a business (World Bank 2006a). India also fared badly in the ease and cost of firing workers and enforcing contracts. Other World Bank surveys of the investment climate in China and India reported on regulatory quality and control of corruption, and the index

Table 12.1 Doing Business Indicators in China and India, 2005

Starting a business				Hiring and firing workers			
Indicator	China	India	OECD average	Indicator	China	India	OECD average
Number of procedures	13	11	6.5	Difficulty of hiring index	11	56	30.1
Time (days)	48	71	19.5	Rigidity of hours index	40	40	50.4
Cost (% of income per capita)	13.6	62.0	6.8	Difficulty of firing index	40	90	27.4
Minimum capital requirement (% of income per capita)	946.7	0	41.0	Rigidity of employment index	30	62	36.1
				Firing costs (weeks of wages)	90	79	40.4
Registering property				**Getting credit**			
Indicator	China	India	OECD average	Indicator	China	India	OECD average
Number of procedures	3	6	4	Legal rights index	2	5	6.3
Time (days)	32	67	34	Credit information index	3	2	5.0
Cost (% of property per capita)	3.1	8.9	4.9	Public credit registry coverage (borrowers per 1,000 adults)	0.4	0	76.2
Protecting investors				Private bureau coverage (borrowers per 1,000 adults)	0	1.7	577.2
Indicator	China	India	OECD average				
Disclosure index	10	7	5.6				
Enforcing contracts				**Closing a business**			
Indicator	China	India	OECD average	Indicator	China	India	OECD average
Number of procedures	25	40	19	Time (years)	2	10	1.7
Time (days)	241	425	229	Cost (% of estate)	22	9	6.8
Cost (% of debt)	25.5	43.1	10.8	Recovery rate (cents on the dollar)	31.5	12.8	72.1

Source: World Bank 2006a.

for each category was about the same for both countries (World Bank 2004c). The government effectiveness index was higher for China than for India. In a separate 2004 World Bank study, Indian hardware firms in particular rated government services as inefficient (4 on a scale of 1 through 5, where 1 was most efficient) (World Bank 2004b).

Firms in both countries found that their interactions with government created bottlenecks to growth (figure 12.1). Corruption and rent-seeking ranked highest among their concerns because of their pervasiveness, which affected many points of interaction with government. In China, tax administration was seen as the second greatest constraint. In India, business regulation and tax administration were

Figure 12.1   Factors Identified as Bottlenecks to Growth in China and India

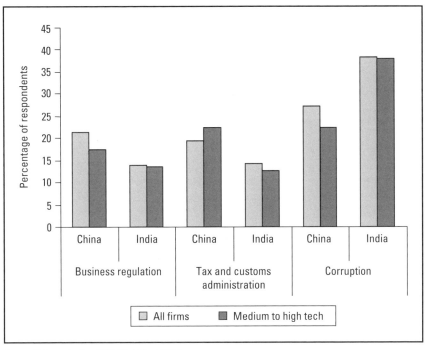

Source: Dollar and others 2003; World Bank 2004b.

seen as equally burdensome. Chinese firms suffered more from multiple inspections, but Indian managers spent more time dealing with regulations. Customs delays were about the same (figure 12.1 and table 12.2).

China. China presents a paradox: It was able to sustain an excellent growth performance despite what many indicators point to as a poor business environment. China's performance shows that the country has developed alternative and less formal ways to provide favorable business environment attributes for private investors as well as state-owned enterprises, despite underdeveloped market institutions.

A good business environment necessarily includes the efficient provision of public services. China's success in maintaining robust growth in private investment despite poor market institutions can be attributed to administrative reforms that aligned the incentives of the bureaucracy with the objectives of rapid, market-based development. For example, China introduced market-based incentives at all levels of the bureaucracy: state employees were allowed to "jump into the sea" and become private entrepreneurs; and government agencies were forced to meet a market test of relevance by selling services to make up for cuts in budget

Table 12.2 **Indicators of Investment Climate Constraints for Medium to High Tech Manufacturing Industries**

Indicators of costs of regulation of business	China	India
Inspections per year (number)	40.3	7.6
Senior management time spent on regulation (percentage)	7.4	12.7
Days to clear customs	8.4	7.1

Source: World Bank 2004a.

allocations. Of great importance, career promotions within the bureaucracy became strictly dependent on market-based criteria of success in promoting development (Tenev 2006).

With such incentives, central and local governments developed the capacity to function as helping hands for economic development by promoting private economic activity. Reform initiatives led to a congruence of interests between various levels of the government and the enterprise sector. This congruence of interests infused reform commitments with credibility and also provided private entrepreneurs in China with de facto protection of their private property rights in the absence of legal and constitutional provisions. The alignment of incentives at all levels of the bureaucracy to promote development went a great distance toward explaining the apparent contradictions between poor institutions and phenomenal growth.

The probusiness role that local governments played in China had its downside. A tendency to overinvest, local protectionism, and fragmented macroeconomic control were the flipside of the local government coin. Opportunities for corruption were abundant when the government was so actively involved in the economy. The interplay of interjurisdictional competition and prodevelopment incentives, however, tended to limit the costs of government activism.

India. In India, a complex web of business regulations and a pervasive culture of government interference imposed serious costs on doing business. Private investors required many approvals from the government of the Indian state in which they were located to start a business and had to interact with their state's bureaucracy in day-to-day operations because of laws governing worker welfare, pollution, sanitation, and the like. Such high levels of government interaction raised the potential for corruption, which World Bank ICA survey respondents regarded as a major problem. The World Bank's Investment Climate Assessments (ICAs) for India showed that the private sector in India was constrained by several policy and regulatory factors, including high and complex taxes and tariffs, restrictions on foreign direct investment (FDI), restrictions on the industrial sector, labor regulations (discussed in chapter 10), and business inefficiencies arising from bureaucratic interference. The adverse effect of an unfavorable investment climate on business growth was demonstrated by its negative correlation with productivity:

Table 12.3   Manufactured Exports by Technology Intensity
(% total exports)

	1985			1996		
Exports	China	India	World	China	India	World
Resource based	11.7	40.3	19.3	9.8	31.1	13.7
Low tech	57.1	46.1	23.4	56.3	52.3	21.3
Medium tech	21.8	10.6	37.3	13.4	13.1	37.3
High tech	9.4	3.0	20.1	20.6	4.4	27.7

Source: Lall 1999.

Table 12.4   Growth Rates of Manufactured Exports
(percentage, 1990–96)

Exports	China	India
Resource based	15.2	9.3
Low tech	18.4	11.8
Medium tech	9.4	12.6
High tech	35.4	14.5

Source: Lall 1999.

productivity was higher in Indian states with better investment climates (World Bank 2004b).

Exports from India's manufacturing sector have been weighted toward resource-based and low technology exports rather than high technology exports. It is possible that the unfavorable aspects of India's business environment had especially adverse effects on medium and high technology exports. Following Indian reform, post-1990 growth was fastest in the high tech segment, although nothing like the pace of growth in China's high tech manufacturing exports (tables 12.3 and 12.4).

Impact of Government Policies on the Hardware Industries in China and India

Government policies affect the hardware industries in China and India in a variety of ways. Some policies, such as tax concessions, research and development (R&D) and marketing support, provision of infrastructure, and some trade and investment policies, promote industry growth. Others, such as high taxes, bureaucracy, low efficiency of government services, lack of provision of infrastructure, travel and visa restrictions, and other trade and investment policies, may unwittingly hinder the growth of the industry. The analysis of the way government policies in China and India might affect the hardware industries in each country led to

Table 12.5   Impacts of Government Policies on Growth

Impact	China	India
Promote growth	3.2	3.1
Hinder growth	2.8	3.6

Source: IFC survey.
Note: Mean of five growth-promoting policies and six growth-hindering policies, where 1 = no impact and 5 = great impact.

the conclusion that Chinese hardware firms in general benefit more and are hindered less from government policies than Indian hardware firms (table 12.5). The balance of policy impacts among Chinese firms is positive while the balance of impacts among Indian firms is negative.

Government Policies That Hinder Growth for Hardware Firms

Specific government policies that hinder the growth of hardware firms were both more numerous and reported to be more harmful by Indian hardware managers than by Chinese hardware managers.

Among hardware firms in particular, Indian firms reported more government policies that hindered growth than did Chinese firms. Excessive government bureaucracy and paperwork and high import tariffs and import restrictions were among the most troublesome; these two hindrances were a statistically significant difference between Indian and Chinese hardware firms in a multivariate analysis. Low efficiency of government services and taxes—corporate income, excise, and sales taxes—were also reported as major hindrances to Indian hardware firms' growth. Taxes were also growth hindering for Chinese hardware firms (table 12.6). Box 12.1 reports one Indian company's experiences with the business environment. The ratings are perceptions of managers, and it is possible that the intercountry comparison does not correspond to an objective measure, if there is one, because Indians typically feel free to criticize their government while Chinese managers may be less willing to do so.

The regulatory burden hardware firm managers face is substantial in both China and India. About 10 percent or more of their time, on average, was spent dealing with regulatory issues, according to the IFC survey (table 12.7).

Restrictive Indian labor laws did not yield a disadvantage for Indian hardware firms compared with their Chinese counterparts. The median firm in both countries was at its desired employment level, while the mean desired level was only slightly below the actual at 98 percent for Chinese firms and nearly 100 percent for Indian firms. The lack of adverse effect of restrictive Indian labor laws that make reductions in employment very difficult might be traced to the preponderance of

Table 12.6   Government Policies with Negative Impact
(scale: 1 = no impact, 5 = great impact)

Finding: *Chinese hardware firms reported less adverse impacts of government bureaucracy and import restrictions than did Indian hardware firms, and these were a statistically significant difference between the two sets of firms when other policies were accounted for; Chinese hardware firms also were less hindered by taxes and low efficiency of government services than were Indian hardware firms in a simple comparison.*

Impact on growth	China	India
Taxes—corporate income, excise, and sales	3.5	4.1
Infrastructure quality and quantity	3.2	3.5
Travel and visa restrictions	2.6	2.1
Bureaucracy and paperwork requirements	*2.8*	*4.0*
Low efficiency of government services	2.8	4.1
High import tariffs and import restrictions	*2.6*	*3.8*

Source: IFC survey.
Note: Policies in italics showed a statistically significant difference between Indian and Chinese firms in a multivariate analysis. All other policy impacts differ between Chinese and Indian hardware firms in simple comparisons except infrastructure quantity and quality.

Box 12.1   Hical: Indian Hardware Supplier

Hical was established in 1988 to make handsets and telephone exchanges for the Indian market, which at the time was protected from imports of these goods. The domestic market was not big enough, however, to achieve economies of scale. Therefore, when import protection policies were changed in the 1990s, the company was unable to compete against imported products. The company then switched to making power converters and transformers for mobile phones, starting as a supplier to Siemens. The relationship with Siemens was important for access to technology, but the company turned down a joint venture offer from Siemens, which allowed the company to supply other customers, such as Nokia. The company aims to add one major customer a year.

Hical has been able to win supply contracts against competitors from China in part because purchasers value diversity of supply. Hical is the only non-Chinese supplier to one particular customer. The company finds it hard to achieve the same scale economies as it might in China because of labor laws that discourage hiring of large numbers of workers. Instead, it focuses on high–value added products that can be produced with a small workforce and on added value through design services. Venture capital investments of equity have supported Hical's growth.

---

small firms in this industry that are exempt from the provisions of the law and to the forecast for accelerating rates of growth of the industry that implies an increase in future demand for labor.

Promotion of Growth in the Business Environment

Governments adopt policies intended to promote the growth of businesses generally. Some policies are targeted to particular industries. Chinese government

Table 12.7 Effects of Regulations

Areas affected	China	India
Management (percentage of time spent dealing with government regulations)		
Mean	10.4	13.9
Median	10.0	9.0
Employment level desired compared with actual (percentage of existing workforce)		
Mean	97.6	99.8
Median	100.0	100.0
Customs clearance time (mean number of days)		
Imports	9.5	4.6
Exports	11.3	3.2

Source: IFC survey.

policies supported the hardware industry directly, but also indirectly, especially via special economic zones (SEZs). The Indian government adopted reforms of trade and investment policies, but they came late in the hardware industry's development.

China. The Chinese government facilitated industrial development by establishing SEZs. A distinctive characteristic of these zones in China was that their legal status more closely resembled that of local governments than of corporations. This status facilitated government support in the form of tax concessions, lending at preferential terms, and assistance with licenses and residence permits. China's SEZs played an important role in providing land, infrastructure, and a low-cost business environment for manufacturers, including hardware manufacturers. The SEZs were particularly attractive for foreign investors because they eliminated the challenge of acquiring sites and services and of navigating the complexities of local regulations. These incentives created the nucleus around which clusters developed (see the Land Use section in chapter 10). Local governments in inland China subsequently adopted similar policies of using SEZs to attract investment; the existence of SEZs became a way to judge the performance of local government officials. The establishment of SEZs away from coastal regions enabled Chinese companies to maintain a labor cost advantage.

The Chinese government was also involved in the hardware industry through state ownership or control. Some state-owned firms, such as Great Wall, were subsequently privatized as successful computer manufacturers.

India. In India, unlike in China, special zones did not play an important role in industrial development. They existed, but did not reduce the complexity of regulations, offer fiscal incentives, or provide superior infrastructure. Instead of offering "one-stop shopping" services to investors, zone administrators became "one more stop" shops. State governments did not prioritize infrastructure services in zones the way China did. Only with the passage of the SEZ Act in 2005 was India able to empower SEZ administrators to cut through government red tape. Even so, India's restrictive labor laws still apply within SEZs (Lall and Mengistae 2005). The percentage of Indian hardware companies in the IFC sample located in SEZs is therefore somewhat lower than in China.[1]

Until economic reform began in 1991, the average import tariff rate in India was more than 90 percent, and only 12 percent of Indian manufacturers could import freely (Topalova 2004). By restricting imports through high tariffs and licensing, India kept the real exchange rate artificially high, deterring exports. In the late 1990s, the Indian government introduced various export incentive schemes to counter this bias against exports. Indian companies that exported a certain proportion of their output were classified as Export Oriented Units (EOUs) and qualified for tax concessions, including duty-free imports and exemption from corporate income tax, which otherwise was 36 percent. Of the hardware firms in the survey, 41 percent were registered as EOUs.

EOU status notwithstanding, trade and tax policy plus lack of access to internationally competitive technology led most hardware companies to focus on the domestic market. In the IFC survey, only 29 percent of telecommunications manufacturers, 19 percent of peripherals firms, 14 percent of components-manufacturing firms, and no computer manufacturers were export oriented.

Government Policies That Promote Growth for Hardware Firms

Both Chinese and Indian hardware managers perceived benefits from specific government policies but the advantage was with the Chinese industry.

The most important government policies reported by Chinese hardware firm managers that promoted the growth of their firms, and which were a statistically significant difference from the Indian industry, were the availability of corporate income tax concessions, marketing support from the government, and R&D support with assistance in accessing technology. Many more Chinese hardware firms (81 percent) than Indian hardware firms (53 percent) received income tax concessions. In addition, the impact of the benefit was seen to be strongly toward the high end of the scale by Chinese managers (mean impact score of 3.7 on a scale where 1 = no impact and 5 = great impact) and also by Indian managers who received such a benefit (the scale score was 4.0) (table 12.8).

In the view of Chinese hardware managers, marketing support from the government provided the single most important benefit to growth. Chinese hardware firms that received more benefit from government marketing support also showed faster short-term sales revenue growth—about 14 percent faster sales growth for a 10 percent greater policy impact. Support for R&D and access to technology was

Table 12.8   Government Policies with Positive Impact
(scale: 1 = no impact, 5 = great impact)

Finding: *Chinese hardware firms reported greater positive impacts of marketing and R&D support from the government, and more benefit from income tax concessions than did Indian hardware firms; all of which were statistically significant differences between the two countries' firms after other policy variables were accounted for. Chinese firms that reported greater impacts from marketing support also showed faster sales revenue growth.*

Impact on growth	China	India
Infrastructure provision	*3.3*	*3.9*
Marketing support	*3.6*	*2.0*
Contribution of marketing support to sales revenue growth	+14%	no effect
R&D support and technology access	*3.4*	*2.7*
Policy liberalization		
Import	2.8	3.7
FDI	2.8	3.0
Firms that benefit from income tax concessions	*81%*	*53%*

Source: IFC survey.
Note: Policies in italics show statistically significant differences between Indian and Chinese firms in a multivariate analysis. All other policy impacts differ between Chinese and Indian hardware firms in simple comparisons except liberalization of FDI.

the other government policy that favored Chinese hardware firms (impact of 3.4 for Chinese firms and only 2.7 for Indian firms), and the difference was statistically significant after accounting for other policies.

Policies in China that promoted government procurement also were a major source of revenue for domestic enterprises (box 12.2). For example, companies that make integrated circuit–based identity cards for the government (Datang and Tsinghua Tongfang, for instance) derived a significant portion of their revenues from government contracts.

There are just two government policies in the growth-promoting arena for which Indian hardware managers reported positive impacts greater than reported by their Chinese counterparts: provision of infrastructure and liberalization of import policies. However, these favorable policies did not give the Indian firms an advantage over Chinese firms; rather, they might be seen as catching up or making up for past deficiencies.

Why India Promoted Software but Not Hardware

The Indian government did not promote its hardware industry, even though it promoted the software industry very actively and directly. Why favor a new and uncertain software industry but not an existing high technology hardware industry? The reasons, the analysis suggests, reflect both history and practical politics.

Beginning with India's First Five-Year Plan, the government pursued an economic development strategy emphasizing import substitution in the agricultural

---

Box 12.2   The Development of the Semiconductor Industry in China: Governments Pitch In

Manufacturing in integrated circuit (IC) intensive industries, including telecom, has grown rapidly in China. In this fast-growing environment, the semiconductor industry became the weakest link in China's electronics industry. China's leaders recognized this constraint and developed policies to support the development of the semiconductor industry as a strategic high-growth industry.

The quickest way to jump-start the development of the industry was to invite outside expertise and investment in the foundry subsector. With the backing of the government, Richard Chang, former chief executive officer of a Taiwanese chipmaker, founded Semiconductor Manufacturing International Corporation (SMIC) in April 2000. SMIC received Chinese renminbi (RMB) 12.3 billion ($1.48 billion) in initial investment. Following SMIC, a larger number of companies shifted production to China or established new foundries in China, including Grace Semiconductor in Shanghai, Huahong in Shanghai, UMC in Suzhou, and TSMC in Ningbo. Between 2000 and 2002, China's IC industry received approximately RMB 29 billion ($3.5 billion) in investment, which in these two years equaled all previous investment in the sector.

The government views semiconductors as a strategic industry and has offered extensive support to companies involved in IC design and manufacturing. The main areas and forms of support are outlined in Document 18, "Policies for Encouraging the Development of Software and Integrated Circuit Industries," published in June 2000. Support includes bank loans subsidized by public authorities, government investments, tax reductions, and the founding of design centers. Local governments often compete with each other to offer better incentives to attract investment in the IC industry.

The government's emphasis on the IC industry is also reflected in China's 10th Five-Year Plan, which identified the time period to 2010 as critical to the Chinese semiconductor industry, and set out the objectives for national IC wafer production to reach RMB 50 billion ($6 billion) by 2010 with sales of RMB 200 billion ($24 billion). The production should constitute 5 percent of world sales and meet 50 percent of domestic demand. To attain these goals, the plan proposed establishment of a national IC R&D center to research and develop large-scale technology production and system-level IC; support to independent design groups; and the building of a number of fabrication plants as well as five or six packaging plants.

Source: IFC survey.

---

and industrial sectors. Import substitution was a common policy response of post–World War II development planners to the breakdown of international trade that occurred in the interwar period. The Nehru government and its successors took up import substitution with particular vigor because it complemented two of the most important influences on political thought: the Ghandian concept of *swadeshi*, or self-reliance, and Fabian socialism, which viewed foreign investment and trade with suspicion. As was common in the state-led planning paradigm of the postwar period, the government saw industry as the leading sector that would drive growth and employment creation.[2] Little consideration was given to the scope for services to add economic value, while financial services were regulated to support greater investment in industry and agriculture, reflecting the historical experience of the industrial revolutions of the United Kingdom, the United States, and Japan, which heavily influenced the thinking of Indian development planners (Government of India Planning Commission 1951). The basis of Indian industrial policy was to develop domestic industries by protecting them from foreign competition in the home-country market. The irony is that the government's intent was to promote manufacturing industries, not to hinder them. The instruments were industrial licensing, directed lending by the domestic banking system, restrictions on capital flows, and quotas or tariffs on imports. Electronic hardware manufacturing was treated like other manufacturing industries. Quotas and high tariffs on imports were introduced after the 1956–57 balance of payments crisis. Tariffs on hardware reached 135 percent by the 1970s, before being reduced to 40 percent to 55 percent after the 1991 liberalization, and then to 20 percent by 2000. High tariffs encouraged "tariff-jumping"—inward investment by multinationals such as IBM, Burroughs, and Texas Instruments, which established computer assembly operations in India. At the same time, all manufacturing industries, including hardware, were subject to the "license raj" regulations and state controls that distorted managerial incentives, diminished competition, and in turn weakened the international competitiveness of Indian hardware firms. Domestic industrial licensing policy encouraged the creation of a few large enterprises in each sector to serve the domestic market, with the aim of exploiting economies of scale and avoiding overcapacity. As a result, IBM gained a near monopoly in the hardware market in India.

However, the 1973 Foreign Exchange Regulation Act required foreign investors to convert their Indian subsidiaries into minority joint ventures, with the foreign ownership stake capped at 40 percent. Some multinationals complied, but concerns about inability to protect their intellectual property as a minority partner in a joint venture led IBM (and, famously, Coca-Cola) to withdraw from India instead. This stimulated the growth of domestic companies such as Wipro and HCL, which then stepped in to assemble computers using imported technology under license. To compensate for lack of access to the latest technology, the government sponsored public investment in hardware development, including a successful supercomputer project. The government also gave more direct support to the development of high technology manufacturing through its sponsorship of public enterprises in the defense and aerospace sectors. The intent, again, was to promote the industries. Nevertheless, Indian hardware manufacturers were handicapped by lack of access to the latest proprietary technologies (Dossani 2005).

Software was not affected in the same way by these policies. As technological change in the computer industry led to the unbundling of hardware and software applications in the 1980s, software became less constrained by the policy-induced barriers to hardware development. The timing was fortuitous, because it coincided with the beginnings of a shift in Indian economic policy under Rajiv Gandhi away from import substitution toward export promotion. Although much of the structure of industrial policy remained in place until the 1991 liberalization and be-yond, the government began to provide incentives for exports. Most important, it exempted profits on export sales from income tax beginning in 1984. This encouraged new export activities to be established.

However, exporting manufacturers still had to comply with the license raj, directed lending, and high tariffs, which biased incentives toward the domestic market. These policy contradictions were only slowly resolved over the following 20 years. The shift happened slowly because vested interests—both incumbent corporations and the public sector bureaucracy—stood to lose from these changes. The political economy of reform was difficult and drawn out, only gaining momentum once the gains from liberalization in some sectors, notably software and telecom, came into view to offset the immediately visible losses. For example, it was easier to provide tax concessions to a new industry such as software (under the 1984 New Computer Policy) than it was to reduce taxation on existing industries, such as hardware, that would result in a fiscal loss. Similarly, it was easier to permit foreign investment in new sectors than to expose profitable domestic incumbents to new competition in long-established industries. Because hardware manufacturing was viewed as part of the wider manufacturing sector, policy toward it remained closely tied to overall industrial policy.

In contrast, the services industry was largely ignored by industrial policy. This had its drawbacks—for example, banks had little incentive to lend to services companies that did not meet any government lending guidelines, and service companies did not qualify for export financing. However, this governmental neglect did have the advantage of shielding software from many of the increased costs and distorted incentives facing the industrial sector. At the same time, Rajiv Gandhi saw potential benefits in actively encouraging software services, both as a new opportunity to generate export revenue, and as a source of domestic productivity gains in the public and private sectors through greater adoption of information technology. In the 1980s, when the New Computer Policy was introduced, domestic penetration of information technology was very low relative to OECD countries. Hence, as well as being in line with the overall policy direction of the Rajiv Gandhi government, it was natural to promote software as an export industry from the start. It was technical-labor intensive, and infrastructure weaknesses could be overcome. The New Computer Policy reduced tariffs on both hardware and software to 60 percent, delicensed the software industry, and permitted enterprises to be 100 percent foreign owned.

Infrastructure and Institutions

Infrastructure and institutions affect the ability of firms in an industry to grow and compete. Their impacts on Chinese and Indian hardware firms are analyzed in this section.

Figure 12.2   Infrastructure as Obstacles to Growth

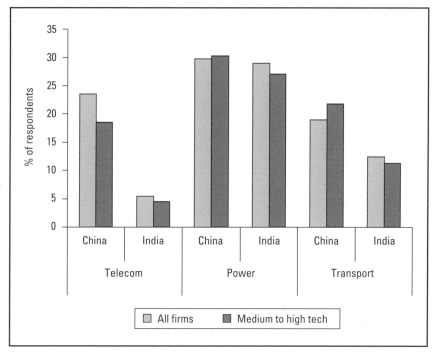

Source: World Bank 2004b; Dollar and others 2003.

Infrastructure

Infrastructure, especially the lack of availability and high cost of electric power, was a major obstacle to growth in both China and India, according to World Bank surveys (figure 12.2).

China. China's infrastructure is not immune from problems. Accelerated growth since the early 2000s has strained China's infrastructure. Power cuts have occurred with some frequency in some eastern and southern provinces, such as Zhejiang, Jiangsu, and Guangdong, where the majority of hardware producers are located, although the problem appears to have subsided with the additional power generation capacity coming onstream. Bottlenecks have occurred, however, on roads and railways and in ports.

China has made significant progress in building modern infrastructure to support economic growth. All indicators show rapid improvement in infrastructure, and in almost all indicators China surpasses India in investments in infrastructure (table 12.9). China's largest city has more than twice the telephone density of the

Table 12.9   Investments in Infrastructure, 1996–2006

($ billions)

Infrastructure	China	India
Telecom	13.0	9.2
Electric power	14.3	7.5
Transport	15.9	2.3

Source: Wolf 2005.

Figure 12.3   Growth in Telecommunications Lines in China

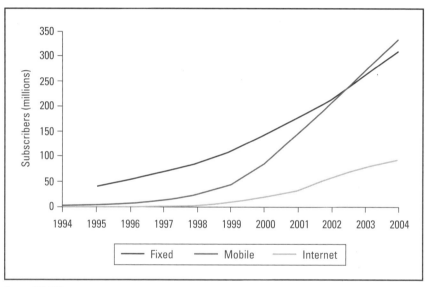

Source: IFC 2005.

largest Indian city. China has four times as many personal computers per 1,000 people as India has. Close to 90 percent of Chinese roads are paved compared with 56 percent in India, and in cost of shipping, China's advantage is pronounced. Despite this remarkable progress, China still lags behind middle-income countries on many aspects of infrastructure development, and more Chinese than Indian respondents to the IFC survey perceived infrastructure to be a constraint to growth.

In 2003, the Chinese mobile phone subscriber base surpassed the fixed subscriber base with fixed-line penetration of 25 percent, and mobile penetration of 26 percent. The number of Internet users reached 94 million at year-end 2004 (figure 12.3). Of these, 26 million were using broadband access, compared with 1.9 million in 2001.

Table 12.10   Computers and Connectivity, China and India, 2002

Indexes of use	China	India
Internet users (millions)	33.7	5.0
Internet bandwidth (Gbps)	7.8	1.4
Installed PC base (millions)	21.7	3.9
Domestic software sales ($ billions)	4.30	2.06

Source: Contractor and Kundu 2004.
Note: Gbps = gigabits per second.

India. In the Indian telecom and ports sectors, the regulatory framework evolved over time and, once stabilized, yielded positive results in an increase in private investment, both domestic and international. In other sectors, such as power, transport, water and sanitation, and solid waste, progress has been negligible. Severe infrastructure bottlenecks in these sectors hamper the efficiency and competitiveness of Indian businesses, particularly of manufacturing firms. Moreover, despite India's prowess in information technology, installed computer capacity and connectivity remain much lower than in China, reducing the prevalence of computer use in business (table 12.10).

In 2003–04, the World Economic Forum rated infrastructure as the most challenging factor in doing business in India. India ranked 82nd in the world out of 104 countries in the quality of its power supply (World Economic Forum 2004). State-owned electricity boards dominate the power sector, the facilities suffer from underinvestment, and cross-subsidies from industrial users support rural consumers. Reliability and availability are low, and prices are high.

Manufacturers in India face an average of 17 severe power outages per month compared with fewer than 5 among manufacturers in China. In India, approximately 9 percent of the total value of output of firms is lost as a result of power breakdowns, compared with 2 percent in China (World Bank 2004b). Moreover, industry is charged tariffs significantly higher than the cost of supply. As a result, a large majority of Indian firms operate their own captive generators. For instance, World Bank surveys indicate that 30 percent of surveyed Chinese firms have their own power generators versus 69 percent of the Indian companies (Dollar and others 2003). Reliance on captive generation increases the Indian industry's cost of power and reduces industrial competitiveness, particularly for power-intensive manufacturing processes (figure 12.4).

India has one of the most extensive transport systems in the world, but severe capacity and quality constraints are numerous. As of 2004, India had no interstate expressways linking the major economic centers (even in 2007, the Mumbai-Pune Expressway stood out as one of a kind) and only 3,000 kilometers of four-lane highways. China, however, has built 25,000 kilometers of four-to-six lane, access-controlled expressways since 1995. Poor ride quality and congestion result in truck and bus speeds on Indian highways that average 30–40 kilometers an hour, about

Figure 12.4   Indicators of Power Supply Deficiency from the Public Grid

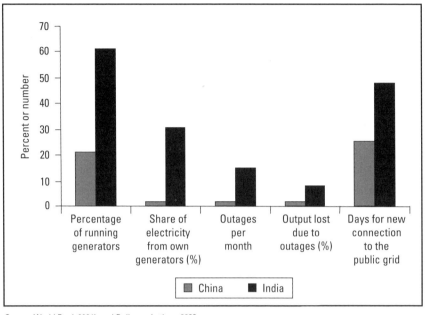

Source: World Bank 2004b and Dollar and others 2003.

half the expected average on major roads in other countries. Notable progress has been made with the Golden Quadrilateral highway project, which links Delhi, Mumbai, Chennai, and Kolkata (completed in 2005) and the North South-East West highway project currently under construction. Even with these upgrades, however, just 22 percent of the country's national highways and none of the state highways, which are in serious disrepair, will be reasonably well-surfaced, four-lane highways.

With a network of 63,000 kilometers, Indian Railways is the second largest rail network in the world, yet this network fails to provide efficient freight transportation. High cargo tariffs arising from cross-subsidization of passenger fares are a key problem and have caused long-haul goods traffic to move steadily away from rail to roads. In addition, serious congestion on main lines is steadily increasing long-haul delivery times and making the railways even more unattractive.

Although there has been a modicum of reform and operational improvement of some of the major ports, airports, and customs procedures and increased private investment in port facilities, costs of importing and exporting are high because of inadequate capacity and slow procedures. The mean delay at customs for imports was still 6.3 days and 5.1 days for exports in 2003 (World Bank 2004b). Manufacturers of garments, leather goods, textiles, pharmaceuticals, and automobile components, which import raw materials and intermediates and export final products, suffer from total delays ranging from 11.8 days to 13.4 days.

Figure 12.5 Indicators of Infrastructure Bottlenecks

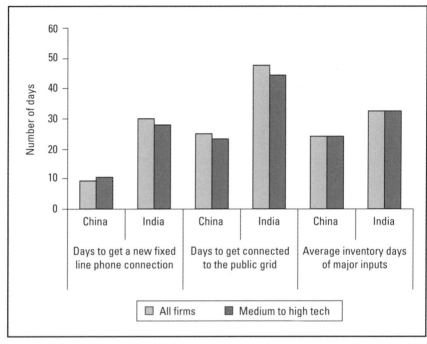

Source: World Bank 2004b; Dollar and others 2003.

Such delays raise working capital requirements and reduce competitiveness. As figure 12.5 shows, Indian firms carry higher input inventory than Chinese firms. These constraints reinforce the tariff- and quota-induced bias in manufacturing toward serving the domestic market, and more specifically, the local market.

Hardware firms, like all manufacturers, need ample and reliable electric power, adequate road and rail networks and services, and to some extent, telecom services. Firms that import components or export products also need efficient port facilities. The top managers of Chinese hardware firms in the IFC survey reported less-adverse impacts on their businesses from infrastructure weaknesses than did the Indian firms' managers.

Chinese hardware firms had an infrastructure advantage over Indian hardware firms because of a more reliable electric power supply and less need to install their own generators, and to a lesser extent, because of a better public transport network.

Indian firms in the survey rated electric power cuts or surges as having a greater adverse impact on their businesses than did Chinese hardware firm man-

Table 12.11   Infrastructure Impacts
(scale: 1 = no problem, 5 = major problem)

Finding: *Chinese hardware firms faced less serious problems than Indian firms from electric power cuts and public transportation failures, but telecom infrastructure problems were not different between the two countries.*

Finding: *Equal numbers of hardware firms in both countries were located in special parks or zones.*

Infrastructure	China	India
Electric power		
Power cuts: seriousness of problem	2.6	3.2
Have own electric power facilities (percentage yes)	48	82
Transportation		
Public transport failures	2.4	2.7
Telecom		
Unavailable telephone service	2.2	2.0
Unavailable Internet broadband service	2.5	2.6
Percentage of firms located in SEZs, STPs, or export-processing zones	47	49

Source: IFC survey.
Note: SEZ = Special economic zone; STP = Software technology park.

agers (see table 12.11), and the difference is statistically significant in univariate and multivariate analyses. Some 82 percent of Indian hardware firms in the survey had their own power generation facilities (a somewhat higher figure than that reported in the World Bank ICA survey for all manufacturing firms; World Bank 2004b) compared with 48 percent of Chinese hardware firms. These findings corroborate the World Bank ICA, in which Indian hardware manufacturers ranked power as the most important infrastructure service. The ICA also found that hardware firms paid 16 rupees (Rs) per kwh (about 3.5 U.S. cents) for public power and Rs50/kwh (about $1.10) for their own power and that cost of power was the most important factor in choosing plant locations for Indian manufacturers.

Indian managers of hardware firms in the IFC survey rated public transport failures as having a greater adverse impact than did Chinese hardware firm managers (2.7 and 2.4, respectively), which was a significant differentiator between the two countries' firms in a multivariate analysis.

Telecom problems were less serious than other infrastructure problems for Indian hardware firms, and no difference was found between Chinese and Indian firms' reports. All of the reports by hardware firm managers about the seriousness of infrastructure problems, except electric power in India, had scores that tended toward the "no problem" side rather than the "major problem" side of the scale. Survey ratings of problems caused by infrastructure failures were not as high as expected, likely because companies found ways to work around these constraints (for example, through batch production processes, captive power supplies, and direct satellite links).

Until the late 1990s, government-owned landline providers predominated in the telecom industry in India. According to the ICA, Indian hardware firms took 73 days to get a phone connection (and 71 days to get a power connection). Only since the early 2000s have privately owned mobile telecom and broadband providers broken through the telecom bottlenecks.

Institutions

Well-developed and high-quality legal, financial, regulatory, and educational institutions contribute to the efficient functioning of markets and the growth and development of firms. Both the government's influence on these institutions and the ways in which markets work differ in China compared with India. In general, India's legal and financial institutions are more highly regarded than China's, although complaints are frequently made about the slowness of India's judicial processes and the high cost of finance in India. However, the burden of government regulation in India is often criticized. The analysis investigated several of the effects of these institutions.

Overall there was little net difference in the impact of institutions on Chinese relative to Indian hardware firms. Chinese hardware managers reported somewhat more effective judicial systems but also somewhat longer delays in customs clearances in simple comparisons. None of the features of the institutional environment are statistically significantly different between the two countries' firms when accounting for other differentiators.

While Chinese hardware and software managers had similar views about the effectiveness of the Chinese judicial system in enforcing their contractual and property rights, Indian hardware managers were somewhat less confident in the judicial system than were their Indian software firm counterparts; the result is that the Indian judicial system was judged less effective for hardware firms than was the Chinese judicial system in a simple comparison (2.9 and 3.4, respectively, when 5 = fully effective and 1 = not at all effective).

Chinese hardware companies met the need for financing by bank borrowing less often than did Indian hardware companies (see the section on capital as a factor of production in chapter 10). This difference does not necessarily mean that financial institutions in China are inferior—most of the Chinese hardware companies that did not have bank lending said they did not need it.

Educational institutions were somewhat less important for hardware than for software companies, at least higher educational institutions, simply because the demand for professional labor is lower in hardware companies. Chapter 10 notes the finding that Chinese hardware firms had lower entry-level educational qualifications for professionals and that the use of professionals was not high in Chinese hardware firms.

Indian hardware firms did not suffer disadvantages from delays at customs. Chinese firms in the IFC survey reported 10–11 days on average for imported inputs and exports to clear customs whereas Indian hardware firms in the survey reported 3–5 days, which is less than reported by all manufacturing firms in the World Bank ICA survey (World Bank 2004b); this difference was statistically significant between the two countries' firms in a multivariate analysis. The figure for China is higher than in surveys conducted before the recent acceleration in growth. The figure for India is likely biased downward because not many Indian hardware firms participate in international trade.

If corruption is indicated in part by the need for firms to make informal payments to public officials to get things done (with regard to customs, taxes, licenses, regulatory approvals, and the like) and if the perceptions of managers are accurately reported, then Chinese hardware firms have an advantage over their Indian counterparts. Chinese managers believed that the median hardware firm spent nothing on informal payments to public officials—the mean was 0.1 percent of its revenue. Indian managers believed the median hardware firm spent 0.5 percent of its revenue—the mean was 1.3 percent. The differences were significant in a simple comparison.

By contrast, corruption (rent-seeking) in India was ranked as the greatest problem in the World Bank ICA for all manufacturing firms, ahead of power failures, tax rates, and government administration (World Bank 2004b).

Market Competitiveness

The more competitive the markets in which a firm participates, the stronger the firm must be to survive and grow (box 12.3). If countries' market competitiveness is measured, and differs systematically across countries, the competitive pressure under which the countries' firms operate can be inferred. Although Chinese hardware firms in the IFC sample had greater export intensity than the Indian hardware firms (23 percent versus 16 percent, on average), the difference was not statistically significant. Therefore, both countries' firms in the sample operate primarily in their home-country markets. Stronger home-country markets are one basis for stronger export performance (Porter 1990). The strength of home-country markets depends on several features, one of which is the rivalry among firms in the industry (in Porter 1996 terminology). Others include the strength of suppliers and distributors, horizontal technology spillovers from related industries, the strength of domestic-market demand, and the productivity and abundance of factors of production, especially created factors in modern high technology industries.

The analysis measured some aspects of market competitiveness among the firms in the IFC survey.

Chinese hardware firms faced less competitive markets by some measures than did Indian hardware firms.

Indian managers reported easier entry into the business than did Chinese hardware company managers. They also reported less pricing power over customers; that is, customers were less willing to accept price increases, and Indian managers appeared to have less pricing power against their competitors (many

---

Box 12.3   China's Hardware Companies Go Global

Increasingly, China's leading domestic vendors have global ambitions for their businesses. Lenovo's 2005 purchase of IBM's PC business for $1.25 billion in cash and stock is the most significant example of a Chinese company expanding overseas, but Lenovo is not alone. In fact, the Lenovo-IBM deal is part of a continuing trend of Chinese firms striking deals to expand their business overseas.

TCL, China's second largest handset maker and one of the largest makers worldwide of consumer electronics, has made a string of overseas deals. In 2002, TCL purchased the bankrupt German television manufacturer Schneider for €8.2 million ($7.4 million). Through the acquisition, TCL hoped to gain access to a recognizable brand to support its entrance into the European market. In November 2003, the company took a larger step into international markets by forming a joint venture with Thomson for its television business. The joint venture is reported to have created the largest television manufacturer in the world—TCL and Thomson TV sold a total of 18 million units in 2003, accounting for 10 percent of the global market. TCL has a controlling stake in the joint venture with 67 percent; Thomson holds the remaining 33 percent. In 2004, TCL formed a joint venture with Alcatel for its handset business; TCL holds a 55 percent in the venture and Alcatel the remaining 45 percent.

Chinese telecom equipment vendors are also moving overseas. Huawei, China's largest telecom equipment vendor with $5.58 billion in sales in 2004, formed a joint venture with 3Com in November 2003. Through the partnership, Huawei assigned most of its Ethernet switch and mid- to low-end router R&D team and network equipment manufacturing to the joint venture and took a 51 percent share of the company; 3Com invested $160 million and licenses for its intellectual property products and took the remaining 49 percent share. Through overseas partnerships and its own overseas sales, Huawei has turned its international business into a multi-billion dollar operation. Huawei generated $2.28 billion in international revenues in 2004, up 117 percent from 2003. The company's international sales span the globe. In early November 2004, Huawei won over $400 million in contracts in Africa from telecom operators in Kenya, Nigeria, and Zimbabwe for 3G equipment, optical transmission, switches, routers, and intelligent networks products. Huawei also won new contracts in Australia and Latin America in November. In 3G, Huawei has won contracts in both developing and developed markets. In October 2004, Huawei signed Africa's first 3G contract with Mauritius operator EMTEL. The company has also sold to Etisalat in the United Arab Emirates. In more developed markets, the company has won contracts for $155 million from Huawei-invested Hong Kong, China mobile operator Sunday. And in December 2004, Huawei broke into the European 3G market by securing a 3G contract valued at approximately €200 million ($252 million) in the Netherlands.

ZTE, China's second largest equipment vendor with contract revenues reaching $4.13 billion in 2004, is also expanding aggressively overseas. The company had $1.64 billion in sales overseas in 2004, representing a year-to-year increase of 169.5 percent. The company's stock was listed on the Hong Kong Stock Exchange in December 2004, raising additional capital to fund its international expansion.

Source: IFC survey.

Table 12.12   Hardware Market Competitiveness

Indicator	China	India
Pricing power with competitors (percentage of competitors that would raise prices to match mine)	31.0	6.3
Pricing power with customers (1 = do not accept, 5 = accept willingly	2.58	2.02
Ease of entry into the industry (1 = very easy, 5 = very hard)	3.50	2.76
Threat from imports (1 = no threat, 5 = big threat)	4.38	2.89
Threat from foreign firms producing in home market (1 = no threat, 5 = big threat)	3.97	2.94
Gross margins compared with other industries in the home country (1 = lower, 5 = higher)	2.80	2.36

Source: IFC survey.
Note: Higher scale scores for variables below the dotted line indicate less market competitiveness. All of these China-India differences are statistically significant between the two countries' firms in a multivariate analysis.

fewer Indian than Chinese managers reported that their competitors would raise prices to match their price increases). There was no apparent difference, however, in the market concentration of firms in the industries in either country.

A manager who feels a substantial threat from imported products or from foreign firms that are producing competitive products in his or her home country is generally a member of a firm that is exposed to foreign trade or investment competition and that is not confident of its ability to withstand the foreign competition. A manager who feels less threat from abroad either works for a strongly internationally competitive firm or a firm that is protected by import or inward FDI restrictions enacted by the government. The IFC survey responses showed that Chinese managers felt significantly more threatened both by imports and by foreign firms producing in China than did the Indian managers (table 12.12). Both import market share and FDI inflows were very much greater in the Chinese hardware industry than in the Indian industry. These outcomes could be partly due to trade and investment restrictions in the past through a legacy effect, even though markets are more open now.

Intercountry comparisons of individuals' judgments, especially across countries that are culturally quite different, might suffer from systematic differences in the tendency to be optimistic or positive versus pessimistic or negative, or to perceive the dynamics of competition systematically differently—that is, to perceive objectively similar market situations either more favorably or unfavorably.

Notes

1. It is likely that the sample overrepresents companies located in Indian Export Processing Zones or software technology parks because these companies are more visible and easier to locate and interview.

2. See, for example, Rostow (1960).

Chapter 13

Summary of Explanations for the Different Outcomes for China's and India's Hardware Industries

This chapter presents the principal findings from the IFC survey of the hardware industry in China and India and, where appropriate, of the analysis of World Bank Investment Climate Assessment data. These conclusions address why the Chinese hardware industry grew so fast, both domestically and internationally, but the Indian industry did not in either domain.

Labor

This factor of production gave no direct economic edge to Chinese hardware firms. Chinese hardware firms had fewer well-educated professionals and paid them higher entry-level wages than did Indian hardware firms. China's labor productivity was not higher than India's, but China's wages were higher. Chinese unit labor cost was higher, therefore, than Indian unit labor cost. Firms in the IFC survey grew faster in both China and India when labor productivity was higher, but this did not favor the Chinese compared with the Indian industry. These apparent Chinese disadvantages in the micro aspects of labor were overcome by other more macro- and management-related aspects of labor. Because labor constitutes a much smaller share of total production cost in hardware than it does in software, labor as a factor of production was less important to the firm's performance.

Capital

The capital intensity of hardware firms in the two countries was not significantly different. Capital is an important input into hardware production, though less important for assembly operations than for manufacturing. A majority of Chinese and Indian hardware companies are primarily assembly operations. China did not have an advantage over India in the cost of physical capital. For financial capital,

Chinese firms had access to capital at lower interest rates, and foreign direct investors supplied capital. Indian hardware firms relied more on bank borrowing and paid higher interest rates, thus raising their costs.

Land

China's Special Economic Zones gave its hardware industry an advantage over India's hardware manufacturers. Clustering of hardware firms in the same geographical area provided benefits for Chinese firms from an expanded labor pool and knowledge sharing among workers. These benefits exceeded those reported by Indian firm managers.

Management

Emphasis on quality certifications and ability to capitalize on cultural traits were among China's leading advantages. Chinese hardware firms had management advantages over Indian hardware firms. For example, China's more flexible labor market, more mobile skilled labor, and less restrictive labor laws were advantageous to management. Indian hardware firms could avoid the effects of the country's restrictive labor laws by staying small, but in so doing they sacrificed scale economies.

Other advantages of Chinese hardware firms over Indian firms derived directly from actions taken by individual managers within the firm, including obtaining quality certifications from international standards organizations and capitalizing on common cultural traits in the workforce. Most Chinese hardware firms but few Indian firms, for example, had International Organization for Standardization quality certifications, which provided a significant advantage for Chinese hardware firms compared with Indian hardware firms. In both countries, however, having quality certifications contributed to a firm's growth. Chinese managers also took advantage of the national culture traits of their workforce that fit well with hardware manufacturing requirements for structure, order, control, and discipline in the workplace.

Technology

China's technology inputs and outputs gave the Chinese hardware industry an advantage over India's. Chinese hardware firms spent more on R&D than did Indian hardware firms, and more Chinese firms filed for patents. These firm-level advantages were consistent with the generally greater amount of technology activity in the Chinese economy compared with the Indian economy as a whole, and some of this advantage was due to government support.

International links

More foreign ownership of Chinese hardware firms was an advantage. The Chinese and Indian hardware industries differed in types of international links, but the difference in the number of links was not large. The single major difference between the two countries was the greater degree of direct foreign investment with management control of hardware firms in China. Foreign direct investors typically bring technology and capital as well as access to markets abroad. Chinese and Indian hardware firms did not differ in their use of nonequity strategic alliances. The contribution of overseas residents was of little importance to the firms in both countries.

Government policies

China's government actions gave Chinese hardware firms a great advantage over Indian firms. More of China's government policies than India's promoted growth, especially in the areas of marketing, technology, and taxes. Chinese hardware firms had the advantage of positive governmental incentives compared with Indian hardware firms, including stronger marketing support, research and development support, and better income tax concessions. The Chinese government aided high technology industries by subjecting them to fewer regulations, granting easier access to land, and providing improved infrastructure and better trade and investment opportunities—all of which were especially attractive to foreign firms. India's attempts to create similar zones for high tech industries came later and did not succeed as well. In addition, many Chinese hardware firms owed their success as startups to state sponsorship.

Fewer Chinese policies than Indian policies hindered growth. Chinese hardware managers reported fewer governmental obstacles to growth than did Indian managers in the areas of government bureaucracy and inefficiency of government services. These differences in positive incentives and negative hindrances were a statistically significant difference between the two countries' firms.

Infrastructure

Chinese hardware firms had an advantage over Indian firms, especially in access to electric power. Infrastructure is important for hardware manufacturing and assembly. Electric power, the most critical component of a country's infrastructure for hardware, is less reliable in India than in China. Consequently, many more Indian hardware firms than Chinese firms installed their own power generators, thus adding to Indian hardware costs.

Institutions

Some institutions provided advantages to Chinese and Indian firms, and others placed firms at a disadvantage. Managers' perceptions of the functioning of institutions that form part of the business environment were divided. Chinese managers believed their judicial system was more effective in protecting property and contract rights than did Indian managers. However, they also reported longer customs clearance times for both import and exports.

Market competitiveness

Chinese managers reported less competitive domestic markets. A sizable majority of both Chinese and Indian hardware firm revenue was earned in their domestic markets. Based on managers' perceptions (but without the benefit of objective measures), it appeared that Chinese managers felt less-competitive dynamics in their markets than did Indian managers. This response may reflect the difference between the two countries in the organization and functioning of markets generally.

Part IV
Summary and Conclusions

Chapter 14

Why Software and Hardware Industries Differed in China and India

The previous chapters have explained in detail the interplay between the investment climates and factor endowments of China and India and their success in promoting the new industries of software and hardware production. This chapter draws together the threads of this analysis to summarize the key differences between the countries that drive their differential performance in software and hardware production.

Software

Because software production does not use capital intensively, has limited infrastructure needs, and has been less affected by government regulation, differences in the use of skilled labor and the quality of management overall were the primary drivers of differences in industry performance.

Labor

Labor is usually the first reason given for Indian software export success. Software production is skilled-labor intensive, and India had a large supply of well-educated workers who were paid low wages in dollar terms—all true. India certainly had a lower cost of production for software than did the United States, its major export market, and India probably had not only absolute advantage but comparative advantage, too. However, labor is not a sufficient explanation for Indian software export success compared with China. China also had an ample supply of educated, low-wage labor. If skilled labor was a critical factor of production, and China had it too, why did China not become a software export powerhouse? Aside from other arguments, such as English language proficiency (taken up later in this section), did Indian software firms have a labor advantage over Chinese software firms? If so, exactly what was it?

Supplies of technically educated labor apparently were ample in both countries, and China in particular increased its supply considerably from the 1980s on. Perhaps India had an edge at the higher end of the educated labor spectrum than China, and perhaps Chinese software engineers were somewhat less suited for employment in multinational corporations than their Indian counterparts. But the analysis in the previous chapters using IFC survey data suggests the story about labor and India's software export success is best found not at a macro labor supply level but rather at a more micro firm level that includes management as well as labor.

The labor story must account for labor skill, labor productivity, wage rates, and at the end, unit labor cost. Labor skill in Indian software firms exceeded that in Chinese software firms. The main difference was that Indian firms employed more professionals, and those professionals had more education. Labor productivity, in turn, was higher in Indian software *services* firms—and these firms were the exporters—than in Chinese software services firms. The Indian labor productivity advantage did not hold, however, for software *products* firms, for which it appears that Chinese firms had a labor productivity edge. Wage rates for equivalent types of workers were not much different between Indian and Chinese software firms; Indian wages (and benefits) certainly were not higher, and may have been slightly lower, than Chinese wage rates. But the unit labor cost of software production was *not* lower in Indian software firms compared with Chinese firms. From the labor perspective, Indian software services firms were successful exporters because the managers of these firms employed more skilled and professional labor, which was more productive, while achieving a unit labor cost that was no higher than the Chinese unit labor cost. In fact, in other ways, the management of Indian software firms was the critical factor in their export success compared with Chinese software firms.

Management

Managers at Indian software firms contributed to the export success of the industry in several ways aside from their use of labor. Their greater international experience compared with that of their Chinese counterparts and their project management know-how enabled them to overcome barriers to export success. Indian software firm managers overcame the liability of foreignness that especially plagued India before their software was well known, in part by promoting the concept of quality certifications for software and by achieving them. This demonstrated to export customers that Indian firms used best practices technologically and followed standard project management practices. Chinese software firms did not pursue quality certifications at that time (although they do now).

To obtain market access for exports, Indian managers forged strategic alliances with U.S. and other foreign firms. These alliances also helped accelerate the adoption of best practice corporate cultures for the production of software services. The national culture of India, more so than China, provided a favorable backdrop for developing appropriate corporate cultures.

Indian software firm managers had two other advantages compared with Chinese managers that contributed to the industry's export success. All Indian managers were English speakers and could deal effectively with export customers. It was not English language proficiency among Indian software engineers that mattered compared with China—it was Indian managers' ability to work in English. In addition, some Indian software firms in the early years of the industry gained the benefit of export market access with the assistance of nonresident Indians. However, entrepreneurship, which is sometimes attributed to Indian managers and professionals, was not more prevalent among Indian than Chinese software firms.

Hardware

Labor and management are also important in successful hardware production, but infrastructure, links to foreign firms, and government policies play a larger role in the performance of the hardware sector.

Labor and Management

China had the right factors of production and the right production environment for rapid growth in the hardware industry. Labor and management taken together are among these factors, but the labor story for Chinese hardware is not one of greater labor skill, higher labor productivity, or lower wages. In fact, Chinese hardware firms had no advantage over Indian hardware firms in any of these dimensions. This analysis estimates that in 2004, Chinese unit labor cost in hardware production was actually higher than Indian unit labor cost, although it was competitive in earlier years. From the labor perspective, Chinese hardware is not the equivalent of Indian software. Of course, labor is a less important factor of production for hardware than it is for software.

Capital is an important factor of production for hardware, unlike for software. But access to capital does not explain Chinese hardware industry growth, nor is it a statistically significant difference between Chinese and Indian hardware firms. The analysis found no important differences in access to capital or use of capital between Chinese and Indian firms, except for the role of foreign investment.

The labor and management story for Chinese hardware has four parts. First is the fit between the cultural context of the Chinese labor force and the appropriate corporate culture for hardware manufacturing. Hardware production requires structure, order, discipline, and control, cultural characteristics that international cultural comparisons have identified to be relatively more prevalent in Chinese society. This corresponds to the software case, with its corporate culture of collaboration, ambiguity, and open-ended work situations that fit well with Indian national cultural traits, and it supports the inference that different national cultural contexts favor the emergence of different industries.

The second part is also comparable to the software case. Chinese hardware firms gained International Organization for Standardization quality certifications more often than did Indian hardware firms, and having these quality certifications contributed to a firm's growth in both countries.

The third labor and management feature was the flexibility of production labor in China that benefited hardware firms. Geographical mobility and clustering of firms, facilitated by the government's creation of Special Economic Zones (SEZs) that enlarged the labor pool, contributed to the growth of hardware firms. Of course, less burdensome labor regulations gave managers in Chinese hardware firms greater freedom to deploy labor flexibly, unencumbered by the regulatory restrictions Indian firms dealt with, and which they could only escape by staying small and thus forgoing scale and scope economies.

Fourth, technology use is determined by management decisions, and Chinese hardware firms were better at creating and using technology than were Indian hardware firms. Reflecting national differences, Chinese managers spent more on research and development (R&D) and more often filed for patents than their Indian counterparts. China's technology advantage in hardware firms might have conferred a modest competitive advantage but not a decisive advantage. Most of the patents were Chinese rather than foreign, much of the Chinese R&D appeared to be adaptive rather than innovative, and not that many new products were actually new to the market.

International Links

Chinese hardware firms were more often owned and controlled by foreign multinational firms than were Indian hardware firms. The capital and technology resources that foreign owners can bring were potentially important in the hardware industry, more so than in the software industry. Hardware is high technology, and the Chinese industry got the technology it needed. Because foreign investment was mostly direct investment, Chinese-located hardware firms also had access to management resources that Indian firms did not have. As was the case for China's software firms, its hardware firms had fewer foreign nonequity strategic alliances than Indian hardware firms, but unlike for software, this difference between the two industries appeared not to be important. Foreign direct investment remains the sole Chinese advantage from international links.

Infrastructure

Infrastructure is important for hardware manufacturing and assembly, and China's infrastructure was better than India's. A reliable electric power supply is the most critical infrastructure requirement for hardware firms, and the power supply in China was more available and reliable than India's. Unlike Chinese firms, most Indian hardware firms installed their own power generation facilities, which added to Indian hardware costs.

Government Support

Government policy in China was favorable to the development of its hardware industry, but the same cannot be said about Indian government policy. China's general policy environment and active promotion measures advanced hardware firm growth.

China's economic reforms began earlier than India's. Because the hardware industry developed earlier than the software industry, it benefited from these earlier reforms. In addition, the Chinese government was quite decentralized, which allowed for local government initiatives and decision making in the promotion of new industries, within an overall policy framework from the center that encouraged industrial development. In addition, bureaucracy was less intrusive in China than in India. The industrial licensing scheme in India, for example, continued during the early years of the hardware industry's development and hampered its growth. Because the Indian hardware industry was protected until the early 1990s, it lost international competitiveness, and the domestic hardware market remained small.

Specific government policies in China, such as marketing and technology support and business income tax concessions, promoted the growth of the hardware industry as well. SEZs conferred advantages that Indian hardware firms did not have—access to land, good infrastructure, and less restricted trade and foreign investment. In addition, Chinese startup companies were sponsored directly by the state and through universities.

Impact of Investment Climate on Industry Development

The comparison of the software and hardware industries in China and India provides insights into which aspects of the investment climate in a country most affect industrial development.

Infrastructure emerges as a key condition for industry growth. Both the software and hardware stories illustrate the importance of addressing infrastructure constraints. India was able to address the more limited, more manageable infrastructure needs of software, but not the larger, more costly needs of hardware manufacturing. China was able to invest enough in infrastructure to compete globally in manufacturing exporting.

The hardware industry story also illustrates the importance of an investment climate that supports flexible labor use. The greater flexibility in the use of labor in China played an important role in the development of the hardware industry, although lack of flexibility was less of a constraint to the development of India's software industry. Labor flexibility involves the ability of labor to move to production locations favored for logistical and clustering reasons and also the ability of firms to deploy labor flexibly without undue government restrictions. Hardware more than software depends on locations with good transportation and sufficient land for plants to achieve economic scale and for related production facilities to be clustered. The provision of industrial land also turns out to be an important enabling factor for industrial growth, whether it is software technology parks in India or SEZs in China.

Access to technology is important for international competitiveness in hardware manufacturing but less so in software production. This is one way in which the Chinese hardware industry experience illustrates the important role that foreign direct investment (FDI) can play in stimulating industrial development. Both China and India had low-cost labor and the potential for scale economies necessary for manufacturing; both countries lacked the latest technologies and the connections to tightly integrated supply chains. FDI supplied these key ingredients in China. Similarly, despite high savings rates, domestic access to capital was limited in both countries, but FDI provided much more capital to China than it did to India. Finally, after long periods of inward-looking economic policies, China and India both needed to reintegrate into global supply chains. FDI provided China with a shortcut to doing so.

The final lesson is the importance of progrowth government policies and incentives in overcoming weaknesses in the investment climate. Both China and India rank poorly on World Bank international comparisons of investment climate indicators, yet both have been able to nurture world-beating industries. The key to this paradox is that governments can continue to work on the first-best solution of improving the overall investment climate, which is a long-term process, while also creating "micro climates" in the short term that boost business through second-best, industry-specific interventions. The software sector policies in India are a clear case of this, as are the promotion of SEZs for manufacturing in China.

In neither of the success cases was industrial growth the result of laissez-faire government. Both benefited from government policies that made key inputs readily available at competitive prices. For software, the key inputs were skilled labor, reliable electric power, and telecommunications connectivity. For hardware, the key inputs were low-cost labor, capital, and technology. In both cases, government policies played an enabling role by providing a low-tax environment and by facilitating access to inputs.

In addition to a favorable investment climate, the macroeconomic conditions for growth should be examined. A long-established finding asserts that countries with strong protection against imports damage their prospects for exporting. Such protection creates an overvaluation of the real exchange rate, provides incentives for producing for the domestic market rather than for exports, and reduces competition that spurs innovation and efficiency among domestic producers. India, which heavily protected the manufacturing sector but not the software-services sector, experienced poor performance in manufacturing exports, including hardware. Similarly, China's industrial growth was supported by macroeconomic policies characterized by low import protection and strong incentives for manufacturers to export, along with a competitive exchange rate. In China, software did not benefit from the same export incentives and hence has grown mainly to serve the domestic market, while hardware manufacturing has been strongly export oriented.

Chapter 15

Emerging Trends in the Chinese and Indian Software and Hardware Industries

The survey data on which much of this study is based were obtained in 2004. The analysis of these data necessarily focused on developments in the software and hardware industries in China and India through that date, although more recent data on the size and growth of these industries were presented throughout the chapters. This chapter offers some observations about the most important new developments and trends since 2004, and relates them to the main findings of the analysis.

Among the two countries and two industries, the most significant new developments are taking place in Indian hardware, and secondarily in Chinese software, the two industries that were previously lagging. This chapter begins with these new developments, and concludes with shorter notes about the other industries.

Indian Hardware

The analysis found that high capital costs, high tariffs, poor infrastructure, and government regulation in India deterred investment in hardware manufacturing. High tariffs encouraged a focus on a small and slow-growing home market and raised production costs, which led to small, subscale operations using obsolete technology. With few exceptions, Indian hardware manufacturers were not competitive internationally, exports were negligible, and profitability was low.

In 2004, this analysis could have applied to many parts of the manufacturing sector in India because the constraints were common to all kinds of manufacturing. The main exceptions were high–value added, engineering-intensive manufacturing such as pharmaceuticals and auto components, in which India's comparative advantage in providing skilled labor and good management outweighed the other constraints on export-oriented manufacturing. These sectors, while small in proportion to India's overall manufacturing sector, provided early evidence that Indian manufacturing could successfully compete internationally.

Since 2004, the rate of growth of manufacturing output increased dramatically, averaging about 8 percent per year compared with 5 percent per year previously. Growth expanded beyond pharmaceuticals and auto components into a broad range of engineering-based products, including hardware manufacturing. What explains this change and the persistence of a bias against low technology, labor-intensive manufacturing? Three factors changed, and two stayed the same: tariffs, the cost and availability of capital, and the level of domestic demand all changed, while the regulatory burden, especially on labor, and poor infrastructure did not.

Tariffs

Tariffs have been steadily decreasing in India and by 2005 average tariffs had fallen to 14 percent—still high relative to global averages, but about at the point where they are not a prohibitive barrier for imports and do not create a major bias against exports. As a result, industry has refocused on export opportunities, and has faced increased domestic competition from imports. These trends have provided a stimulus to invest and reorganize to achieve international competitiveness.

Capital

Since 2004, rapid increases in global liquidity and India's increasing rate of economic growth encouraged greater capital inflows into India. At the same time, government efforts to reduce the fiscal deficit began to bear fruit, with the consolidated deficit (central government plus state governments) falling from over 10 percent of GDP at its peak in 2002 to 5.9 percent by 2008. The combination of greater capital inflows and reduced government borrowing to fund its fiscal deficit strengthened India's creditworthiness, and its public debt achieved investment grade in 2006. Domestically, financial capital inflows were partly sterilized (leading to growth in foreign exchange reserves to over $300 billion by April 2008), and partly fed through into rapid expansions of domestic credit (expanding about 30 percent annually since 2005). This led to sharp decreases in interest rates (the real interest rate on 10-year government bonds fell from 9 percent in the mid-1990s to 3 percent in 2007), which enabled banks and financial institutions to book windfall gains as their large holdings of government securities gained in value. This recapitalization further encouraged banks to expand lending. The net effect of these mutually reinforcing trends was to reduce the cost and increase the availability of capital to the industrial sector, including hardware manufacturing companies. As a result, private fixed capital formation grew about 15 percent per year during 2004–08 (table 15.1). Investment increased from 24 percent of GDP in fiscal 2002/03 to 36 percent of GDP in fiscal 2007/08. In 2005/06, the Indian electronics industry as a whole achieved sales of $11 billion and was growing by over 20 percent a year.

Table 15.1   China and India: Selected Macroeconomic Trends
(annual percentage growth rates, except for exchange rate)

China	2004	2005	2006	2007	
Real GDP growth	10.1	10.4	11.1	11.4	
Industrial production	31.1	29.5	16.6	18.5	
Gross fixed investment	12.4	11.5	11.2	11.1	
Price inflation, consumer	3.9	1.8	1.5	4.8	
Renminbi/$ exchange rate (average)	8.28	8.07	7.97	7.61	

India	2003/04	2004/05	2005/06	2006/07	2007/08
Real GDP growth	8.5	7.5	9.4	9.6	8.7
Industrial production growth	6.0	8.5	8.1	10.6	8.6
Private fixed capital formation growth	14.7	23.6	17.1	14.5	17.5
Credit to commercial sector growth	13.0	31.0	27.1	25.9	20.3
Prices, GDP deflator	3.4	6.4	3.9	5.6	4.1
Rupee/$ exchange rate (average)	46.0	44.9	44.3	45.2	40.3

Sources: IMF (www.imf.org); Economist Intelligence Unit (www.eiu.com); Institute for International Finance (www.iif.com).

Economic Growth

The third change was the easiest to foresee. Inevitably, sustained economic growth in India would reach the point at which consumer spending would pick up rapidly. With economic growth averaging about 8 percent annually since 2004, approximately 30 million Indians enter the middle class each year, with a corresponding increase in consumption of goods and services. By 2006/07, domestic consumption growth accounted for half of GDP growth. This trend led to rapid increases in demand for consumer goods and consumer durables, such as mobile telephones (by 2007 there were 166 million subscribers; Oxford Analytica 2007), color televisions, and two-wheelers (motorcycles and scooters). This increase in domestic consumption, along with the pick-up in industrial investment, stimulated domestic demand for hardware. For example, in 2006/07 personal computer sales in smaller towns increased by 33 percent, and accounted for 27 percent of the growth in the domestic market (Oxford Analytica 2007). As a result, hardware manufacturers are now starting to locate production in India for India-specific goods as well as for exports.

The two factors that did not change much are the quality of infrastructure and the regulatory burden of employing labor. As a result, it is the more capital-intensive aspects of manufacturing that are showing the most rapid growth. Conversely, in the hardware sector, labor-intensive assembly operations have not shown much growth.

Nevertheless, compared with 2004, there are signs of increasing investment in hardware production in India. For example, China's Lenovo now produces 3 million personal computers a year in India, and Dell produces 400,000 units a year (Oxford Analytica 2007). The government is making strenuous efforts to overcome the weakness in infrastructure and to ease the regulatory burden on business through the creation of Indian Special Economic Zones. If successful, this will further reduce the constraints to hardware manufacturing. Hence, it would be wrong to write off the prospects for India emerging as a major source of hardware manufacturing based on the poor performance through 2004. Instead, developments since 2004 show that the constraints on the growth of the sector are not insurmountable, and are being reduced over time.

Chinese Software

Two new developments are beginning to reshape the nature of the Chinese software industry, and both are stimulating exports of software services, the previously lagging business.

Indian and Other Foreign Investment

One of these developments is foreign direct investment in China by Indian software companies. Most major Indian firms recently opened businesses in China.[1] Apprehensions in India about future labor shortages of qualified technically educated professionals, rising wages among these workers, and high turnover—coupled with, at worst, no unit labor cost disadvantage in China—motivate Indian software firms to start operations in China. For customized software services, the Chinese weakness in project management skill is being overcome by expatriate Indians who relocate to the Chinese operations. For example, Infosys opened its first China operation in 2003 and in 2008 had 800 employees in three locations. Infosys China achieved Capability Maturity Model Integration (CMMI) Level 5 quality certification in 2007; the business is primarily customized software services exports, and also includes business process outsourcing (www.infosys.com/china). Tata Consultancy Services, the largest Indian software company, first established operations in China in mid-2002.

Investment by non-Indian multinational information technology (IT) firms also is taking place. For example, software giants such as IBM, Microsoft, and SAP recently acquired minority stakes (less than 10 percent) in sizable, established Chinese software firms—Kingdee, Chinasoft International, and Neusoft. To the extent that these relatively small investments result in greater export orientation by Chinese firms, as is intended, they constitute a new development in the Chinese software industry.

Outsourcing from Japan

The second emerging trend that affects Chinese software is the export of customized software services to Japanese customers. In 2006, more than 60 percent of all Japanese software outsourcing was supplied by Chinese software firms (www. xinhuanet.com). Although the languages are not the same, many characters are shared, and Chinese software engineers who do entry-level work can quickly and easily learn to read and write enough Japanese to allow them to write and test lines of code for Japanese customers. Cultural similarity facilitates business dealings. In addition, the Chinese government promotes this business by offering tax incentives for firms that locate in Special Economic Zones.

Both of these export trends for Chinese software services are aided by the rapid growth in the number of companies operating in China that are gaining high-level CMMI quality certifications (A.T. Kearney, Inc. 2004). After many years of disregard for quality certifications, Chinese software managers are now seeking them.

The rate of growth of the Chinese software industry continues at a rapid pace. According to official Chinese government statistics, the Chinese industry in 2007 was substantially bigger than the Indian industry (see table 4.1). However, the comparison might not be accurate; figures from NASSCOM (2007), the Indian industry association, show a much smaller Chinese industry, smaller than that in India.

Indian Software

The software industries in both China and India are continuing along their previous development paths. Growth in revenue continues to be rapid but not quite as fast as in the early 2000s. Indian IT sector revenues grew 28 percent in fiscal 2007 (NASSCOM 2007). The growth rate of exports of software services from India is slowing down somewhat due to slower rates of GDP growth in the United States and the strengthening of the Indian rupee against the U.S. dollar, yet exports to the United States continue to dominate Indian software firms' revenue. But domestic sales are increasing much faster than in previous years as Indian economic growth and hardware industry growth both accelerate. The domestic sales growth rate was 21 percent in fiscal 2007. Multinational corporations such as IBM and Microsoft that have long been established in India now are finding that the Indian domestic market is among their fastest growing.

The largest firms are leading the industry's growth, gradually moving into higher–value added segments of the business. The intent to move toward more higher-margin software consulting services is not new, but the rate of transition might not be as fast as desired as software firms in other countries become competitors for Indian firms' usual entry-level business (*Economist* 2007b). Firms in some countries, such as Vietnam, Brazil, and notably China itself, compete on the basis of labor cost. Other countries, such as the Russian Federation, compete on the basis of labor. The Indian software sector remains overwhelmingly focused on services, with only gradual expansion into software products.

Perhaps the most important new development in the Indian software industry is the renewed question about labor supply and labor wages. By 2007, labor shortages were starting to create wage pressures and excessive employee turnover. However, given the relatively small size of the industry relative to the Indian labor market as a whole, these shortages will not necessarily become critical. Only a small increase in university graduates would meet the staffing needs of the software sector. The Indian government is supporting substantial expansion of the higher education sector, and private universities and business schools, albeit with many quality concerns, are rapidly expanding. IT firms themselves, facing rising wages and labor shortages, are emphasizing labor supply; NASSCOM has noted the growing emphasis by its members on education.

Chinese Hardware

The main macroeconomic trends in China that affect manufacturing are the strengthening of the renminbi and the acceleration of price inflation that began in 2007 and was still accelerating in 2008. Both trends are harmful to Chinese manufacturing, and some observers report a loss of manufacturing competitiveness (Knowledge @ Wharton 2008). But the hardware industry is affected less than the manufacturing industry generally.

In July 2005, the Chinese renminbi was devalued 2.5 percent and the fixed peg to the dollar was broadened to include other currencies. Since that time the Chinese government has allowed the renminbi to appreciate faster. The stronger Chinese currency hampers the efforts of exporters whose prices to foreign customers rise or profit margins narrow. However, to the extent Chinese exporters assemble products from imported components, that element of their costs goes down. For the Chinese hardware industry, exports are a majority share of their business, while assembly from imported components has been substantial. The absolute net effect on the Chinese hardware industry is therefore somewhat mixed though on balance probably not favorable. Relative to other hardware manufacturing countries that do not have strengthening currencies, the Chinese industry is certainly worse off.

Price inflation in China, for both purchased inputs and labor wages, most adversely affects the competitiveness of unskilled-labor-intensive, low-margin products, and hampers export-oriented firms more than firms whose primary market is domestic. Chinese hardware is medium in its unskilled-labor intensity (less than toys or clothing, for example), and a majority of its revenue is derived from exports; thus, high price inflation is a problem for Chinese hardware firms. Because Chinese price inflation began to exceed price inflation in most of its major export markets in mid-2007, the real renminbi exchange rate from that point onward tended to get stronger, hampering exports even more than the strengthening nominal renminbi implies. This is the case for exports to the United States and all countries whose currencies are pegged to the dollar, but not for exports to Euro Area countries or Japan, against whose currencies the nominal renminbi is weakening, not strengthening, as of late 2008.

Inflation and rapid growth are beginning to apply pressure on China's labor markets. Media reports about labor shortages on the coast are more numerous. With rising food prices, the flow of farm workers to the manufacturing centers of coastal China is slowing down. This is pushing up wages and eroding China's traditional comparative advantage based on cheap labor. Demographic trends are also contributing to China's gradual transformation from a labor-surplus to a labor-shortage economy (Fangchao 2008).

In sum, recent trends tend to diminish some of the differences observed in earlier years. Indian hardware manufacturing is growing more competitive, while Chinese software is also growing strongly. This reflects convergence in economic policies and investment climates, and the gradual overcoming of the initial obstacles to industrial growth. The signs are that both China and India will become important global suppliers of both hardware and software in the future. If these trends continue, China and India may end up at similar destinations having followed very different routes for the development of their software and hardware industries.

Note

1. The timing may have been partly related to the desire to be eligible for Chinese government contracts relating to the 2008 Olympics.

References and Other Resources

Accenture. 2002. "Making Indian Manufacturing Globally Competitive." Unpublished, New Delhi.

Ahluwalia, M. S. 2002. "Economic Reforms in India Since 1991: Has Gradualism Worked?" *Journal of Economic Perspectives* 16 (3): 67–88.

Ahya, C., and A. Xie. 2004. "India and China: A Special Economic Analysis." Morgan Stanley.

Aggarwal, A., and A. Pandey. 2004. "The Next Big Opportunity: Moving up the Value Chain from BPO to KPO." Evalueserve Report.

Amano, Akihiro. 1977. "Specific Factors, Comparative Advantage and International Investments." *Economica* 44 (174): 131–44.

Ambastha, Ajitabh, and Kirnakumar Momaya. 2004. "Challenges for Indian Software Firms to Sustain Their Global Competitiveness." *Singapore Management Review* 26 (2): 65–77.

Amsden, Alice. 2001. *The Rise of "The Rest": Challenges to the West from Late-Industrializing Economies.* New York: Oxford University Press.

Analysys International. 2005. "IT Products and Services—Quarterly Tracker on China Software Market 05Q2." Guang Zhou, China. www.english/analysys.com.cn.

Arora, Ashish, V. S. Arunachalam, Jai Asundi, and Ronald Fernandes. 2001. "The Indian Software Services Industry." *Research Policy* 30 (8): 1267–87.

Arora, Ashish, and Suma Athreye. 2002. "The Software Industry and India's Economic Development." *Information Economics and Policy* 14 (2): 253–73.

Arora, Ashish, and Alfonso Gambardella. 2005. *From Underdogs to Tigers: The Rise and Growth of the Software Industry in Brazil, China, India, Ireland and Israel.* Oxford: Oxford University Press.

Athreye, S. 2005. "The Indian Software Industry and Its Evolving Service Capability." *Industrial and Corporate Change* 14 (3): 393–418.

A.T. Kearney, Inc. 2004. "The Changing Face of China: China as an Offshore Destination for IT and Business Process Outsourcing." A.T. Kearney, Inc., Chicago, IL.

Baark, Eric. 1987. "Commercialized Technology Transfer in China 1981–86: The Impact of Science and Technology Policy Reforms." *The China Quarterly* 111: 390–406.

Bajpai, Nirupam, and Vanita Shastri. 1999. "Software Industry in India: A Case Study." HIID Discussion Paper No. 667, Harvard Institute for International Development.

Balasubramanyam, V. N., and Ahalya Balasubramanyam. 1997. "International Trade in Services: The Case of India's Computer Software." *World Economy* 20 (6): 829–43.

Baldwin, Richard, and Anthony Venables. 1994. "International Migration, Capital Mobility and Transitional Dynamics." *Economica* 61 (243): 285–300.

Basant, Rakesh, and Uma Rani. 2004. "Labour Market Deepening in India's IT." *Economic and Political Weekly*, December 11, 5317–26.

Basu, P. 2005. *India's Financial Sector: Recent Reforms, Future Challenges.* New Delhi: Macmillan.

Batra, Geet, Daniel Kaufmann, and Andrew H. W. Stone. 2003. *Investment Climate around the World.* Washington, DC: World Bank.

Batra, Reveendra, and Prsanta K. Pattanaik. 1970. "Domestic Distortions and the Gains from Trade." *Economic Journal* 80 (319): 638–49.

Bernard, Andrew, and J. Bradford Jensen. 1999. "Exporting and Productivity." NBER Working Paper No. 7135, National Bureau of Economic Research, Cambridge, MA.

Besley, Timothy, and Robin Burgess. 2004. "Can Labor Regulation Hinder Economic Performance? Evidence From India." *Quarterly Journal of Economics* 119 (1): 91–134.

Bhagwati, Jagdish, and Robert Hudec. 1997. *Fair Trade and Harmonization.* 2 vols. Cambridge, MA: MIT Press.

Bhide, A. 2004. "Tax & Spend (Please)." Online article at Project Syndicate Web site, Frontiers of Growth series. http://www.project-syndicate.org/commentary/bhide2/.

Borchers, G. 2003. "The Software Engineering Impacts of Cultural Factors on Multi-Cultural Software Development Teams." In *Proceedings of the 25th International Conference on Software Engineering, 2003*, 540–5.

Bosworth, Barry, and Susan Collins. 2003. "The Empirics of Growth: An Update." *Brookings Papers on Economic Activity* 34 (2003-2): 113–206.

Brizendine, Thomas. 2002. "Software Integration in China." *The China Business Review* (March-April): 26–31.

BusinessWeek. 2005. "A New World Economy." August 22.

Carmel, Erran. 2003. "Taxonomy of New Software Exporting Nations." *Electronic Journal of Information Systems in Developing Countries* 13 (2): 1–6.

Cater-Steel, A., and M. Toleman. 2008. "The Impact of National Culture on Software Engineering Practices." *International Journal of Technology, Policy and Management* 8 (1): 76–90.

CCID (China Center for Information Development). 2002. "Proposal for 10th Five-Year Plan for Software Industry." http://software.ccidnet.com/pub/disp/Article?articleID=11883&columnID=329.

Chandra, Aruna, Tim Fealey, and Pradeep Rau. 2006. "National Barriers to Global Competitiveness: The Case of the IT Industry in India." *Journal of Global Competitiveness* 16 (1): 12–9.

Chandra, Pankaj, and Shastry Trilochan. 2002. "Competitiveness of Indian Manufacturing: Finding of the 2001 National Manufacturing Survey." IIMA Working Paper No. 2002-09-04, Indian Institute of Management, Ahmedabad.

Chen, Chong, and Kunshan Hu. 2002. "Status Quo and Development Trends for China's Software Industry." Paper presented at the China Software International Forum, Nanjing, April 24. http://www0.ccidnet.com/news/analyseobserve/2002/05/08/109_65165. html.

Chen, Stephen. 1995. "From Software Art to Software Engineering." *Engineering Management Journal* 7 (4): 23–8.

Chenery, Hollis, Sherman Robinson, and Moshe Syrquin. 1986. *Industrialization and Growth: A Comparative Study*. Washington, DC: World Bank, and New York: Oxford University Press.

Child, John, and Malcolm Warner. 2003. "Culture and Management in China." In *Culture and Management in Asia*, ed. Malcolm Warner. London: Routledge.

Chi-Ming, Hou. 1963. "Economic Dualism: The Case of China 1840–1937." *Journal of Economic History* 23 (3): 277–97.

Commander, Simon. 2005. *The Software Industry in Emerging Markets*. Cheltenham, UK: Edward Elgar.

Commander, Simon, Rupa Chanda, Mari Kangasniemi, and L. Alan Winters. 2004. "Who Gains from Skilled Migration? Evidence from the Software Industry." Center for Economic Performance, London School of Economics.

Contractor, Farok, C. C. Hsu, and S. Kundu. 2005. "Explaining Export Performance: A Comparative Study of International New Ventures in Indian and Taiwanese Software Industry." *Management International Review* 45 (Special Issue): 83–110.

Contractor, F., and S. Kundu. 2004. "The Role of Export-Driven Entrepreneurship in Economic Development: A Comparison of Software Exports from India, China, and Taiwan." *Technological Forecasting and Social Change* 71 (8): 799–822.

———. 2005. "Testing the Three-Stage Theory in an Emerging Market Context: The Case of Indian Firms." Prepared for an AIB Panel Workshop: "Research on Multinationality-Performance Relationship: Current Status & New Directions." Quebec City, July 8–12.

Correa, Carlos M. 1996. "Strategies for Software Exports from Developing Countries." *World Development* 24 (1): 171–82.

Costello, Donna. 1993. "A Cross-Country, Cross-Industry Comparison of Productivity Growth." *Journal of Political Economy* 101 (2): 207–22.

Dahlman, Carl, and Jean-Eric Aubert. 2001. *China and the Knowledge Economy: Seizing the 21st Century*. World Bank Institute. Washington, DC, World Bank.

Dahlman, Carl, and Anuja Utz. 2005. *India and the Knowledge Economy: Leveraging Strengths and Opportunities*. World Bank Institute. Washington, DC: World Bank.

Das, D. K. 2003. "Quantifying Trade Barriers: Has Trade Protection Declined Substantially in Indian Manufacturing?" Working Paper No. 105, Indian Council for Research on International Economic Relations, New Delhi.

Datamonitor. 2003. "Global Software and Services." Datamonitor Industry Market Research, October 1.

———. 2008. "Global Software & Services." Datamonitor, April.

Dataquest. 2003. Vol XXI, no. 13. CyberMedia, New Delhi.

———. 2005. Vol XXIII. CyberMedia, New Delhi.

———. 2006. Vol XXIV. CyberMedia, New Delhi.

D'Costa, Anthony, and E. Sridharan, eds. 2004. *India in the Global Software Industry*. Basingstoke, UK: Palgrave Macmillan.

De Filippo, Giuseppe, Jun Hou, and Christopher Ip. 2005. "Can China Compete in IT Services?" *McKinsey Quarterly,* Issue 1.

De Long, J. Bradford, and Lawrence Summers. 1991. "Equipment Investments and Economic Growth." *Quarterly Journal of Economics* 10 (2): 445–502.

Desai, Ashok V. 2003. "The Dynamics of the Indian Information Technology Industry." DRC Working Paper No. 20, Centre for New and Emerging Markets, London Business School.

———. 2005. "India." In *The Software Industry in Emerging Markets,* ed. Simon Commander. Cheltenham, UK: Edward Elgar.

Desai, M. 2003. "India and China: An Essay in Comparative Political Economy." Paper prepared for conference "A Tale of Two Giants: India's and China's Experience with Reform and Growth," New Delhi, November 14–16.

Dollar, David, Mary Hallward-Dreimeier, Anqing Shi, Scott Wallsten, Shuilin Wang, and Lixin Colin Xu. 2003. "Improving the Investment Climate in China." Investment Climate Assessment, World Bank, Washington, DC.

Dossani, R. 2005. "Origins and Growth of the Software Industry in India." Asia-Pacific Research Center, Stanford University, Stanford, CA.

Economist. 2006. "The Search for Talent: The World's Most Valuable Commodity Is Getting Harder to Find." October 5.

———. 2007a. "Entrepreneurship." November 22. http://www.economist.com/displaystory. cfm?story_id=10180767&fsrc=RSS.

———. 2007b. "Gravity's Pull: Is India's Computer-Services Industry Headed for a Fall?" December 15.

Economist Intelligence Unit. 2006. "Country Risk—Chinese Historical GDP Growth Rates Revised." Country Briefing. www.riskcenter.com/story.php?id=12085.

Ernst, Dieter. 2005. "Complexity and Internationalisation of Innovation: Why Is Chip Design Moving to Asia?" *International Journal of Innovation Management* 9 (1): 47–73.

Evalueserve. 2004. "Offshoring of IT Services—Present and Future." Evalueserve Business Research Report. www.evalueserve.com.

Fangchao, Li. 2008. "Nation May Face Labor Shortage in 2010." *China Daily*, April 28.

Feenstra, Robert. 1998. "Integration of Trade and Disintegration of Production in the Global Economy." *Journal of Economic Perspectives* 12 (4): 31–50.

Garnaut, R., L. Song, S. Tenev, and Y. Yao. 2005. *China's Ownership Transformation: Process, Outcomes, Prospects.* Washington, DC: World Bank.

Gartner Dataquest database. www.gartner.com.

Ghemawat, Pankaj. 2002. "The Indian Software Industry in 2002." Product No. 9-700-036, Harvard Business Online.

Global Entrepreneurship Monitor. 2004. "Summary Results." www.gemconsortium.org.

———. 2006. "Summary Results." www.gemconsortium.org.

Goel, Abhishek, Neharika Vohra, Liyan Zhang, and Bhupinder Arora. 2007. "Attitudes of Youth towards Entrepreneurs and Entrepreneurship: A Cross-Cultural Comparison of India and China." W. P. No. 2007-01-06, Indian Institute of Management, Ahmedabad.

Gong, Xiaofeng, and Fang Cao. 2002. "Distance between China and India Software Industries." *Economic Daily*, June 13.

Goswami, Omkar, A. K. Arun, Srivastava Gantakolla, Vishal More, Arindam Mookherjee, David Dollar, Taye Mengestae, Mary Hallward-Dreimeier, and Giuseppe Iarossi. 2002. "Competitiveness of Indian Manufacturing: Results from a Firm-Level Survey." Working Paper No. 31797, Confederation of Indian Industry and World Bank, Washington, DC.

Government of India Planning Commission. 1951. *First Five Year Plan.* New Delhi.

Gregory, N., S. Tenev, and D. Wagle. 2000. *China's Emerging Private Enterprises: Prospects for the New Century.* Washington, DC: International Finance Corporation.

Gu, Wulong, Frank Lee, and Jianmin Tang. 2000. "Economic and Productivity Growth in Canadian Industries." *American Economic Review* 90 (2): 168–71.

Hall, Edward T. 1976. *Beyond Culture.* Garden City, NY: Anchor Press.

Harrigan, J. 1997. "Technology, Factor Supplies, and International Specialization: Estimating the Neoclassical Model." *American Economic Review* 87 (4): 475–94.

———. 1999. "Estimation of Cross-country Differences in Industry Production Functions." *Journal of International Economics* 47 (2): 267–93.

Heeks, Richard. 1996. *India's Software Industry: State Policy, Liberalisation, and Industrial Development.* New Delhi: Sage Publications.

———. 1999. "Software Strategies in Developing Countries." Working Paper No. 6, Development Informatics, Institute for Development Policy and Management, University of Manchester, UK.

Heeks, Richard B., and Brian Nicholson. 2004. "Software Export Success Factors and Strategies in 'Follower' Nations." *Competition & Change* 8 (3): 267–303.

Helpman, Elhanan. 1999. "The Structure of Foreign Trade." *Journal of Economic Perspectives* 13 (2): 121–44.

Hofstede, Geert. 1980. *Culture's Consequences: International Differences in Work-Related Values.* London: Sage Publications

———. 1991. *Cultures and Organizations: Software of the Mind.* Maidenhead, UK: McGraw-Hill.

Hu, Hongli, Zhangxi Lin, and William Foster. 2003. "China's Software Industry: Current Status and Future Developments." Paper prepared for Global Information Technology Management conference, Calgary, June.

Hu, Hongli, and Jie Sheng. 2004. "Development Trends and Prospects of China's Software Industry in 2004." *China Information World,* February 2. http://linux.ccidnet.com/pub/article/c14_a88211_p1.html.

Huang, Yasheng. 2006a. "China Could Learn from India's Slow and Quiet Rise." *Financial Times* Jan 23.

———. 2006b. "Do Financing Biases Matter for the Chinese Economy?" *Cato Journal* 26 (2).

Huang, Yasheng, and Tarun Khanna. 2003. "Can India Overtake China?" *Foreign Policy* 137 (July/August): 74–81.

IDC (International Data Corporation). 2006a. "China IT 2006–2010 Forecast and Analysis." Doc # CN381101N.

———. 2006b. "Worldwide Software 2006–2010 Forecast Summary." Report #203224.

IFC (International Finance Corporation). 2005. "The ICT Landscape in the PRC: Market Trends and Investment Opportunities." Washington, DC: IFC.

IFC and Booz Allen Hamilton. 2003. "Electronics Manufacturing in Emerging Markets." Unpublished.

IIPA (International Intellectual Property Alliance). 2004. "China WTO: Comments Regarding Copyright Protection and Services/Market Access in China in Response to the 'Request for Comments and Notice of Public Hearing Concerning China's Compliance with WTO Commitments,' " October 12. IIPA, Washington, DC. www.iipa.com/country reports.html.

———. 2005. "Testimony of Eric H. Smith, President International Intellectual Property Alliance (IIPA) before the Subcommittee on Courts, the Internet, and Intellectual Property, United States House of Representatives, 'Intellectual Property Theft in China,' " May 17. IIPA, Washington, DC. www.iipa.com/countryreports.html.

IMF (International Monetary Fund). 2006. "India: Selected Issues." IMF Country Paper No. 06/56, IMF, Washington, DC.

Irwin, Douglas. 2000. "How Did the United States Become a Net Exporter of Manufactured Goods?" NBER Working Paper No. 7639, National Bureau of Economic Research, Cambridge, MA.

Kapur, Devesh. 2001. "Diasporas and Technology Transfer." *Journal of Human Development* 2 (2): 265–86.

———. 2002. "The Causes and Consequences of India's IT Boom." *India Review* 1 (2): 91–110.

Kapur, Devesh, and Ravi Ramamurti. 2001. "India's Emerging Competitive Advantage in Services." *Academy of Management Executive* 15 (1): 20–33.

Kelkar, V. L. 2003. *Reports on India's Tax Reforms.* Ghaziabad, India: Academic Foundation.

Kennedy, Scott. 1997. "The Stone Group: State Client or Market Pathbreaker?" *The China Quarterly* 152: 746–77.

Kennedy, Robert E. 2000 (Revised 2001). "Tata Consultancy Services: High Technology in a Low-Income Country." Case 9-700-092, Harvard Business School, Cambridge, MA.

Khanna, Tarun. 2004. "India's Entrepreneurial Advantage." *McKinsey Quarterly* (Special Edition): China Today: 111–14.

———. 2008. *Billions of Entrepreneurs: How India and China Are Reshaping Their Futures . . . And Yours.* Cambridge, MA: Harvard Business School Press.

Khanna, Tarun, and Yasheng Huang. 2003. "Can India overtake China?" *Foreign Policy* July/Aug.

Khanna, Tarun, and Krishna G. Palepu. 2004. "Globalization and Convergence in Corporate Governance: Evidence from Infosys and the Indian Software Industry." *Journal of International Business Studies* 35 (6): 484–507.

Knowledge at Wharton. 2008. "New Challenges for Foreign Producers: China's Manufacturing Competitiveness Is at Risk." http://www.knowledgeatwharton.com.cn/index.cfm?fa=printArticle&articleID=1812&languageid=1.

Kochhar, Kalpana, Utsav Kumar, Raghuram Rajan, Arvind Subramanian, and Ioannis Tokatlidis. 2006. "India's Pattern of Development: What Happened, What Follows?" IMF Working Paper WP/06/22, IMF, Washington, DC.

Kostova, Tatiana. 1999. "Transnational Transfer of Strategic Organizational Practices: A Contextual Perspective." *Academy of Management Review* 24 (2): 309–24.

Kraemer, Kenneth L., and Jason Dedrick. 2001. "Liberalization and the Computer Industry: A Comparison of Four Developing Countries." Center for Research on Information Technology and Organizations, University of California, Irvine.

Krueger, Anne O. 2002. *Economic Policy Reforms and the Indian Economy*. Chicago: The University of Chicago Press.

Krugman, P. R. 1980. "Scale Economies, Product Differentiation, and the Pattern of Trade." *American Economic Review* 70 (5): 950–9.

———. 1998. "Space: The Final Frontier." *Journal of Economic Perspectives* 12 (2): 161–74.

Kuijs, Louis. 2005. "Investment and Saving in China." Policy Research Paper Series No. 3633, World Bank, Washington, DC.

Kumar, Nagesh. 2001. "National Innovations Systems and the Indian Software Industry Development." Background paper for World Industrial Development Report 2001, UNIDO.

———. 2002. "Towards an Asian Economic Community: The Relevance of India." Discussion Paper No. 34, Research and Information Systems for Non-Aligned and other Developing Countries (RIS), New Delhi.

Kuemmerle, Walter, and William Coughlin. 2004. "Infosys: Financing an Indian Software Start-Up." Case No. 9-800-103, Harvard Business School, Cambridge, MA.

Kuznets, Simon. 1966. *Modern Economic Growth: Rate, Structure, and Spread*. New Haven and London: Yale University Press.

Lall, S. 1999. "India's Manufactured Exports: Comparative Structure and Prospects." *World Development* 27 (10): 1769–86.

Lall, Somik V., and Taye Mengistae. 2005. "The Impact of Business Environment and Economic Geography on Plant-Level Productivity: An Analysis of Indian Industry." Policy Research Working Paper No. 3664, World Bank, Washington, DC.

Licht, Walter. 1995. *Industrializing America: The Nineteenth Century (The American Moment)*. Baltimore and London: The Johns Hopkins University Press.

Maddison, Angus. 2001. *The World Economy: A Millennial Perspective*. Paris: OECD Development Centre.

Malenbaum, Wilfred. 1982. "Modern Economic Growth in India and China: The Comparison Revised, 1950–1980." *Economic Development and Cultural Change* 31 (1): 45–84.

Maneschi, Andrea. 2004. "The True Meaning of David Ricardo's Four Magic Numbers." *Journal of International Economics* 62 (2): 433–43.

Martin, Will, and Vlad Manole. 2004. "China's Emergence as the Workshop of the World." Working Paper No. 216, Stanford Center for International Development, Stanford University, Stanford, CA.

Mao Zedong. 1956. "On the Ten Major Relationships." Speech delivered to the Politburo on April 25. http://www.marxists.org/reference/archive/mao/selected-works/volume-5/mswv5_51.htm.

McDowell, Stephen D. 1995. "The Decline of the License Raj: Indian Software Export Policies." *Journal of Communication* 45 (4): 25–41.

McKinsey Global Institute. 2001. "Bridging the Digital Divide: Lessons from India." National Institute of Advanced Study, Bangalore.

Meng, Qingxuan, and Mingzhi Li. 2002. "New Economy and ICT Development in China." *Information Economics and Policy* 14 (2): 275–95.

Miles, Grant, Charles Snow, and Mark Sharfman. 1993. "Industry Variety and Performance." *Strategic Management Journal* 14 (3): 1963–77.

Milgrom, Paul, and John Roberts. 1990. "The Economics of Modern Manufacturing: Technology, Strategy, and Organization." *American Ecnomic Review* 80 (3): 511–28.

Miller, Robert R. 2001. "Leapfrogging? India's Information Technology Industry and the Internet." Discussion Paper No. 42, International Finance Corporation, Washington, DC.

Ministry of Information Industry and State Statistical Bureau of China. 2002. "White Paper on China's Software Industry in 2002."

Mitra, Arup, Aristomene Varoudakis, and Marie-Ange Veganzones-Varoudakis. 2002. "Productivity and Technical Efficiency in Indian States' Manufacturing: The Role of Infrastructure." *Economic Development and Cultural Change* 50 (2): 395–426.

Mitra, Jay, and Jun Li. 2002. "The Evolution of the IT Software Industry and Technological Entrepreneurship in India." Enterprise Research and Development Centre, Business School, University of Central England, Birmingham.

Mokyr, Joel. 1977. "Demand vs. Supply in the Industrial Revolution." *Journal of Economic History* 37 (4): 981–1008.

Moylan, Carol E. 2004. Data table for "GDP and Final Sales of Software" in "Prices and Output for Information and Communication Technologies" series. Bureau of Economic Analysis, U.S. Department of Commerce. www.bea.gov

Mukand, Sharun, and Dani Rodrik. 2005. "In Search of the Holy Grail: Policy Convergence, Experimentation, and Economic Performance." *American Economic Review* 95 (1): 374–83.

Mukherji, Joydeep. 2002. "View from the Silk Road: Comparing Reform in China and India." *Standard & Poor's Credit Week*, February 6, 32–43.

Nanda, Ashish, and Thomas DeLong. 2002. "Infosys Technologies." Case 9-801-445, Harvard Business School, Cambridge, MA.

Nanda, Ramana, and Tarun Khanna. 2007. "Diasporas and Domestic Entrepreneurs: Evidence from the Indian Software Industry." Working Paper 08-003, Harvard Business School.

NASSCOM (National Association of Software and Service Companies). 2004. "Strategic Review 2004: The IT Industry in India." Delhi.

———. 2005. "Strategic Review 2005: The IT Industry in India." Delhi.

———. 2006. "Strategic Review 2006: The IT Industry in India." Delhi.

———. 2007. "Strategic Review 2007: The IT Industry in India." Delhi.

National Bureau of Statistics of China. 2003. *China Statistical Yearbook 2003.*

Naughton, Barry. 2007. *The Chinese Economy: Transitions and Growth.* Cambridge, MA: MIT Press.

Neelankavil, James P., Anil Mathur, and Yong Zhang. 2000. "Determinants of Managerial Performance: A Cross-Cultural Comparison of the Perceptions of Middle-Level Managers in Four Countries." *Journal of International Business Studies* 31(1): 121–40.

NeoIT. 2005. "Mapping Offshore Markets Update 2005." Offshore Insights Market Report Series, vol. 3, no. 8. www.neoIT.com.

Oxford Analytica. 2007. "India: Hardware Sector is Poised for Revival." August 29.

Paine, Lynn Sharp, Carin-Isabel Knoop, and Suma Raju. 2001. "Wipro Technologies (A)." Harvard Business School Case 9-301-043, Harvard Business School, Boston, MA.

Panagariya, Arvind. 2004. "India in the 1980s and 1990s: A Triumph of Reforms." Working Paper WP/04/43, International Monetary Fund, Washington, DC.

Pandey, A., A. Aggarwal, R. Devane, and Y. Kuznetsov. 2004. "India's Transformation to Knowledge-Based Economy: Evolving Role of the Indian Diaspora." Evalueserve, Gurgaon, India.

Parker, Jesse. 2002. "The Lotus Files: The Emergence of Technology Entrepreneurship in China and India." *Fletcher Forum of World Affairs* 26 (2).

Parnell, John A., Steven Shwiff, Lei Yaline, and Hal Langford. 2003. "American and Chinese Entrepreneurial and Managerial Orientations." *International Journal of Management* 20 (2): 125–37.

Patibandala, Murali, and Bent Patersen. 2002. "Role of Transnational Corporations in Evolution of a High-Tech Industry: The Case of India's Software Industry." *World Development* 30 (9): 1561–77.

Perkins, Dwight. 1975. *China's Modern Economy in Historical Perspective*. Stanford, CA: Stanford University Press.

Perlow, Leslie, and John Weeks. 2002. "Who's Helping Whom? Layers of Culture and Workplace Behavior." *Journal of Organizational Behavior* 23 (4): 345–62.

Porter, Michael. 1990. *The Competitive Advantage of Nations*. New York, NY: Free Press.

———. 1996. "What is Strategy?" *Harvard Business Review* November-December: 61–78.

Puga, Diego, and Anthony J. Venables. 1999. "Agglomeration and Economic Development: Import Substitution vs Trade Liberalization." *Economic Journal* 109 (455): 292–311.

Reilly, Frank, and Eugene Drzycimski. 1974. "Alternative Industry Performance and Risk." *Journal of Financial and Quantitative Analysis* 9 (3): 423–46.

Reuters. 2000. "Rupee Fall Has Adjusted Real Exchange Rate." July 25. www.rediff.com/money.

Rivkin, Jan. 2000. "Imitation of Complex Strategies." *Management Science* 46 (6): 824–44.

Rodrik, Dani, and A. Subramanian. 2004. "From 'Hindu Growth' to Productivity Surge: The Mystery of the Indian Growth Transition." Working Paper No. 04/77, IMF, Washington, DC.

Rostow, W. W. 1960. *The Stages of Economic Growth: A Non-Communist Manifesto*. Cambridge, UK: Cambridge University Press.

Roy, T. 2002. "Economic History and Modern India: Redefining the Link." *Journal of Economic Perspectives* 16 (3): 109–30.

Saxenian, AnnaLee. 2000. "The Silicon Valley-Hsinchu Connection: Technical Communities and Industrial Upgrading." *Industrial and Corporate Change* 10 (4): 893–920.

———. 2002. "Bangalore: The Silicon Valley of Asia?" In *Economic Policy Reforms and the Indian Economy*, ed. Anne O. Krueger, 169–210. Chicago: University of Chicago Press.

————. 2005. "Government and Guanxi: The Chinese Software Industry in Transition." In *The Software Industry in Emerging Markets*, ed. Simon Commander. Cheltenham, UK: Edward Elgar.

Saxenian, AnnaLee, and X. Quan. 2005 "Government and Guanxi: The Chinese Software Industry in Transition." In *The Software Industry in Emerging Markets*, ed. Simon Commander. Cheltenham, UK: Edward Elgar.

Schneider, S. C., and J. L. Barsoux. 2003. *Managing Across Cultures*. New York: Prentice Hall.

Sethi, B. S. 2002. "Report on Visit to China from 6th to 16th April 2002." *ELCINA Electronics Outlook*. Unpublished, ELCINA, New Delhi.

Shirk, Susan. 1993. *The Political Logic of Economic Reform in China*. Berkeley, CA: University of California Press.

Siddharthan, N. S., and Stanley D. Nollen. 2004. "International Growth by Networking But Not M&A: The Counter Example of Indian Software." In *Global Corporate Evolution: Looking Inward or Looking Outward?* ed. Michael A. Trick, 53–60. Pittsburgh: Carnegie Mellon University Press.

Spencer, Michael, and Sanjeev Sanyal. 2002. "Will India Challenge China?" Deutsche Bank Global Markets Research, Frankfurt.

Srinivasan, T. N., and S. Tendulkar. 2003. *Reintegrating India with the World Economy*. Washington, DC: Peterson Institute for International Economics.

Steinfeld, Edward. 2004. "Chinese Enterprise Development and the Challenge of Global Integration." In *Global Production Networking and Technological Change in East Asia*, ed. by Shahid Yusuf, M. Anjum Altaf, and Kaoru Nabeshima. Washington, DC: World Bank.

Sundrum, R. M. 1985. "Modern Economic Growth in India and China: Comment." *Economic Development and Cultural Change* 34 (1): 157–60.

Tendulkar, Suresh D. 2003. "Organized Labour Market in India: Pre- and Post-Reform." Delhi School of Economics.

Tenev, Stoyan. 2006. "Why China Grows from Below." *Far Eastern Economic Review* 169 (1): 22–5.

Tenev, Stoyan, and Omar Chaudry. 2004. "Scaling Up Private Sector Models for Poverty Reduction: A Report on the Field Visit to Sichuan and Zhejiang Provinces, China." Prepared for the Shanghai conference on Scaling Up Poverty Reduction, May 2004. International Finance Corporation, Washington, DC.

Timmons, J. 1994. *New Venture Creation*, 4th ed. Burr Ridge, IL: Irwin.

Topalova, Petia B. 2004. "Trade Liberalization and Firm Productivity: The Case of India." Working Paper No. 04/28, International Monetary Fund, Washington, DC.

Tsang, Denise. 2007. "Leadership, National Culture and Performance Management in the Chinese Software Industry." *International Journal of Productivity and Performance Management* 56 (4): 270–84.

Tschang, Ted. 2003. "China's Software Industry and Its Implications for India." Presentation at International Conference on IT/Software Industries in Indian and Asian Development, Chennai, November 11–12.

Tschang, Ted, and Lan Xue. 2002. "The Emergence of China's Software Industry." Presentation at The Global IT Industry: The Future of India and China, University of California at Santa Cruz, May 30.

————. 2005. "The Chinese Software Industry." In *From Underdogs to Tigers: The Rise and Growth of the Software Industry in Brazil, China, India, Ireland and Israel*, ed. Ashish Arora and Alfonso Gambardella, 131–70. Oxford: Oxford University Press.

Tyers, R., J. Golley, Y. Bu, and I. Bain. 2006. "China's Economic Growth and Its Real Exchange Rate." ANUCBE School of Economics Working Papers No. 2006-476. Australian National University, Canberra.

Upadhya, Carol. 2004. "A New Transnational Capitalist Class? Capital Flows, Business Networks, and Entrepreneurs in the Indian Software Industry." *Economic and Political Weekly*, November 27, 5141–52.

U.S. Central Intelligence Agency. *World Factbook*. www.cia.gov.

Vedwa, Niraj. 2004. "Indian IT: Challenges for Global Competitiveness." IIFT-NASSCOM Seminar, New Delhi.

Wadhwa, Vivek, and Gary Gereffi. 2005. "Framing the Engineering Outsourcing Debate." Pratt School of Engineering, Duke University, Durham, NC.

Wang, Tao. 2005. "Sources of Real Exchange Rate Fluctuations in China." *Journal of Comparative Economics* 33 (4): 753–71.

Wei, Shang-Jin. 2000. "Why Does China Attract So Little Foreign Direct Investment?" In *The Role of Foreign Direct Investment in East Asian Economic Development*, ed. Takatoshi Ito and Anne O. Krueger, 239–61. Chicago: University of Chicago Press.

Wei, Yingqi Annie. 2004. "Foreign Direct Investment in China." In *Foreign Direct Investment: Six Country Case Studies*, ed. Yingqi Annie Wei and V. N. Balasubramanyam, 9–46. Cheltenham, UK: Edward Elgar.

Wei, Yingqi Annie, and V. N. Balasubramanyam, eds. 2004 *Foreign Direct Investment: Six Country Case Studies*. Cheltenham, UK: Edward Elgar.

Wolf, M. 2005. "Asia's Giants Take Different Routes." *Financial Times*, February 22nd.

World Bank. 2002. "Investment Climate Surveys: Knowledge for Change." World Bank, Washington, DC.

————. 2004a. *Doing Business in 2004: Understanding Regulation*. Washington, DC: World Bank.

————. 2004b. "India: Investment Climate and Manufacturing Industry." Investment Climate Assessment, World Bank, Washington, DC.

————. 2004c. *World Development Report 2005: A Better Investment Climate for Everyone*. Washington, DC: World Bank.

————. 2006a. *Doing Business 2006: Creating Jobs*. Washington, DC: World Bank.

————. 2006b. *World Development Indicators*. World Bank, Washington, DC.

World Economic Forum. 2003. "Global Competitiveness Report." Geneva, Switzerland.

————. 2004. "Global Competitiveness Report." Geneva, Switzerland.

Yang, Deli, Pervez Ghauri, and Mahmut Sonmez. 2005. "Competitive Analysis of the Software Industry in China." *International Journal of Technology Management* 29 (1/2): 64–91.

Yong, Zhang. 2004. "Chip Consumption to Rise 30% in 2004." *China Daily* March 3. http://www.chinadaily.com.cn/english/doc/2004-03/03/content_311262.htm.

Young, S., and P. Lan. 1997. "Technology Transfer to China through Foreign Direct Investment." *The Journal of the Regional Studies Association* 31 (7): 669–79.

Zagha, Roberto. 1998. "Labor and India's Economic Reforms." *Journal of Economic Policy Reform* 2 (4): 403–26.

Index

Boxes, figures, notes, and tables are indicated by *b*, *f*, *n*, and *t*, respectively.

241

attitudes of students toward
entrepreneurship, 92–93
link to software industry, 116, 117*b*7.1
researchers' affiliation with, 173

V
value added
hardware industry, 155–56
software industry, 72–78, 86*nn*1–3
venture capital
in hardware industry, 162–63, 165–66
in software industry, 83

W
wages
hardware industry, 155–57
software industry, 78–79, 131, 225–26

Western India Vegetable Products (Wipro),
122*b*7.2
Wipro Infotech, 122*b*7.2
workforce. *See* labor
World Bank Investment Climate
Assessment surveys, overview, 10,
11, 12*t*1.6, 20*n*6
World Economic Forum, 66
World War II, pre-WWII period in China
and India, 31–32, 51*n*2

Y
Y2K, 115, 128–29, 135

Z
ZTE, 206*b*12.3